Have You Ever Wondered?

Questions about Christianity

Fritz E. Barton, Jr. MD

WESTBOW PRESS®
A DIVISION OF THOMAS NELSON & ZONDERVAN

WestBow Press books may be ordered through booksellers or by contacting:

WestBow Press
A Division of Thomas Nelson & Zondervan
1663 Liberty Drive
Bloomington, IN 47403
www.westbowpress.com
844-714-3454

ISBN: 978-1-9736-9878-4 (sc)
ISBN: 978-1-9736-9879-1 (hc)
ISBN: 978-1-9736-9880-7 (e)

Library of Congress Control Number: 2023909458

Print information available on the last page.

WestBow Press rev. date: 08/24/2024

Table of Contents

1. Where Did Time Come From? 1
2. Why Did God Pick Planet Earth? 5
3. How Did the Nation of Israel Come to Exist? 10
4. Who Was Elijah? 16
5. Why Did God Require Genocide of All Inhabitants of the Promised Land? 24
6. How Was the New Testament Assembled? 35
7. What Is Lower Criticism of the Bible? 39
8. What Is Higher Criticism of the Bible? 46
9. What Happened to Trust in the Bible? 52
10. The Abiathar Confusion: Was Mark Mistaken? 56
11. Israel and the Church: How Do They Relate? 62
12. How Did Understanding of the Soul and Afterlife Develop? 70
13. Body, Soul, and Spirit: What's the Difference? 83
14. Christian Heresies: Was Jesus God or Man? 90
15. Why Did God Wait Thousands of Years to Send Christ to Earth? 93
16. How Do You Reconcile the Different Stories of Jesus's Birth? 99
17. Was Jesus Born at Christmas? 103
18. What Was the Christmas Star of Bethlehem? 114
19. Why Was Herod Fearful of Jesus's Birth? 121
20. Did Jesus Actually Claim to Be God? 125
21. Did the Voice at Jesus's Baptism Adopt Him into Deity? 134

22. When Did Jesus Become the Son of God? 138
23. What Is the Begotten Controversy? 143
24. Why Did a Sinless Jesus Need to Be Baptized? 149
25. What Was the Chronology of Jesus's Ministry? 154
26. Who Were the Women Who Supported Jesus's Ministry? 163
27. Calling of the Twelve: Why Did They Respond? 170
28. Why Did Jesus Command People Not to Tell Who He Was? 176
29. Who Was John the Disciple? 179
30. Who Was Peter the Disciple? 184
31. What Are the Kingdoms? 192
32. Why Did Jesus Start Speaking in Parables? 198
33. When Was Jesus's Last Supper? 203
34. Did Jesus Really Sweat Blood at Gethsemane? 206
35. Why Did Jesus Have to Die? 208
36. What Day Did Jesus Die? 214
37. What Was the Time of Jesus's Crucifixion? 229
38. How Many Ascensions? 234
39. Was Jesus in the Grave for Three Days? 237
40. Where Is Paradise? 243
41. Did Jesus Really Go to Hell? 249
42. Who Is Satan? 258
43. Was the Resurrection a Surprise? 262
44. Where Did Easter Come From? 268
45. Why Did Miracles Cease after the First Century? 271
46. What Was the Chronology of Jesus's Post-Resurrection Appearances? 275
47. Why Did History Not Better Record the Crucifixion and the Resurrection? 281
48. What Happened to the Apostles? 297
49. Who Was the Apostle Paul? 312
50. Why Is the New Heaven on Planet Earth? 319
51. Who Was John Mark? 322

52. Why Was Augustine So Influential? 328
53. Does Man Have Free Will? 333
54. What Is the Role of Grace? 342
55. What is a Personal Relationship With Jesus? 351
56. Are There Messianic Prophecies in Matthew? 358
57. Did Daniel Prophesy the Future? 370
58. Did Scribes Write the Bible? 379
59. How Did the Popes Dominate Christianity? 385
60. How Did the Gospel Writers Remember The Exact Quotes Of Jesus? 389

PROLOGUE

The difficulty in studying the Bible is that the story is scattered among sixty-six different books. Sorting out the "big picture" is challenging.

Having come from an academic background, I tend to think of things in topics. The selection of a topic for study often begins with the question,"Have you ever wondered……."? Then, the investigation begins, gleaning a piece here and a piece there throughout the books of the Bible.

Personally, I had hoped that these questions would be taught in "Sunday School". After all, what is more important to understand than eternal fate?

Then, I hoped to find the answers in seminary, but many of these questions are too insignificant for higher education. Some, perhaps, seem irreverent.

Asking questions to "seek understanding" in no way means that you are challenging doctrinal validity. In my previous career training surgeons, I encouraged them to know "why" as well as "what" they were doing. It is the basic Socratic method of education.

In *Seeking Understanding Faith*, I reversed Anselm's classic quote of "faith seeking understanding". Understanding is a requisite to believing.

That book dealt with the questions of God and interactive faith. This book is a collection of questions about the Bible and Christianity.

I will agree, up front, that this list of scattered questions has no cohesion. Some are bigger questions than others. This collection represents many of the questions that have intrigued me personally. Maybe you have thought about them too.

Have you ever wondered..........?

Fritz E. Barton, Jr, M.D.

1

Where Did Time Come From?

History

Both Genesis 1:1 in the Old Testament and John 1:1 in the New Testament start with "In the beginning." Biblically, time began at the creation of the universe. The first chapter of Genesis defines time into "days." Of course, there is debate over the exact length of a biblical "day," but nevertheless, it established the existence of time measurement.

The Garden of Eden contained the "tree of life" (Gen. 1:8; 3:22). Apparently, eating of the "tree of life" resulted in living forever (Gen. 3:22), which God forbade Adam and Eve from doing. In Genesis 3:19, God decreed that "man," who was made from dust, would return to dust—that is, have a limited, not forever, life span. Then, in Genesis 6:3, the longevity of humanity was limited to 120 years.

Measuring Time

From humanity's standpoint, it was noticed that conditions changed: light/dark, temperature with seasons, growth, and aging. So time was evidenced in more than cosmological rotations and exposure to sunlight. Earthly living things changed with time.

The measurement of time began sometime before 1500 BC. The Egyptians likely were the first to develop methods of measuring time. At first, it was one-twelfth of daylight, but of course, the length of daylight varied with seasons. More accurate measurements followed with sandglasses, water clocks, and candles.[1]

With the invention of the mechanical clock in the thirteenth century, the unit of time moved from days to hours.

When Did Time Start?

Before Einstein, astronomers (for the most part) understood the universe in terms of three laws of motion presented by Isaac Newton in 1686. These three laws follow:[2] (1) Objects in motion (or at rest) remain in motion (or at rest) unless an external force imposes change. (2) Force is equal to the change in momentum per change of time. For a constant mass, force equals mass times acceleration. (3) For every action, there is an equal and opposite reaction.

Philosophers and scientists until the time of Albert Einstein concluded that the universe was both static and eternal. Even Einstein initially agreed. But with the development of the big bang beginning and evidence of an expanding—not static—universe, Einstein reluctantly changed his mind.

But how did the concept of time fit into all this?

In 1905 Einstein conceived of the theory of special relativity, which defined the relationship between matter, energy, and the speed of light. Hence the famous formula $E = MC^2$. "Simply put, as an object approaches the speed of light, its mass becomes infinite, and it is unable to go any faster than light travels."[3]

But the theory of special relativity also dealt with time. He determined that space and time were intertwined into a single continuum known as space-time. Time changed as objects moved through space.[4]

For the next fifteen years, Einstein pondered the implications of special relativity and finally added the effects of gravity and acceleration, leading to his theory of general relativity in 1915. He concluded that massive objects warp the fabric of space-time because of the effect of gravity.

So if time is a space-time entity, did it always exist or did it have a beginning?

Some have proposed that while not exactly known, string theory suggests that there has always been time.[5] Conversely, Stephen Hawking's "no boundary" proposal concludes the universe has not existed forever. Rather, the universe, and time itself, had a beginning in the big bang, about fifteen billion years ago.[6]

Think about that mind-boggling concept. That time itself had a beginning! Maybe Genesis 1:1 and John 1:1 are more informative than just an introductory phrase.

What Is the Significance of Time?

The answer lies in two forces: (1) entropy of all elements of the universe, and (2) the aging process of all living things on earth.

All living tissues are composed of cells, and living cells divide and multiply, replacing themselves in a process called mitosis. So what keeps them from multiplying over and over so that the plant or animal goes on forever? That takes us back to the telomere. Due to the telomere, the number of replications is fixed. As the rattles of the telomere are used up, the cells age. While the rate of aging can be influenced by environmental factors or disease, there remains a maximum number of replacement cells, after which the organism dies.

So the main significance of time on living things is its effect on aging.

But nonliving matter—rocks, liquids, gases—also changes with time. Atoms function with energy, but they tend to get out of coordination in a process called entropy. Without getting too much into the weeds of thermonuclear physics, entropy generally means that the heat energy of atoms composing minerals and gases tends to get out of sync, leading to irreversible deterioration with time. This process has apparently been present since the beginning of the universe.

Interestingly, the human mind seems to be incapable of escaping the reference of time. *The Cambridge English Dictionary* describes eternity as "time that never ends or that has no limits." *Meriam-Webster* defines eternity as "infinite time." The Google Dictionary uses the terms "infinite or unending time." Even dictionaries cannot describe the absence of time.

But what about the spiritual world? If God and heaven are not composed of matter and energy controlled by the laws of physics, are they subject to time? Is the spiritual world subject to entropy?

But what if time is just the measurement of change (entropy)? And what if change (entropy) only started with the beginning of the universe?

We measure the physical world by height, width, and length (space), with the fourth dimension now to include time. Perhaps before entropy started, there were no time and no space limitations.

Perhaps modern cosmological physics, in fact, allows that before the beginning of the physical universe and its laws of physics, there could have been eternity, with the immutability and omnipresence of God.

2

Why Did God Pick Planet Earth?

Why would God focus on just the tiny planet Earth within the vastness of the universe?

At Oxford University, on October 22, 2009, Richard Dawkins, the polemical atheist evolutionary biologist, debated John Lennox, the Oxford mathematician and evangelical Christian. The topic was "Has Science Buried God?" During the debate, Dawkins commented,[7]

> He [Lennox] believes that the Creator of the universe, the God who devised the laws of physics, the laws of mathematics, the physical constants, who devised the precepts of space, billions of light years of space, billions of years of time, that this paradigm of physical science, this genius of mathematics, couldn't think of a better way to rid the world of sin than to come to this little speck of cosmic dust, and have Himself tortured and executed so that He could forgive himself. That is profoundly unscientific—not only is it unscientific, it

also doesn't do justice to the grandeur of the universe.
It is petty and small minded.

According to the Bible, God sent His only Son to planet Earth to communicate with the human race. And in Revelation, prophecy proclaims that after a period of judgment, God will come and dwell on a "New Earth" (Rev. 21:1–22:6).

Is Christianity really "petty and small-minded"?

This mystery has perplexed those considering Christianity since Copernicus discovered that earth was, indeed, not the center of the universe. Why would the Creator of the vast universe seem to focus His attention on a tiny planet (Earth), in one of at least five hundred solar systems, in a galaxy (the Milky Way) that is but one of between two hundred billion and two trillion known galaxies in the currently observable universe, and leave the rest of the universe just for the recreational night viewing of earthly humans?

To create a living object, you really need only four elements: carbon, hydrogen, oxygen, and nitrogen, plus small amounts of sulfur, phosphorous, calcium, and iron. All are in plentiful amounts on earth. That's not to say that it's easy to get from these elements to reproductive metabolic life, but their presence is evidence of necessary building blocks.

In 1969, a meteorite crashed to earth in Murchison, Australia, north of Melbourne. Researchers from the Ames Research Center in California examined the meteorite rocks and found the presence of polyols—a complex string of sugars made with a carbon backbone. Other carbon-containing rocks—carbonaceous chondrites—have also impacted earth. In 2000, one such meteorite landed at Tagish Lake in Canada. It is now thought that Halley's Comet contains 255 organic molecules. Suffice it to say, there is increasing evidence that organic matter is plentiful in the universe.[8]

The noted astrophysicist Fred Hoyle solved the riddle of how the larger atoms could have arisen from the single proton hydrogen, which was the dominant atom (92 percent) present shortly after the big bang. Hoyle developed the process of nucleosynthesis whereby the heat of fusion sequentially developed heavier (more protons and neutrons) atoms. Hydrogen to helium to carbon and oxygen, then carbon to nitrogen.[9] That being discovered, it is not surprising that those building blocks of life (carbon, hydrogen, oxygen, nitrogen, and a few minor others) are scattered throughout the universe already.

If those elements were found elsewhere in space, would that be a clue that life might be elsewhere in the universe as well as on earth?

Hoyle and a small number of other scientists have proposed the theory of "panspermia." That is, that primitive life initially formed elsewhere in the universe and seeded earth via meteorites. Remember that the basic definition of life, rather than pure organic chemistry, is the ability to have two functions: metabolism (production of energy for function) and reproduction (the ability to multiply). According to Hoyle, primitive life-forms seeded earth, then evolved into to more complex life-forms.

Of course, Hoyle's theory of panspermia and the meteorite evidence of organic compounds present in space do not begin to answer how that initial life was formed, but it does create suspicion that earth may not be the only location of life in the universe.

Scientists from the SETI Institute, in collaboration with NASA and GAIA (the European Space Agency), have analyzed data from the Kepler space telescope. They estimate that there may be as many as three hundred million potentially inhabitable planets in our galaxy alone. Some are within thirty light-years alone.[10]

Frank Drake is an astrophysicist and one of the SETI (Search for Extraterrestrial Intelligence) projects. In 1961, in setting the agenda for the first SETI meeting, Drake constructed a multifaceted formula to estimate the possibilities of life on other planets of our solar system, the Milky Way.[11] While the accuracy of the mathematical assumptions within the formula have generated debate, it does illustrate the enormity of possibilities.

The Drake equation is where …

N = the number of civilizations in our galaxy with which communication might be possible (i.e., which are on our current past light cone):

and

R_* = the average rate of star formation in our galaxy
f_p = the fraction of those stars that have planets
n_e = the average number of planets that can potentially support life per star that has planets
f_l = the fraction of planets that could support life that develop life at some point
f_i = the fraction of planets with life that develop intelligent life (civilizations)
f_c = the fraction of civilizations that develop a technology that releases detectable signs of their existence into space
L = the length of time for which such civilizations release detectable signals into space

Under Drake's equation you divide the number of stars in a selected portion of the universe by the number of stars that are likely to have planetary systems; divide that the number of planetary systems that could theoretically support life; divide that by the on which life, having arisen, advances to a state of intelligence; and so on … even with the most conservative inputs the number of advanced civilizations in just the Milky Way always works out to be somewhat in the millions.[12]

Even Stephen Hawkins, the noted astrophysicist and atheist, concedes, " It is estimated that one star in five has an Earth-like planet orbiting at a distance from the star to be compatible with life as we know it."

So where does that leave us?

Obviously, our understanding of the universe so far cannot confirm that there is another life system, similar to earth, located elsewhere. But the previously discussed evidence of extraterrestrial organic substances indicates the possibility.

Stephen Hawking, in his last book, *Brief Answers to the Big Questions*, postulates "there are other forms of intelligent life out there, but that we have been overlooked."[13]

And how does all this effect Dawkins's conclusion that a creator God of the universe would not exclusively confine His interaction with His creation to the tiny planet Earth? Well, maybe earth isn't the only interaction God has. An omnipotent creator, with omnipresent capability could have created an "earth" scenario an unlimited number of times.

Perhaps we are one of many. Does that make our interaction with the Creator less relevant?

3

How Did the Nation of Israel Come to Exist?

The story of modern human population resets with Noah's great flood. All humans are descendants of one of the three sons: Ham, Shem, or Japeth.

> The sons of Noah who came out of the ark were Shem, Ham and Japheth. (Gen. 9:18)

Japeth's descendants settled Eurasia; Ham's descendants settled north Africa and the Arabian peninsula; Seth's descendants settled what is now known as the Middle East.

Shem (Middle East)

Shem (Heb. "Name") was Noah's oldest son and part of Noah's family of eight who survived the great flood. Shem was the father of the nations of the ancient Near East, including the Israelites. The Jewish religion (Judaism), Christianity, and Islam sprang from the line of Shem. The Semites were particularly known for their religious zeal.

Ham (Africa and Arabian Peninsula)

Ham (Heb. "hot" or "Black") was Noah's second oldest son. Ham and his wife bore four sons who became the fathers of the nations of Africa. Ham's fourth son, Canaan, was prophetically cursed because he gazed at his father's nakedness while he was drunk (Gen. 9:22). This curse would mean later that Canaan would lose his land to the Hebrews and would be subservient to the descendants of Shem. The Hamites were known for their physical endurance.

Japheth (Eurasia)

Japheth (Heb. "God will Enlarge") was Noah's third oldest son. Japeth's descendants settled the European (Caucasian) nations. The Japhethites were known for their intellectual activity.

As the nations developed after Babel, the Middle Eastern populations concentrated around water supplies. These were the Mediterranean coast (Levant), the Nile River delta, and the Tigris-Euphrates River pathway from what is now Turkey to the Adriatic Sea.

It was from Ur in Chaldes (modern-day Iraq), located in the Tigris-Euphrates watershed, that Abram was called by God in approximately 2000 BC. God promised Abram (the Abrahamic Covenant) that his descendants would inherit the Promised Land:

> On that day the Lord made a covenant with Abram and said, "To your descendants I give this land, from the Wadi[a] of Egypt to the great river, the Euphrates—the land of the Kenites, Kenizzites, Kadmonites, Hittites, Perizzites, Rephaites, Amorites, Canaanites, Girgashites and Jebusites." (Gen. 15:18–21)

This boundary included the territories occupied by the tribes of the "Canaanite Nations" plus the Hittites in modern-day Turkey.[14, 15]

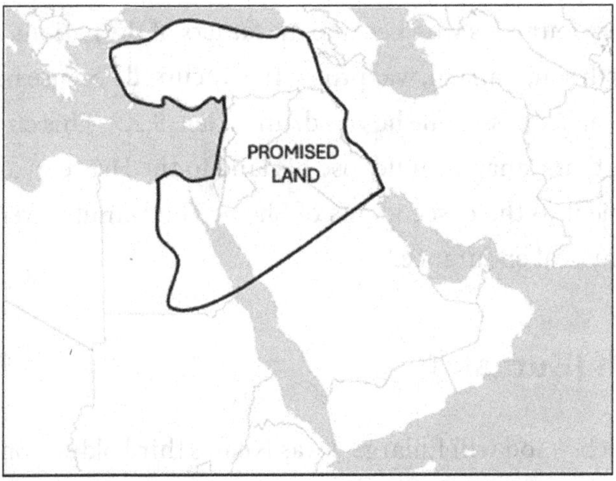

However, the immediate implementation of the covenant was delayed for four hundred years due to the Israelites' rebellion, illustrated by Sodom and Gomorrah (Gen. 19). As a result of worldwide famine (Gen. 42:57), Jacob's sons moved to Egypt, where grain was plentiful. There they multiplied and served in bondage for four hundred years.

Moses led the Exodus in approximately 1440 BC. After forty more years in the wilderness, Joshua entered Canaan in about 1400 BC. The Israelites demanded to have a king like the surrounding nations, and between 1200 to 1000 BC, Saul became the first king of the nation of Israel. He was then followed by David, then Solomon. So a formal nation of Israel, headed by a king, was established in what was previously Canaan by 1000 BC.

An interesting sidelight is the story of Ishmael. Ishmael, the son of Abram and his concubine Hagar, pursued a rebellious path. God said to Hagar,

> The angel of the Lord also said to her:
> "You are now pregnant

and you will give birth to a son.
You shall name him Ishmael,
for the Lord has heard of your misery.
He will be a wild donkey of a man;
his hand will be against everyone
and everyone's hand against him,
and he will live in hostility
toward all his brothers." (Gen. 16:11–13)

The descendants of Ishmael apparently migrated into upper Arabia and evolved into the Midianites, one of the Arab factions.[16]

The Midianites intersect the history of the Israelites. First, they were the nomadic merchants who bought Joseph for twenty shekels and took him to Egypt (Gen. 37:28). Second, after Moses slew the Egyptian taskmaster, he wandered in the desert (Exod. 2:15). While in exile, he married a Midianite woman, Zipporah (Exod. 2:21). Finally, as Moses was leading the new generation toward entrance to the Promised Land, the Midianites joined the Moabites to attack the Israelites. Balaam devised a plan to undermine the morality of the Israelites by enticing them to engage in sex with Moabite and Midianite women, leading to worship of their gods (Num. 25:13). God instructed the Israelites to kill the Midianites. (Num. 25:16)

At about the same time Joshua entered Canaan, a mysterious sea people, perhaps from Macedonia, entered southern Canaan. The exact date is not specifically known but is estimated to be around 1200 BC.[17] If so, the twelve Israelite tribes had already colonized Canaan. It was, of course, about 1200 BC when David slew the Philistine giant, Goliath.

It is important to realize at this point in the history of the Levant (previously Canaan), that at the time of Philistine invasion, the Israelites may already have had an established nation with Saul as the inaugural king. The Philistines, by contrast, were a tribal people settling in the southern Levant.[18] The name "Palestine" was previously derived by the

Greeks as the "land of the Philistines" or "Philistia" and was in a small area of the southern coast of the Levant between modern-day Tel Aviv-Yafo and Gaza.[19] Although there was no independent government, a geographic area known as Palestine was established.

The Philistines, intermixed with other descendants of Ham, and later Ishmael (Midianites), were the precursors of modern Palestinians. Interestingly, the Philistines were apparently separate from Arabs. "Arabs" are first mentioned in the Bible during the period of the divided kingdom in 2 Chronicles 17:11:

> Some Philistines brought Jehoshaphat gifts and silver as tribute, and the Arabs brought him flocks: seven thousand seven hundred rams and seven thousand seven hundred goats.

The first use of the term *Arab* was apparently about 853 BC,[20] and the place-name "Arabia" occurs for the first time in the Greek Herodotus (484–425 BC).[21]

After Solomon, Israel split into two kingdoms: the upper maintained the name Israel, and the lower became Judah. The upper kingdom was destroyed in 722 BC by the Assyrians, and most of the Israelites were dispersed from the land. Then in 586 BC, the Babylonians destroyed Judah and took the Israelites into exile for seventy years. With the rise of the Persian empire, King Cyrus allowed the Israelites (now called "Jews") to return to the Levant and rebuild Jerusalem and the Temple. The Jews had been able to return to the Holy Land, but they had no independent nation. They became subservient to whichever colonizing power dominated the region.

The Persians defeated the Babylonians in 539 BC and ruled the levant until defeated by Alexander the Great in 334 BC. After the death of Alexander the Great in 323 BC, his empire was divided among his generals—Seleucis and Ptolomy being the most relevant. The Seleucids were in the north, and the Ptolomys were in the south. The Seleucids and Egyptians conquered back and forth during the six Syrian wars of the third to first centuries BC. The Seleucids were most responsible for Hellenization of Jerusalem, with Antiochus IV erecting a statue of Zeus in the Temple.

The Maccabean Jews revolted against Seleucid Hellenization in 165 BC and established a semi-independent nation once more. This national independence was short-lived, and the Greeks ruled the Levant until conquered by the Romans in 63 BC. The lineage from the Maccabees became the Hasmonaean dynasty, which controlled the high priesthood. The Hasmonaeans were "client rulers" under first the Seleucids, and then the Romans, until the arrival of the Herodian dynasty in 37 BC.

Herod (the Great) was appointed provincial governor of Galilee by Julius Caesar in 47 BC. In 36 or 37 BC, Herod became king of Judea. His reign lasted until his death in 4 BC. He was succeeded by his three sons. Herod Antipas ruled Galilee from 4 BC to 39 BC. He is the Herod referred to in the Gospels. Antipas maintained his power as tetrarch during the ministries of both John the Baptist and Jesus of Nazareth. He was even involved in the trial of Jesus later in history.

The Romans continued their rule throughout the period of Jesus in the first century AD. The Jews rebelled again in AD 63, followed by the destruction of the Temple in AD 70 by the Roman general Titus.

4

Who Was Elijah?

Biography

Elijah, also spelled *Elias* or *Elia*, Hebrew *Eliyyahu* (flourished ninth century BCE). The name Elijah is a combination of the Hebrew words El (God) and Yah (Jehovah).[22]

Historically, Elijah was from Tisbe in Gilead, which was located just east of the Jordan River in what is now Jordan. He first appears in 1 Kings 17:1

> Now Elijah the Tishbite, from Tishbe in Gilead, said to Ahab, "As the Lord, the God of Israel, lives, whom I serve, there will be neither dew nor rain in the next few years except at my word."

Not much is known about Elijah's background. He may have been thirty to fifty years old when he first appeared in Old Testament scripture.

His story starts with God telling him to go live by the stream in Cherith, where ravens brought him food. He was then sent to Zarapeth, where he encountered the starving widow and God provided food (1

Kings 17:9–16). Finally, when the widow's son became ill and died, Elijah called on the Lord and brought the child back to life (1 Kings 17:17–23).

Elijah was a prophet primarily in the upper kingdom of Israel, where he prophesied judgment against Ahab and his wife, Jezebel. Jezebel was a follower of the cult of Baal and was influential in turning the northern kingdom Israelites from Yahweh to Baal.

Elijah is perhaps most famous for confronting the 450 prophets of Baal on Mount Carmel, where both were trying to summon the gods to bring rain. Elijah demonstrated the sovereignty of Yahweh by calling fire on his alter (1 Kings 18:38), followed by rain, to end the three-year drought. The episode ended with the Israelites slaying the Baal priests.

As a result, Jezebel became enraged at Elijah, who then fled to the wilderness of Judah. Wishing to die under a juniper tree, he was assuaged by an angel (1 Kings 19:4–8). Journeying to a cave in Mount Horeb in the Southern Kingdom Sinai, Elijah once again petitions God to take his life. But God tells him to go anoint a new king of Israel and to anoint Elisha as his successor.

Elijah then prophesies that King Ahab's sons would be destroyed (1 Kings 12:22); Ahaziah would die of his illness (2 Kings 1:16–17); Jezebel would be eaten by dogs (1 Kings 21:23); calling fire on fifty-one soldiers (2 Kings 1:10,12); parting of the Jordan with Elisha (2 Kings 2:8); promising that Elisha would get a double portion of his spirit (2 Kings 2:10); prophesying Jehoram would die a horrible death (2 Chron. 21:12–15.).[23]

Finally, Elijah *never underwent physical death.* He was carried directly to heaven in a whirlwind accompanied by a chariot of fire (2 Kings 2:11):

> As they were walking along and talking together, suddenly a chariot of fire and horses of fire appeared and separated the two of them, and Elijah went up to heaven in a whirlwind.

Expecting Messiah

The Jews of the first century were expecting a Messiah. When Moses was about to leave the Exodus Israelites, he said God would send a series of prophets to lead them in his absence:

> The Lord your God will raise up for you a prophet like me from among you, from your fellow Israelites. You must listen to him. (Deut. 18:15)

Devout Jews remembered that Elijah had never died but rather had been taken directly to heaven. They therefore thought that he might be the prophet who returned to announce the end of time.[24]

The prophet Malachi, writing two hundred years after Elijah, foretold the return of a new Elijah, presumably Jesus:

> See, I will send the prophet Elijah to you before that great and dreadful day of the Lord comes. He will turn the hearts of the parents to their children, and the hearts of the children to their parents; or else I will come and strike the land with total destruction. (Mal. 4:5–6)

Revered in Jewish Custom

Due to the reference in Malachi (4:5-6), traditional Jews in modern times look for Elijah to return and announce the earthly arrival of the Messiah.

In Judaism, Elijah's name is invoked at the weekly Havdalah ritual that marks the end of Shabbat, and Elijah is invoked in other Jewish customs, among them the Passover Seder and the Brit *milah* (ritual circumcision). He appears in numerous stories and references in the Haggadah and rabbinic literature, including the Babylonian Talmud.[25]

Every Passover, Jews set an extra cup of wine on the dinner table and open the door for the enigmatic prophet Elijah, hoping he will enter.[26]

Even in modern times, there is an empty chair and a table setting for Elijah whenever Passover is celebrated. Little children also go to the door of the home and open it in anticipation of Elijah's coming. The Old Testament prophets had said that God would send Elijah before the coming of the Messiah (Mal. 3:1; 4:5–6). According to these calculations, John the Baptist was born at Passover. Remember the angel's words to Zechariah? The angel said that John the Baptist was to come "in the spirit and power of Elijah" (Luke 1:17). Elijah came at Passover![27]

John the Baptist

The abrupt appearance of John the Baptist with his ministry of repentance was a radical movement against the law-laden culture of the Pharisees. It would not be surprising to conclude that John the Baptist was the reincarnate Elijah.

First, there was a similarity in *eccentric appearance*. Elijah is described as wearing a hairy garment with a leather girdle:

> They replied, "He had a garment of hair and had a leather belt around his waist."
> The king said, "That was Elijah the Tishbite." (2 Kings 1:8)

This correlation is striking because of the appearance of John the Baptist.

> John wore clothing made of camel's hair, with a leather belt around his waist, and he ate locusts and wild honey. (Mark 1:6)

Second, the *message* of Elijah, as well as for John the Baptist, was the need for repentance. Elijah preached repentance to the Israelites of the Northern Kingdom who turned from God to Baal. John the Baptist preached repentance to the Israelites who had turned from God to Greek paganism.

Luke quotes the angel as telling the role of John the Baptist being like Elijah's by referring to Malachi 4:5–6:

> And he will go on before the Lord, in the spirit and power of Elijah, to turn the hearts of the parents to their children and the disobedient to the wisdom of the righteous—to make ready a people prepared for the Lord. (Luke 1:17)

Jesus, Himself, refers to John the Baptist as like Elijah:

> For all the Prophets and the Law prophesied until John. And if you are willing to accept it, he is the Elijah who was to come. (Matt. 11:13–14)

> As they were coming down the mountain, Jesus instructed them, "Don't tell anyone what you have seen, until the Son of Man has been raised from the dead." The disciples asked him, "Why then do the teachers of the law say that Elijah must come first?" Jesus replied, "To be sure, Elijah comes and will restore all things. But I tell you, Elijah has already come, and they did not recognize him, but have done to him everything they wished. In the same way the Son of Man is going to suffer at their hands." Then the disciples understood that he was talking to them about John the Baptist. (Matt. 17:9–13)

Even though John the Baptist denied that he was the reincarnated Elijah,

> They asked him, "Then who are you? Are you Elijah?"
> He said, "I am not."
> "Are you the Prophet?"
> He answered, "No." (John 1:21)

The Archetype of Christ

The importance of Elijah is demonstrated by the many references to him in the New Testament.

When announcing his ministry in Nazareth, he referred to Elijah as an example of a specific mission:

> I assure you that there were many widows in Israel in Elijah's time, when the sky was shut for three and a half years and there was a severe famine throughout the land. Yet Elijah was not sent to any of them, but to a widow in Zarephath in the region of Sidon. (Luke 4:25–26)

Herod, when hearing of Jesus's miracles, wondered if he was Elijah returned:

> Others said, "He is Elijah."
> And still others claimed, "He is a prophet, like one of the prophets of long ago." (Mark 6:15)

At Caesarea Phillipi, when Jesus asked the disciples who people thought He was, their reply included reincarnate Elijah:

> They replied, "Some say John the Baptist; others say Elijah; and still others, Jeremiah or one of the prophets." (Matt. 16:14)

> They replied, "Some say John the Baptist; others say Elijah; and still others, one of the prophets." (Mark 8:28)

> They replied, "Some say John the Baptist; others say Elijah; and still others, that one of the prophets of long ago has come back to life." (Luke 9:19 NIV)

And at the Crucifixion, the crowd questioned if Jesus was calling for Elijah to deliver him:

> When some of those standing there heard this, they said, "He's calling Elijah."
> Immediately one of them ran and got a sponge. He filled it with wine vinegar, put it on a staff, and offered it to Jesus to drink. The rest said, "Now leave him alone. Let's see if Elijah comes to save him." (Matt. 27:47–49)

Two other New Testament references illustrate Elijah's importance:

> God did not reject his people, whom he foreknew. Don't you know what Scripture says in the passage about Elijah—how he appealed to God against Israel. (Rom. 11:2)

> Elijah was a human being, even as we are. He prayed earnestly that it would not rain, and it did not rain on the land for three and a half years. Again he prayed, and the heavens gave rain, and the earth produced its crops. (James 5:17–18)

Transfiguration

There is no greater indication of the importance of Old Testament figures than who was chosen to be present at Jesus's transfiguration: Moses and Elijah.

> Just then there appeared before them Moses and Elijah, talking with Jesus. (Matt. 17:3–13)
>
> And there appeared before them Elijah and Moses, who were talking with Jesus. (Mark 9:4)
>
> Two men, Moses and Elijah, appeared in glorious splendor, talking with Jesus. (Luke 9:30)

Conclusion

Elijah was probably the most famous prophet of the Old Testament, even though no book is authored in his name. He preached repentance to the kings of the Northern Kingdom but is perhaps best known for the Jewish expectation that he would return either as the Messiah or as the forerunner of the Messiah. His accompanying Moses to be present at Jesus's transfiguration cements his importance in Jewish faith.

5

Why Did God Require Genocide of All Inhabitants of the Promised Land?

One of the great mysteries of the Bible is why the God of the Old Testament seems to be so violent, whereas the Son of God, Jesus the Christ, teaches benevolence to one's enemies.

Admonition for Peaceful Treatment of Enemies

Multiple times in the Old Testament, God teaches against violent activities. God specifically prohibits the Israelites to murder:

> You shall not murder. (Exod. 20:13)
> You shall not murder. (Deut. 5:17)

The writer of Proverbs, possibly Solomon, admonishes,

> Do not rejoice when your enemy falls,
> And do not let your heart be glad when he stumbles.
> (Prov. 24:17)

> If your enemy is hungry, give him food to eat;
> And if he is thirsty, give him water to drink. (Prov. 25:21)

At the birth of Jesus, an angel proclaims,

> Glory to God in the highest,
> And on earth peace among men with whom He is pleased. (Luke 2:14)

Then, in the New Testament, Jesus is quoted:

> "But I say to you, love your enemies and pray for those who persecute you." (Matt. 5:44)
>
> "But I say to you who hear, love your enemies, do good to those who hate you, bless those who curse you, pray for those who mistreat you. Whoever hits you on the cheek, offer him the other also; and whoever takes away your coat, do not withhold your shirt from him either. Give to everyone who asks of you, and whoever takes away what is yours, do not demand it back." (Luke 6:27–30)

Finally, in the book of Romans, the apostle Paul preaches,

> "But if your enemy is hungry, feed him, and if he is thirsty, give him a drink; for in so doing you will heap burning coals on his head." (Rom. 12:20)

Old Testament Violence

Yet the Old Testament is filled with violence. God killed millions of people, not even counting the masses killed by Noah's flood.

People Directly Killed by God

Many people were killed either directly or indirectly by God in the Bible. The following is summarized by Biblestudy.org (revised partially by this author):[28]

Genesis 19:17, 26: Lot's wife was executed by being immediately turned into a pillar of salt when she disobeyed the command to not view the destruction of Sodom and Gomorrah. She is the first person in the Bible named as receiving the death penalty from God.

Genesis 38:7: Er, the firstborn child of the patriarch Judah, was put to death by the Eternal for his unspecified wickedness. Onan, the second son of Judah, was executed for refusing to fulfill his duty to produce children with his dead brother's widow (Gen. 38:8–9).

Genesis 38:7: Abihu and Nadab, the sons of Aaron the high priest, were specially called to serve in the tabernacle in the wilderness (Exod. 28:1). One day, they offered before the altar "strange fire" (KJV translation) before God and were immediately executed for their foolishness (Lev. 10:1–2). Biblical commentaries vary regarding their interpretation of what is meant by "strange fire," the offering of which brought about the swift deaths of these two priests.

Second Samuel 6:7: Uzzah, a Levite who was helping escort the Ark of the Covenant for King David, was killed instantly when he rashly tried to steady it as it traveled toward Jerusalem.

Jeremiah 28:12–17: Hananiah, a false prophet who led the people to believe lies, is executed within a year after he is told by the prophet Jeremiah he will be punished for his sins.

First Samuel 25: Nabal was a wealthy but harsh man. He refused, when asked, to provide desperately needed supplies for David (the future king of Israel) and his men. God, ten days after he refused his help, executed him for his wicked behavior.

Second Chronicles 13:20: Jeroboam, the first king of the Northern

Ten Tribes of Israel, was struck down because of his many sins, chief of which were leading the people away from the true God.

Second Chronicles 21:18–19: King Jehoram (also called Joram), the fifth ruler of the Kingdom of Judah, is allowed to contract a fatal bowel disease due to his disobedience.

God also directly executed New Testament individuals:

Acts 5:1–10: Ananias and his wife, Sapphira, were New Testament believers. After selling some land, they decided to give the church part of the proceeds but tell everyone that they were donating the entire amount of the sale. The apostle Peter, however, saw through their mutually agreed ruse. After confronting each one separately regarding their lie and selfish attitudes, they were executed through the power of the Holy Spirit.

Acts 12:23: The angel of the Lord is sent to kill Herod Agrippa, a man who murdered the apostle James and tried to kill Peter, for elevating himself like a god. All these, and no doubt countless others we are not aware of, were personally executed by God for their sins!

In addition, God *indirectly* killed several individuals by specifically commanding the execution:

Numbers 15:32–36: The Lord commanded the Israelites to stone to death an unnamed man found breaking the Sabbath.

First Samuel 4:1–11: Phinehas and Hophni, sons of Eli the high priest, served as priests at the tabernacle in Shiloh. They took advantage of their authority by coercing those who came to offer an animal sacrifice to give them whatever part of the beast they demanded (1 Sam. 2:12–17). They also had illicit sex with some of the women who came to worship (1 Sam. 2:22). God declared, through an unnamed prophet, that he would have the two men executed on the same day because of their many sins (1 Sam. 2:25, 34). This prophecy was fulfilled when the Philistines not only killed them during a battle but also took from under their care the Ark of the Covenant.

First Chronicles 10:13–14: Because Saul, Israel's first king, disobeyed

God, he was allowed to lose a fierce battle with the Philistines so that he would lose his life.

Brian Patrick Byrne, Leon Markovitz, Jody Sieradzki, and Tal Reznik have tallied the total God-directed deaths in the Bible.[29] They purport that, excluding Noah's flood, there are 160 killing "sprees" in the Bible attributable to God. Including the books of the Roman Catholic Apocrypha, the authors count 2,821,364 deaths. By comparison, they attribute only ten kills to Satan.

According to Byrne et al., 2 Chronicles records the most deaths with 1,620,006, followed by Apocrypha (268,913), Judges (252,735), 2 Kings (185,263), 2 Samuel (152,470), 1 Kings (127,457), 1 Samuel (84,094), Esther, Job, Jeremiah, and Ezekiel (75,825), Numbers (38,972), Joshua (12,015), Exodus (3,600), and the remainder (14).[30]

The Promised Land

The Promised Land was defined and bounded by God when He promised it to Abraham and his descendants (Gen. 13:14–17) as part of the Abrahamic Covenant (Gen. 15:18–21).

Who Were the Canaanites?

Ham was one of Noah's three sons. Ham defiled Noah (Gen. 9:22), and as a result, Noah cursed Ham's youngest son, Canaan (Gen. 9:25). Canaan's heirs were the Hittites,[16] Jebusites, Amorites, Girgashites,[17] Hivites, Arkites, Sinites,[18] Arvadites, Zemarites, and Hamathites. (Gen. 10:15–18). These tribes settled along the Levant.

The area of the Levant came to be known as "Canaan" around the year 1552 BCE, when Egypt conquered the Levant. They labelled the region of Phoenicia and southern Palestine as Canaan,[31] likely because the descendent tribes of Canaan inhabited the area.

What Was So Bad about the Canaanites?

God established the nation of Israel by calling a pagan, Abram, to follow Him (Gen. 12:1–3; 15:6). Up until that time, people worshiped multiple pagan gods, particularly Molech (Lev. 18:21; 21:2) and Baal (Num. 25:1–3), which were associated with bizarre rituals, including child sacrifice, incest, and bestiality. The Israelites had a long history of succumbing to pagan influences (Exod. 33:19; Amos 5:26). God warned that if the inhabitants of Canaan were to be allowed to survive, they would intermix their pagan cultures and lead the Israelites away from God (Lev. 18:21; Deut. 12:30–31), a prophecy that would later come to fruition.

As the Israelites were about to cross the Jordan, Moses reminded them that God was not driving out the pagans because they were consistently righteous but rather because the pagans were so wicked (Deut. 9:4–6).

The initial order from God to capture Canaan is given in the books of Exodus, Numbers, and Deuteronomy:

> For My angel will go before you and bring you in to the land of the Amorites, the Hittites, the Perizzites, the Canaanites, the Hivites and the Jebusites; and I will completely destroy them. (Exod. 23:23)

> Then you shall drive out all the inhabitants of the land from before you, and destroy all their figured stones, and destroy all their molten images and demolish all their high places … But if you do not drive out the inhabitants of the land from before you, then it shall come about that those whom you let remain of them will become as pricks in your eyes and as thorns in your sides, and they will trouble you in the land in which you live. (Num. 33:52, 55)

> When the Lord your God brings you into the land where you are entering to possess it, and clears away many nations before you, the Hittites and the Girgashites and the Amorites and the Canaanites and the Perizzites and the Hivites and the Jebusites, seven nations greater and stronger than you, and when the Lord your God delivers them before you and you defeat them, then you shall utterly destroy them. You shall make no covenant with them and show no favor to them. (Deut. 7:1–2)

Only in the cities of these peoples that the Lord your God is giving you as an inheritance, you shall not leave alive anything that breathes. But you shall utterly destroy them, the Hittite and the Amorite, the Canaanite and the Perizzite, the Hivite and the Jebusite, as the Lord your God has commanded you, so that they may not teach you to do according to all their detestable things which they have done for their gods, so that you would sin against the Lord your God. (Deut. 20:16–18)

> This is how you will know that the living God is among you and that he will certainly drive out before you the Canaanites, Hittites, Hivites, Perizzites, Girgashites, Amorites and Jebusites. (Josh. 3:10)

The Strategy

Bowman observes that "God's law in the Pentateuch distinguished at least four different categories of non-Israelites and required Israel to act in markedly different ways toward each group. We may call these four categories indigenous peoples, border peoples, protected peoples, and sojourners."[32]

By *indigenous peoples* I mean the people groups that inhabited the land of Canaan, specified in various texts as the Amorites, Hittites, Girgashites, Perizzites, Canaanites, Hivites, and Jebusites (Gen. 15:19-21; Ex. 3:8, 17; 13:5; 23:23, 28; 34:11; Num. 13:29; Deut. 7:1; 20:17; Josh. 3:10; 9:1; 11:3; 12:8; 24:11; Judg. 1:3–35; 3:5;1 Kings 9:20–21; Ezra 9:1; Neh. 9:8). The dominant tribe or nation among these peoples was the Canaanite people, which is why the land was called Canaan and why the Canaanites are mentioned more than any of the others.

Border peoples lived in cities and villages on the outer edges of Canaan, who were not part of the seven or so indigenous tribes of Canaan. Cities outside the region inhabited by the Canaanites and other condemned peoples, but within the land designated as belonging to Israel, were first to be offered terms of peace, in which its people would become forced labor and serve the Israelites. If a city refused, Israel was to make war against it, kill all its men, and allow the women and children to live (Deut. 20:10-15). The distinction drawn between the outlying cities of the land and the cities of the Canaanites and other peoples clustered within the land reflects the belief that the indigenous peoples were too far gone to be shown any mercy, while other people groups were not deemed similarly degenerate.

The *protected peoples* were tribes or nations in the region that Israel was to leave alone. The most significant of these was Edom. When Israel sought to pass through the territory of Edom—even promising to pay for the use of its water—and Edom refused, Israel simply went another way (Num. 20:14–21). Yet when Sihon, the king of the Amorites, refused to grant the Israelites safe passage, Israel conquered and possessed the Amorite cities (Num. 21:21–32), destroying every man, woman, and child (Deut. 2:32–34). The reason for the differing treatments was that Israel considered the Edomites (who were descendants of Jacob's brother Esau) brothers (Num. 20:14).

Sojourners were individuals or families whose tribal origins were from outside the land but who had immigrated into the land of Canaan. The Old Testament refers to such persons as sojourners, aliens, or strangers (the terms are roughly if not entirely synonymous). Israelites were forbidden to wrong a stranger or oppress him (Ex. 22:21; 23:9).

Execution of the Invasion—Failure to Comply

The varied terrain of Canaan made conquering difficult. The hill country was vulnerable, but conquering the area of the plains was less successful because of Canaanite iron chariots.[33] Rather than following God's instruction to obliterate the populations, the Israelites conquered the area but made the same mistake that the Egyptians had made centuries earlier—they enslaved the people, rather than exterminating them as God directed. Disobedience had delayed their siege of the Promised Land. Now disobedience led to military defeats, rebellions, and cultural contamination.

Their failure was admonished by the angel:

> The angel of the Lord went up from Gilgal to Bokim and said, "I brought you up out of Egypt and led you into

> the land I swore to give to your ancestors. I said, 'I will never break my covenant with you, and you shall not make a covenant with the people of this land, but you shall break down their altars.' Yet you have disobeyed me. Why have you done this? And I have also said, 'I will not drive them out before you; they will become traps for you, and their gods will become snares to you.'" (Judg. 2:1–3 NIV)

The Consequence

Leaving scattered Canaanite tribes within the population of the new Land of Israel had the predicted consequences. Saul had to continue to battle the Amalekites (1 Sam. 15:2–3). Pagan religion persisted. Later in Judah, Ahaz sacrificed his son in fire (2 Kings 16:3). Isaiah condemned the sacrifice of children and adopting stone idols (Isa. 57:5–6). Ezekiel chastised the Israelites for sacrificing their children as food for idols (Ezek. 16:20-21). Jeremiah, prophesying from Judah, reported that children were sacrificed to Baal and Molech (Jer. 7:31; 19:5; 32:37). Jeremiah and Ezekiel cited these pagan practices as the reason Judah was thrown into captivity in Babylon.[34]

Interestingly, there were a few exceptions to Canaanite paganism. Rahab believed in God and was spared (Josh. 6:25). Moses's father-in-law, Jethro the Midianite, became a follower of Yahweh (Exod. 18:11). During the period of the judges, Ruth, the Moabite, married Boaz, who was the grandfather of David (Ruth 4:10).

Conclusion

The goal of mass removal of the inhabitants of the Promised Land was not just a ruthless genocide. Rather, God knew the Israelites were prone to apostacy when exposed to paganistic influences. He therefore commanded the Israelites to purge the culture to separate themselves from temptation. Their failure to do so eventuated in the foretold consequences of conflict and apostacy, eventuating in the destruction of the northern and southern kingdoms.

6

How Was the New Testament Assembled?

The New Testament was assembled over nearly four hundred years. Harry Y. Gamble, associate professor of religious studies, has chronicled New Testament history in his book, *The New Testament Canon: Its Making and Meaning.*[35]

The following is a summary of salient points from Professor Gamble's book.

Terminology

"The English word 'canon' is a transliteration of the Greek *kanon* … meaning an authoritative collection of writings."[36] "The word 'canon' did not begin to be applied to Christian writings until the mid- fourth century when it appeared in the Decrees of the Council of Nicaea by Athanasious, bishop of Alexandria, soon after 350 [AD]."[37]

When did the canon become *scripture*, a term designating religious authority? It was a gradual acceptance of frequent usage.

The term *New Testament* is a latinized rendering of the Greek "new covenant" (*kaine diatheke*). The "new covenant" of Christianity refers to God making a new covenant with Israel (Jer. 31:31). It appears to have been Clement of Alexandria (ca. 180–200) who first referred to the authoritative scriptures as "covenant," and Origen, his successor, who formalized the writings into the so-called old covenant and new covenant.[38] It was apparently Tertullian of Carthage who translated the Greek *diatheke* as *testamentum*, with the New Testament called *novum testamentum*. Gamble points out, "The ruling idea is no longer that these are the scriptures that pertain to the covenant but rather that these scriptures constitute God's testament—that is, the final and authoritative statement of the divine will, on the order of the 'last will and testament' of a human person."[39]

Assembly of Documents

Since the church left no definite record on how the New Testament canon was assembled, Gamble identifies three types of useful evidence:[40]

1. Documents by Christian writers of the second through fifth centuries
2. Explicit discussions and judgements, either by individuals or by ecclesiastical councils, about documents whose authority is either accepted or rejected
3. Ancient manuscripts, mostly form the fourth century and later

The Gospels (Matthew, Mark, Luke) did not attain clear prominence until the late second century. In fact, the word *gospel* referred to the "good news," a theological term rather than a document, hence the Gospel of Mark and so on. "Thus, there are not, strictly speaking, four Gospels but a fourfold gospel."[41]

The first evidence of knowledge and use of the group of the three Gospels (the Gospel of John was not yet included) was by Justin Martyr, who taught in Rome between 150 and 165.[42] Justin viewed the Gospels as historical records, not inspired scripture.[43] The first evidence of the four Gospels collection, with assertion of their exclusive authority, was by Irenaeus, bishop of Lyons, Gaul, in 180.

The Acts of the Apostles, although composed as a companion piece to the Gospel of Luke, had a separate history from Luke and did not come into any broad currency until later. Justin Martyr, near the midsecond century, is the first writer to show any knowledge of Acts.[44]

Many of the early letters of Paul likely were lost. The first solid evidence of an extensive collection is provided by Marcion near the middle of the second century. The collection included Galatians, 1 and 2 Corinthians, Romans, 1 and 2 Thessalonians, Ephesians, Colossians, Philippians, and Philemon.[45] The letters to Timothy and Titus were accepted later.

"The so-called 'catholic epistles' (James, 1 and 2 Peter, 1, 2, and 3 John, and Jude) were little used in the second century. Only 1 Peter had much currency."[46]

Hebrews was not accepted by the church until the late fourth century.[47]

Even though written about 96, there is no clear use of Revelation in the first half of the second century.[48]

The final resolution of what we would identify as the New Testament began to take shape at the Council of Laodicea in AD 363. Twenty-six of the books were included, with the exception of Revelation. Athenasius, bishop of Alexandria, was the first to authoritatively define the full twenty-seven books of the New Testament in AD 367. Finally, at the Council of Hippo (AD 393) and the Council of Carthage (AD 397), all twenty-seven books of the Western New Testament were codified into the canon.[49]

Criteria for Inclusion

One of the interesting elements of canon assembly was the criteria used for acceptance and inclusion. These included the following:[50]

1. Apostolicity: written by an apostle or someone with close contact with an apostle
2. Catholicity: recognized as authoritative and used by the church
3. Orthodoxy: agreement with the faith of the church
4. Traditional usage: commonly used in church services

Surprisingly, inspiration was not a criterion for inclusion. Gamble explains, "The reason for this was simply the conviction that the church as a whole was inspired by the Spirit, so that the concept of inspiration was very much broader that the concept of scripture and offered no leverage on the question of the authority of various writings. ... The NT writings did not become canonical because they were inspired; rather they were judged to be inspired because they had previously commended themselves to the church for other, more particular, and practical reasons."[51]

Recorded as Codices

Gamble summarizes the effect of technical recording on the assembly of the canon:[52]

> Virtually from the beginning, Christianity made use of the codex (leaf book) rather than the roll (or scroll). But the codex was in the first century something of an innovation and not yet well developed, so that its capacity was small and long remained limited. It was not until the fourth century that the technology of bookmaking produced codices capable of containing the whole of the Christian scriptures. It is probably not a mere coincidence, therefore, that the NT acquired a relatively fixed content only when codices became large enough to permit these various writings to be transcribed into a single book.

7

What Is Lower Criticism of the Bible?

Biblical criticism is a broad term that includes studying the Bible as historical literature unrelated to theological considerations. There are two major types of biblical criticism. Lower criticism is the study of the transmission and preservation of the writings. Higher criticism is the study of the origination of the writings—sources, authorship, and historical accuracy.

In this section, we will consider *lower criticism* of the New Testament.

History of Transmission

To date, there are 5,725 known Greek manuscripts of the New Testament present in variable forms of completeness.[53] While none of the original writings—known as the autographs—have been preserved, copies date back to the second century in a few cases. While Jesus, as well as some of the early Christians, likely also spoke Aramaic (the language of the common people), the earliest New Testament manuscripts are in Greek (the language of the educated).

Peter van Minnen charts the most significant extant manuscripts from the first five centuries:[54]

> Numbers preceded by a P refer to papyri, the letters refer to parchment manuscripts. The manuscripts Sin. (Sinaiticus), A (Alexandrinus) and B (Vaticanus) are almost complete parchment manuscripts.

Ca AD	**200**	**250**	**300**	**350**	**450**
Matthew		P45	B	Sin	A
Mark		P45	B	Sin	A
Luke		P4, P45, P75	B	Sin	A
John	P66	P45, P75	B	Sin	A
Acts			B	Sin	A
Romans-Hebrews	P46		B	Sin	A
James-Jude			B	Sin	A
Apocalypse		P47	P72,B	Sin	A

As you can see, from the fourth century onward, the material base for establishing the text of the Greek New Testament is very good indeed.

It must be remembered that in first-century Palestine, only about 10 percent of the population could read, and even fewer could write. So most transcription was done through dictation to an amanuensis (scribe). The scribe was given some degree of leeway in grammar and style. Enns describes this process as "historiography," which he defines as "not the mere statement of facts but the shaping of these facts for a particular purpose. To put it another way, historiography is an attempt to relay to someone the significance of history."[55] After completion, the actual author would proofread the text, commonly add an introductory salutation, and often add a terminal benediction associated with his signature. Mounce concludes, "Paul used Tertius to write Romans (16:22) and Peter may have used Silas (also named Silvanus) the write

1 Peter (1 Pet 5:12). I am also convinced that Paul used Luke to write 1 Timothy, since Luke was a physician."[56]

Given the intense labor necessary for reproducing copies, few existed in the late first and early second centuries, and most of those were in the hands of the church or the very wealthy.

The first writings were on papyrus scroll, but these scrolls were then supplanted by leaf books, called codices, in the second century. Papyrus was then supplanted by parchment, which could be written upon both sides. The two oldest parchment manuscripts that have survived to modern times are Codex Vaticanus and Codex Sinaiticus.[57]

With the official sanction of Christianity as the state religion of the Roman Empire by Constantine in the fourth century, commercial reproduction began. Scribes would sit in a workroom of *scriptorias* and write copies, listening to the reading by a lector. This method allowed multiple copies to be produced simultaneously but also was more prone to transcription errors.[58]

A brief history of the transmission of the New Testament can be summarized:

By the end of the first century AD, all the Greek manuscripts comprising the New Testament had been completed. However, it was not until AD 367 that the full twenty-seven books of the modern New Testament were defined by Athenasius, bishop of Alexandria.

When Constantine certified Christianity as the official religion of the Roman Empire in AD 315, with Latin as the language of the Roman Empire, Jerome was commissioned to translate the Hebrew (Septuagint) and New Testament (Greek) into the Latin Vulgate in AD 382. Due to the dominance of the Catholic Church controlling dissemination of the scriptures, the Vulgate was the dominant translation for over one thousand years of the Dark Ages. During this era, the language of ancient Greece was nearly extinguished, such that little progress in reviewing the ancient Greek scriptures occurred.

With the onset of the Renaissance period (1300–1600), several events coalesced to advance scriptural knowledge. Scholars returned to correct the Latin Vulgate with the original Greek.

John Wycliffe translated the Vulgate into middle English in 1384. The invention of the printing press, by Gutenberg in 1455, facilitated mass production of the Bible. Martin Luther started the Protestant Reformation in 1517, which released the stranglehold of the Roman Catholic Church on accessing the Bible.

Erasmus, a Dutch scholar, translated the Latin Vulgate into Greek in 1516. Erasmus reviewed available twelfth-century Greek manuscripts to edit the Vulgate into the *Novum Instrumentum.* While hastily produced, and with some typographical errors, this revolutionary volume was used by Luther and Tyndale for their German (1522) and English translations (1526) respectively.[59] Erasmus revised his text through five editions, culminating in the 1535. Later modifications of Erasmus's Greek New Testament by Stephanus and by Beza led to the "Textus Receptus," or the "standard text" in 1633.[60]

The most prominent English translation of the Bible was the Geneva Bible, published in 1557. Feeling the need to construct a new English language Bible free of "corruption," James 1 of England convened the largest assembly of translators since the construction of the Septuagint. Forty-seven translators in 1604. In 1611, the King James Version of the Bible was published.[61]

The King James Version remained dominant until publication of the English Revised Version in 1885. This was followed by the American Standard Version (ASV) in 1901, the New American Standard Version (NASB) in 1971, the New International Version (NIV) in 1973, the English Standard Version (ESV), and the New English Translation (NET) in 1996.[62]

Accuracy of Transmission

With the onset of the Enlightenment period of the eighteenth century, the formal discipline of biblical textural criticism arose. Johann Jakob

Griesbach laid the foundation for textural criticism with his fifteen canons.[63] It then expanded into the twenty-first century in seminaries and university religion departments across the world.

There apparently are about 300,000–400,000 variants among the manuscripts,[64] although only 1 percent are deemed substantive.[65] But it must be clarified that the figure does not mean there are that many variants in each modern translation; rather that is 300,000–400,000 variants among over 5,600 different manuscripts, which comprise over 2.5 million pages of texts.[66]

Modern translations have variably dealt with apparent variant verses. Variants are verses or phrases that appear in later manuscripts but are not found in earlier manuscripts. The following is a list of verses that are present in the older English translations (mainly the KJV) but began to be omitted with more modern versions, exhibited by the Revised Version (RV) of 1881 and the later versions, especially the NIV. These are presumed to have been added to the original text. Some have been deleted, some bracketed but left, and some are merely identified by footnotes. In many cases, variant verses are duplicated in other scriptures.

Examples of variants are listed below. A detailed explanation of each is provided by the reference:[67]

The sixteen most commonly omitted verses follow:

1. Matthew 17:21 (similar to Mark 9:29)
2. Matthew 18:11 (similar to Luke 19:10)
3. Matthew 23:14 (similar to Mark 12:40 and Luke 20:47)
4. Mark 7:16 (same as verses 4:9; 4:23)
5. Mark 9:44
6. Mark 9:46 (duplicates and repeated in 9:48 of main text)
7. Mark 11:26 (similar to Matt. 6:15)
8. Mark 15:28 (similar to Luke 23:37)

9. Luke 17:36 (similar to Matt. 24:40)
10. John 5:3–4
11. Acts 8:37
12. Acts 15:34
13. Acts 24:6–8
14. Acts 28:29
15. Romans 16:24
16. 1 John 5:7–8

Some other omitted verses follow:

1. Matthew 20:16(b) (present in Matt. 22:14)
2. Mark 6:11(b) (present in Matt. 10:15)
3. Luke 4:8(b) (same as Matt. 4:10, Matt. 16:23, and Mark 8:33)
4. Luke 9:55–56
5. Luke 23:17 (similar to Matt. 27:15 and Mark 15:6)
6. Acts 9:5–6
7. Acts 13:42
8. Acts 23:9(b) (also found in Acts 5:39)

Not omitted but boxed text follows:

1. Mark 16:9–20 (the long ending in Mark)
2. John 7:53–8:11 (the adulteress)

Versification differences (slight differences in wording) follow:

1. Romans 14 and 16
2. Corinthians 13:14
3. John 15
4. Revelation 12

Perhaps the most significant and most discussed omission is 1 John 5:7–8, the so-called *Johannine Comma*. This pericope is the most explicit definition of the three members of the Trinity. It apparently first appears in a fifth-century Confession of Faith.

Conclusion

So what is the significance of these translational variants? As the reader can see, almost all are either repeated elsewhere or are doctrinally insignificant.

The big question is, do minor transcription errors in the modern Bible translations discredit the central story of Jesus's incarnation, ministry, and resurrection?

Using World War II as an example, while mass mechanical printing better preserves manuscript integrity, historiography yields slightly different compositions of the events. But do those slightly different perspectives mean the war didn't happen? Of course not.

Likewise, the historiographic and edited variants within the modern Bible translations do not diminish the story basics.

8

What Is Higher Criticism of the Bible?

While critical evaluation of the accuracy and validity of the New Testament was present since the second century, the formal questioning of the historical accuracy of the New Testament surged forward with the mass publication of the text in Greek in 1514. Interestingly, even though the Gutenberg movable type printing press was constructed in AD 1440, the difficulty and expense of developing Greek characters took another sixty years before the first New Testament could be widely produced.[68]

In the late eighteenth and early nineteenth centuries, as part of the Enlightenment movement, a group of biblical scholars in Tubingen, Germany, began to analyze the historical records of the Middle East in search of independent confirmation of the biblical events. This convalesced the new discipline of *higher criticism*.[69]

Higher criticism "generally takes a secular approach asking questions regarding the origin and composition of the text, including when and where it originated, how, why, by whom, for whom, and in what circumstances it was produced, what influences were at work in its production, and what original oral or written sources may have been used in its composition; and the message of the text as expressed in its language, including the meaning of the words as well as the way in which they are arranged in meaningful forms of expression. The principles of higher criticism are based on reason rather than revelation."[70]

The higher criticism curriculum focused on several areas: the authorship of the texts, sources of text material, the validity of miracles, and most especially, the historical Jesus—deity of and quotations from. The authorship of the texts is covered in other topics, so we will focus this study on miracles and the historical Jesus.

Authorship of the Texts

Among the issues of authorship of the New Testament, the two most studied follow: (1) who were the actual authors, and (2) what were their sources?

The questions of apostle literacy capacity and writing in the third person is answered by the common use of an amanuensis (scribe). A more complicated issue is the apparent duplication among the Gospel texts. This topic will be considered in detail in other chapters.

Sources of Text Material

The question of duplication of verses among the Gospels has been explained in several different ways. It is called the "synoptic problem." The currently dominant theory is that the first Gospel written—Mark—was used for the construction of Matthew and Luke. Other duplication within Matthew and Luke is explained by use of "quelle" ("Q"). The synoptic problem is discussed in more detail in another chapter.

The Historical Jesus

The identity of Jesus and His deity was debated within the church for four centuries, with various heresies proposed. But in the view of the church, the incarnate deity of Jesus was confirmed at the Council of Nicaea in AD 325, and the role of the members of the Trinity confirmed at the Council of Chalcedon in AD 451.

But the rise of naturalism in the Enlightenment period of the seventeenth and eighteenth centuries led to investigation of the historical Jesus. The most prominent early proponent of this investigation was Hermann Samuel Reimarius of Germany. He proposed that Jesus was an earthly apocalyptic Messiah who, having tried to establish his reign and failed, was finally executed.[71] This became what has come to be known as the first quest for the historical Jesus. The movement lasted until 1910, when Albert Schweitzer criticized the quest's pursuit of the apocalyptic Jesus.[72]

A second quest began in 1953 and lasted until 1988. "This quest focused largely on the teachings of Jesus as interpreted by existentialist philosophy."[73]

In 1985, a group of scholars was convened under the name the "Jesus Seminar." This has been termed the third quest.[74] The group uses colors to indicate reliability of the historicity of Jesus's statements: *red*—Jesus did say the passage; *pink*—probably said; *gray*—didn't say but contained Jesus's ideas; *black*—did not say, probably added later to text.[75]

The theme of all these quests was to show Jesus as an apocalyptic teacher who was purely human. A modern illustration of this concept is provided by Ehrman's *Jesus: Apocalyptic Prophet of the New Millennium*[76] and Meier's five-volume series, *A Marginal Jew*.[77]

Miracles

Of course, the overriding premise of evaluating the historical Jesus is that He was merely mortal. To justify that assumption, evidence of Jesus's deity must somehow be dismissed. The obvious illustration of Jesus's deity was the miracles, the greatest of which was the resurrection.

While deism had been present since antiquity, it had a resurgence in England and France in the seventeenth and eighteenth centuries. Deism then morphed into the naturalism of the Enlightenment period of the nineteenth century. Central to the philosophy was that God did not interfere with natural laws by supernatural events. Therefore, miracles did not actually exist. They were either myths, illusions, or hallucinations.

The most influential critic of miracles was the Scottish philosopher David Hume. Hume's main criteria for refuting miracles follows:[78]

> For first, there is not to be found, in all history, an miracle attested by a sufficient number of men, of such unquestioned good-sense, education, and learning, as to secure us against all delusion in themselves; of such undoubted integrity as to place them above all suspicion of an design to deceive others; of such credit and reputation in the eyes of mankind, as to have a great deal to lose in case of their being detected in any falsehood; and at the same time, attesting facts performed in such a public manner and in so celebrated a part of the world, as to render the detection unavoidable: All which circumstances are requisites to give us a full assurance in the testimony of men.

> Thirdly, it forms a strong assumption against all supernatural and miraculous relations, that they are observed chiefly to abound among ignorant and barbarous nations; or if a civilized people has ever given admission to any of them, that people will be found

> to have received them from ignorant and barbarous ancestors …

Hume's first assertion is countered by the fact that there are at lease fifteen documented post appearances of Jesus. Even if one were to dismiss appearances to the apostles, Paul documents Jesus's appearances to "more than 500 brethren at one time, most of whom remain until now" (1 Cor. 15:6). Clearly Paul was indicating that many of the five hundred were still alive to be interviewed. For Hume to argue that all these witnesses were not of "unquestioned good sense, education, and learning" and were among the "ignorant and barbarous" displays an arrogance that disqualifies serious consideration.

Hermann Samuel Reimarus argued that the disciples had hoaxed the resurrection by stealing the body. Heinrich Paulus argued that the disciples had been mistaken—that Jesus only appeared to be dead. David Friedrich Strauss argued that the miraculous events were myths that didn't happen, or they were hallucinations.[79] These theories have each been thoroughly discredited by Haberman,[80] Craig,[81] and Ross (Morison).[82]

Finally, it seems patently obvious that a God who could have created the universe and the natural laws would be able to abrogate those laws at His will.

Conclusion

The academic exercise of determining the sources of text information—other Gospels, the Sayings Gospel "Q" or the "M" source—is a legitimate endeavor.

However, the investigation of the historical Jesus is a thinly veiled effort to refute the deity of Jesus. Further, in doing so, the movement challenges the existence of God. The deism theology of a God creator, who did not interact with the universe after initial creation, gradually morphed into naturalism, in which laws of nature were inviolate. Inviolate laws of nature therefore precluded miracles. Finally, the Enlightenment movement of rationalism and existentialism concluded that these laws of nature were eternally preexistent. Following that thought conclusion, these laws of nature were capable of self-creation of the universe—a creator God is unnecessary. Atheism is the ultimate intellectual goal.

9

What Happened to Trust in the Bible?

To understand the current trend to distrust the fallibility of the Bible, you must look back into the history of western civilization and the church.

After the Crucifixion of Jesus in approximately AD 30, Christianity spread throughout the Mediterranean. But the theology was unclear, and multiple heresies were proposed. After nearly a twenty-year hiatus, the first documents that would later constitute the New Testament canon were initiated by the apostle Paul from his missionary trips.

It was not until the midfifth century that the New Testament canon was finalized. At that time, the Catholic Church controlled both the documents as well as the interpretation. This was because reproduction of the loose-leaf copies (codices) was by hand, which made limited copies available. Furthermore, since very few common people could read or write, interpretation was controlled by the educated priests.

After the fall of Rome in AD 476, not much happened for the next one thousand years of the Middle Ages. Pandemics, regional wars, and the Muslim invasions of Europe prevailed. The Roman Empire no longer controlled territorial authority, but it did control Christian theology. The church also controlled understood science.

From the fourteenth through the seventeenth centuries, there was an awakening in philosophy, literature, art, and science—the period known as the Renaissance. Part of this movement was the birth of humanism in fourteenth-century Italy. The concept was that God was no longer in charge—man was the center of his own universe.[83]

The invention of the Gutenberg printing press in 1450, associated with the new literacy of the Renaissance, allowed access of information to reach the masses. Widespread access to the printed Bible led to resentment of the control of the Catholic Church for biblical interpretation as well as charging money. This no doubt led to Martin Luther stimulating the Protestant Reformation.

This movement of intellectual independence led to the Enlightenment period of the late seventeenth and early eighteenth centuries. It was characterized by the philosophy of naturalism. Naturalism is the philosophy that all of science can be explained through the action of natural laws of nature. The key figures in this tumultuous period were William Paley, Benedict Spinoza, David Hume, Charles Darwin, and Sir Isaac Newton.

From a scientific standpoint, Sir Isaac Newton's 1687 formulation, the three laws motion, fit with the naturalism philosophy that the universe functions autonomously without the need for divine participation. Charles Darwin's 1859 biologic evolutionary theories in *Origin of the Species* gave an additional naturalist mechanism.

From a theological viewpoint, the Enlightenment period hatched the theology of deism.

Popularized by Edward Herbert in England,[84] deism proposed that God created the universe with fixed laws of physics and biology, then withdrew to allow autonomous progression. Specifically, no supernatural intervention (miracles) is thought to occur. The theists, who believed in God's active participation in design and miracles, were represented by William Paley's *A View of the Evidences of Christianity* (1794). The deists, who deny active supernatural interventions (miracles), were represented by Benedict Spinoza's (1670) *Tractatus Theologico-Politicus* and David Hume's (1779) *Of Miracles.*

The deist movement spread from England and France to Germany. William Lane Craig summarizes:[85]

> The flood of Deist thought and literature that poured into eighteenth-century Germany from England and France wrought a crisis in German orthodox theology. That theology had been characterized by an extremely rigid doctrine of biblical inspiration and infallibility and by a devotional pietism. The critique of the Deists undermined the faith of many in the inerrancy of Scripture, but their piety would not allow them to join themselves to the Deist camp and reject Christianity. This group of scholars, generally, called Rationalists, therefore sought to resolve the crisis by forging a new way between orthodoxy and Deism; namely, they loosed the religious meaning of a text from the historicity of the events described therein.

Thus, the evolution from rejection of supernatural influence by Deism to Rationalist separation of Biblical revelation historicity from religious piety led to deterioration of allegiance to infallibility of the scriptures.

The philosophy of Biblical criticism was then imported to Harvard University and Andover Seminary in the early 1800's. It then spread to liberal seminaries such as Princeton Theological Seminary in the 20th century.

Biblical Criticism basically entails two categories of investigation. *Lower Criticism* focuses on preservation or modification of existing manuscripts. *Higher Criticism*, on the other hand, focuses on the sources and influences in preparation of the original writings.

Interestingly, the Rationalist movement not only led to resistance of theological influence, but at the same time gave rise to the concept of socialism as a means of ideal government. Following the influence of John Locke, in the 17th century, Marxism as a socialist form of government was formalized in the 19th century in Germany.

Conclusion

From the time of the Crucifixion until the fall of the Roman Empire in AD 476, Christianity was unchallenged in the western world. Not much is known about religious acceptance during the next one thousand years of the Dark Ages. Beginning with the renaissance of the fourteenth to seventeenth centuries, the philosophy of humanism focused on the independence of the individual with less dependence on God. The Enlightenment period of the seventeenth and eighteenth centuries replaced God with science—all actions could be explained by natural laws (naturalism); no divine intervention was needed. Naturalism led to deism (God was passive) and on to rationalism (biblical accounts viewed through a historical lens) in the nineteenth century. The final evolution away from godly influence led to socialism (Marxism) in the nineteenth and twentieth centuries. The outcome was the system of lower and higher criticism of the Bible as purely a text.

10

The Abiathar Confusion: Was Mark Mistaken?

In Mark 2:23–27, the Pharisees were condemning Jesus's disciples for eating grain from the fields on the Sabbath. Jesus explains to the Pharisees that "the Sabbath was made for man; not man for the Sabbath" (Mark 2:27). However, in referencing the episode of David's men eating from the consecrated temple bread, Jesus was reported as saying (Mark 2:26 NIV),

> In the days of Abiathar the high priest, he entered the house of God and ate the consecrated bread, which is lawful only for priests to eat. And he also gave some to his companions.

> How he entered the house of God In the days of Abiathar the high priest, and ate the consecrated bread, which is not lawful for anyone to eat except the priests, and he also gave it to those who were with him? (NASB 1995)

Judea (the location of Bethlehem and Jerusalem) due to the presence of Herod's son Archelaus, who was reigning. They went northward to settle around Galilee at Nazareth. Galilee was in Samaria, north of Judea.

Luke explicitly states the angel Gabriel visited Mary at her home of Nazareth to inform her of her impending immaculate pregnancy. So why did the couple go to Bethlehem to pay taxes? Luke answers that question, that Joseph was from the house of David and likely had property there. David, the youngest son of Jesse, was born and raised in Bethlehem (1 Sam. 16).

Was there really a census and taxation necessitating the Bethlehem visit?

Critics like Bart Ehrman argue that there is not historical evidence of a census with taxation and that Quirinius was not governor of Syria until ten years after King Herod's death.[142]

As to the taxation question, Robert Hunt reports a different history.[143] Beginning with Pompey the Great (63 BC), Rome established patronage with its subject nations—financial "tribute," as instituted in Judea. King Herod, to maintain the favor of the Roman Emperor Cesar Augustus, enforced the taxation. Even women above the age of twelve were required to pay a poll tax.[144] The presence of a taxation system is further evidenced by the occupation of Matthew (Levi).

Regarding the census, Matthew 2:2 states, "This was the first census taken while Quirinius was governor of Syria." This suggests that there was a subsequent census under Quirinius. The NIV Study Bible notes indicate that Quirinius probably had two terms as governor of Syria. The first term was 6–4 BC, and the second was AD 6–9. A census was used for military conscription. This topic is covered more extensively in chapter 18.

The "Star in the East"

Also, Matthew's account is the only one to mention the "star in the east" (Matt. 2:2, 9–10). The star is first mentioned in Matthew 2:2, where the magi from the east apparently saw the star and followed it to Jerusalem. It is suggested that the magi were astrologers, likely from Babylon, where Daniel had prophesied the coming of a Jewish Messiah (Dan. 9:25–26).[145] The magi were also likely to be aware of the prophecy of the Messiah to be born in Bethlehem (Mic. 5:2).

The timing and duration of the star is unclear. On the one hand, the magi had traveled approximately 538 miles, from Babylon to Jerusalem.[146] At the rate of twenty-five miles per day,[147] it would have taken the magi at least three weeks to make the journey to Jerusalem. So apparently, the star was present and visible for at least that duration of time.

The biblical references in Matthew are unclear over whether the star persisted between the magi's journey to Jerusalem (Matt. 2:2), then led them on their journey to Bethlehem (Matt. 2:9). The fact that Herod had to ask when the star had originally appeared suggests that it did not persist. It also seems likely that if the star was still present when Herod interrogated the magi, then Herod would not have needed the magi to go find the Jesus child. Herod could have simply sent his soldiers to follow the star to find the child.

Then, in Matthew 2:9–10, the star leads the Magi to the location of the Jesus child. It appears that the star reappears to lead the magi, but the interval between when the magi arrived in Jerusalem at Herod's court and when they set out again to find the Jesus child appears to be short. So did the star persist for at least three weeks, then disappear for several days, then reappear?

The topic of the star of Bethlehem is covered in detail in chapter 18.

Conclusion

While Matthew (writing to a Jewish audience) and Luke (writing to a Gentile audience) emphasize different details of Jesus's birth story, the two accounts are not incompatible.

17

Was Jesus Born at Christmas?

Significant controversy surrounds the actual date of Jesus's birth. The only chronological reference to the time of year occurs in Luke. Two references give clues:

> (This was the first census that took place while Quirinius was governor of Syria.) (Luke 2:2)

> And there were shepherds living out in the fields nearby, keeping watch over their flocks at night. (Luke 2:8)

There are three questions to be answered:

1. What year was Jesus born?
2. What time of year was Jesus born?
3. Why do we celebrate Christmas Day on December 25?

There are several reference points to be considered:

1. The year of Herod's death (Matt. 2:19)
2. Shepherds out in the fields (Luke 2:8)
3. The date and cause of the star (Matt. 2:2)
4. The time of the census ordered by Quirinius (Luke 2:2)
5. The date of Abijah's temple service (Luke 1:5)
6. The Feast of the Tabernacles (John 1:14)

What Year Was Jesus Born?

The Gospels record Jesus's birth as occurring during the reign of Herod the Great. It is generally accepted that Herod died just after Nissan 1, two weeks before Passover, in the spring of 4 BC, as is exhaustedly researched by Lanser.[148, 149] The date of Herod's death establishes a historical anchor date, since Jesus was born sometime in the two years before the death of Herod.

Interestingly, there is a difference in terminology between Luke's account and that of Matthew. Luke describes the angels seeing the baby Jesus lying in a manger (Luke 2:16). The account of the visit of the magi in Matthew describes Jesus as a "child" (Matt. 2:9, 11, 13, 14), which might suggest that Jesus was older. This age difference is further suggested by the fact that when Herod finally discovered that the wise men had not returned to identify the location of Jesus, he ordered all male children aged two and under around Bethlehem to be killed (Matt. 2:16). Of course, Mary and Joseph had taken Jesus to safety in Egypt, where they stayed until Herod's death. This interval suggests that it was two years between Jesus's birth and the death of Herod.

But the exact year of Jesus's birth must be established by other criteria.

What Time of Year Was Jesus Born?

The actual time of year of Jesus's birth has been the subject of intense debate for centuries. A variety of references give clues.

Shepherds out in the Fields

The issue regarding the shepherds is the weather in the Bethlehem. Luke 2:8 makes the point that shepherds were out in the fields at night.

Bethlehem is in the Judean highlands at 2560 feet above sea level.[150] During winter months, known as the Jewish month of Chislev (corresponding to November/December), the weather in the land of Israel is typically cold and rainy (Ezra 10:9,13; Jer. 36:32).[151, 152] Temperatures dip into the high thirties (Fahrenheit) at night, but more commonly are in the mid to low forties.[153]

Some argue that the fall, rainy season was when the grass grew best in the highlands of Bethlehem, and thus, the flocks could have been out in December.[154]

Kay makes a detailed argument that Jesus's birth would not have been in December:[155]

> Israeli meteorologists tracked December weather patterns for many years and concluded that the climate in Israel has been essentially constant for at least the last 2,000 years. *The Interpreter's Dictionary of the Bible* states that, "broadly speaking, weather phenomena and climatic conditions as pictured in the Bible correspond with conditions as observed today."
>
> The temperature in Bethlehem in December averages around 44 degrees Fahrenheit (7 degrees Celsius) but can drop to well below freezing, especially at night. Describing the weather there, Sara Ruhin, chief of

the Israeli weather service, noted in a 1990 press release that the area has three months of frost: December with 29 F. [minus 1.6 C.]; January with 30 F. [minus 1.1 C.] and February with 32 F. [0 C.].

Snow is common for two or three days in Jerusalem and nearby Bethlehem in December and January. These were the winter months of increased precipitation in Messiah's time, when the roads became practically unusable, and people stayed mostly indoors.

This is important evidence to disprove a December date for Messiah's birth. Note that, at the time of Messiah's birth, the shepherds tended their flocks in the fields at night. *"Now there were in the same country shepherds living out in the fields,"* wrote one Gospel writer, *"keeping watch over their flock by night"* (Luke 2:8). A common practice of shepherds was keeping their flocks in the field from April to October, but in the cold and rainy winter months they took their flocks back home and sheltered them.

It thus seems most likely that the shepherds being out in the fields indicates either fall or spring, but not the December winter season.

The Date and Cause of the Star of Bethlehem

This fact is a discussion of its own, which will be considered separately in chapter 18.

Lansing concludes that the "star" places the date in the spring, March 20, 6 BC (Julian), which is March 18 (Gregorian).[156]

The Time of the Census

The census reference in Luke 2:2 has created controversy for centuries.

Amazingly, the number of Roman censes and the dates are not historically established.

Lanser's extensive research[157] is summarized as follows: The Romans carried out censes of their subject states at various times for various reasons. Lansing summarizes: In 11 BC, Caesar Augustus decreed that he and the Roman Senate were to register themselves. Then in 8 BC, Caesar decreed a census for all citizens under Roman control. Finally, in 6 BC, Caesar directed Quirinius to carry out another census for the purposes of taxation—a census that created great unrest in Judea. The reference from Luke 2:2 is translated in most Bibles (NIV, NASB) as "while Quirinius was governor of Syria." As Lanser points out, the actual Greek word is <u>*hēgemoneuontos*</u> (ἡγεμονεύοντος), which is strictly translated "was governing."[158] This is significant because Quirinius apparently ruled in Judea different times in different capacities. Lanser references the historian Tertullian's report that Jesus was born while Saturninus was governor of Syria (9–6 BC). Apparently near the end of Saturninus's rule as governor, Quirinius was directed by Caesar to carry out the census of 6 BC. Quirinius was thus "governing" under the orders of Caesar, even though he was not the actual governor. Lansing explains, "There were two distinct positions of authority in Syria at this time, the imperial representative—a procurator, such as Pontius Pilate was—and a governor proper. Quirinius held both positions at different times."

The editors of the NIV Bible apparently agree with Lanser's conclusion. The footnote to Luke 2.2 in the NIV Bible[159] reads, "Quirinius. This official was possibly in office for two terms, first in 6–4 BC and then AD 6–9. A census is associated with each term. This is the first; Acts 5:37 refers to the second.

Evangelical New Testament scholar Daniel Wallace disagrees with the accuracy of the historical reference to Quirinius's census in Luke 2:2. He argues,[160]

> The text casts serious doubt on Luke's accuracy for two reasons: (1) the earliest known Roman census in Palestine was taken in AD 6-7, and (2) there is little, if any, evidence that Quirinius was governor of Syria before Herod's death in 4 BC. Considering this, many scholars believe that Luke was thinking about the census in AD 6–7, when Quirinius was governor of Syria.
>
> So how do we reconcile the historical confusion over the timing of the census of Quirinius? These historical opinions conflict, but some are suggestive of 6 BC being the census dating the year of Jesus's birth. Confirmation of the exact year will require still additional criteria.
>
> The main value of the census reference, then, may be that it provides a clue to the time of year of Jesus's birth. Since travel was difficult during the cold, rainy, winter months, any census was likely in either the spring or fall of the year. The actual year of Jesus's birth can be established by other criteria.

The Date of Abijah's Temple Service

The episode of the angel's visit to Zacharias announcing the pregnancy of Elizabeth is temporally referenced to Zacharias's service in the temple as part of his responsibility as a priest of the division of Abijah (Luke 1:5, 8–9). After exhaustive historical research, Lanser concludes that Zacharias's service was November 29 to December 6, and John was conceived in early January of 7 BC. Based upon the timing of Mary's visit when Elizabeth was six months' pregnant, he calculates that Mary became pregnant in June, 7 BC. That leads him to date Jesus's birth as Nissan 1, which was March 20, 6 BC.[161]

Kay calculates it differently, pointing out that Zacharias's service would be twice a year. Nine months after one of the terms when John the Baptist was born would have been either March or September. Kay arbitrarily chooses the first term (Sivan 12–18), which would have been May–June, resulting in John the Baptist being born at Passover (March). By these calculations, Jesus would have been conceived at the time of Hanukkah (December), with his birth September 29.[162]

While both calculations would be compatible with a March birth, they are not conclusive.

The Feast of the Tabernacles

Kay finds a clue to Jesus's birth in John 1:14: "And the Word became flesh and *dwelt* (eskēnōsen [ἐσκήνωσεν]) among us."

Kay quotes Bacchiocchi as commenting, "The Greek verb skenoo used by John means "to pitch tent, encamp, tabernacle, dwell in a tent." The allusion is clearly to the Feast of Tabernacles when the people dwelt in temporary booths. This suggests an association between the autumn Feast of Tabernacles and the time of Jesus's birth.

Lanser, however, counters that Joseph would have had to be in Jerusalem to celebrate the Feast of the Tabernacles, precluding him being in Bethlehem at the time of Jesus's birth.

Why Do We Celebrate Christmas Day on December 25?

If the actual date of Jesus's birth was either September 29 or March 20, why do we celebrate it on December 25?

The history of adopting December 25 is reviewed by Kay:[163]

In the first 200 years of Christian history, no mention is made of the calendar date of Yeshua's birth. Not until the year 336 do we find the first mention of a celebration of His birth.

Why this omission? In the case of the Church fathers, the reason is that, during the three centuries after Messiah's life on earth, the event considered most worthy of commemoration was the date of His death. In comparison, the date of His birth was considered insignificant. As the *Encyclopedia Americana* explains,

"Christmas ... was, according to many authorities, not celebrated in the first centuries of the Christian church, as the Christian usage in general was to celebrate the death of remarkable persons rather than their birth ..." (1944 edition, "Christmas").

Speculation on the proper date began in the 3rd and 4th centuries, when the idea of fixing Messiah's birthday started. Quite a controversy arose among Church leaders. Some were opposed to such a celebration. Origen (185–254) strongly recommended against such an innovation. "In the Scriptures, no one is recorded to have kept a feast or held a great banquet on his birthday. It is only sinners who make great rejoicings over the day in which they were born into this world" (*Catholic Encyclopedia*, 1908 edition, Vol. 3, p. 724, "Natal Day").

During this time eight specific dates during six different months were proposed by various groups. December 25, although one of the last dates to be proposed, was the one finally accepted by the leadership of the Western church.

A summary of the debate on the dates of Messiah's birth appears in *The Oxford Dictionary of the Christian*

Church: "Though speculation as to the time of year of Messiah's birth dates from the early 3rd century, Clement of Alexandria suggesting the 20th of May, the celebration of the anniversary does not appear to have been general till the later 4th century. The earliest mention of the observance on Dec. 25th is in the Philocalian Calendar, representing Roman practice of the year 336. This date was probably chosen to oppose the feast of the Natalis Solis Invicti [nativity of the unconquerable sun] by the celebration of the birth of the 'Sun of Righteousness' and its observance in the West, seems to have spread from Rome. (1983 edition, Oxford University Press, New York, 1983, p. 280, "Christmas").

In Rome December 25 was made popular by Pope Liberius in 354 and became the rule in the West in 435 when the first "Christ mass" was officiated by Pope Sixtus III. This coincided with the date of a celebration by the Romans to their primary god, the Sun, and to Mithras, a popular Persian sun god supposedly born on the same day. The Roman Catholic writer Mario Righetti candidly admits that "to facilitate the acceptance of the faith by the pagan masses, the Church of Rome found it convenient to institute the 25th of December as the feast of the birth of Messiah to divert them from the pagan feast, celebrated on the same day in honor of the 'Invincible Sun' Mithras, the conqueror of darkness" (Manual of Liturgical History, 1955, Vol. 2, p. 67).

Protestant historian Henry Chadwick sums up the controversy:

"Moreover, early in the fourth century there begins in the West (where first and by whom is not known) the celebration of December 25th, the birthday of the

Sun-god at the winter solstice, as the date for the nativity of Messiah. How easy it was for Christianity and solar religion to become entangled at the popular level is strikingly illustrated by a mid-fifth century sermon of Pope Leo the Great, rebuking his over-cautious flock for paying reverence to the Sun on the steps of St. Peter's before turning their back on it to worship inside the westward-facing basilica" (*The Early Church,* Penguin Books, London, 1967, p. 126).

The *Encyclopedia Americana* makes this clear: "In the fifth century, the Western Church ordered it [Messiah's birth] to be observed forever on the day of the old Roman feast of the birth of Sol [the sun god], as no certain knowledge of the day of Messiah's birth existed" (1944 edition, "Christmas").

Conclusion

We are left with two possible scenarios.

Glen Kay concludes the date is September 29, 5 BC,[164] the first day of the Feast of the Tabernacle, the date in large part chosen because of John 1:14, "And the Word became flesh and tabernacled among us, full of grace and truth; we have beheld his glory, as of the only Son from the Father," as well as calculation of Zechariah's date of service in the temple marking the date of Elizabeth's conception, which would have been May–June, resulting in John the Baptist being born at Passover (March). By these calculations, Jesus would have been conceived at the time of Hanukkah (December), with his birth September 29.

Rick Lanser concludes the date to be March 20, 6 BC (Julian), which is March 18 (Gregorian).[165] His conclusion is based upon dating Mary's visit to Elizabeth in late September, dating Abijah's division (Zechariah) term of service to be November 29–December 6, Jesus conceived on about June 7, 6 BC, and Jesus born on March 20, 5 BC.

While the issue is not settled, it seems that the cold, rainy season of December likely rules out December 25 based upon the shepherds being out with their sheep. The September 29 date remains a possibility, but the March 20, 6 BC, date is most likely. Not only from the shepherds and the dating of Zechariah's service in the Temple but also the coincidence with the meteor date theory of the Bethlehem star.

18

What Was the Christmas Star of Bethlehem?

The Gospel of Matthew references a star leading the magi:

> And asked, "Where is the one who has been born king of the Jews? We saw his star when it rose and have come to worship him." (Matt. 2:2)

> After they had heard the king, they went on their way, and the star they had seen when it rose went ahead of them until it stopped over the place where the child was. When they saw the star, they were overjoyed. (Matt. 2:9–10)

Who Were the Magi?

The suggestion that the magi were kings is probably erroneous.

These magi probably came to Babylonia to perform religious rituals for the Persians and Medes who stayed in that country as royal officials and soldiers. According to Herodotus (1.101), magi were one of six

Median tribes and formed the hereditary priestly clan. He adds that they occupied an influential position at the Median court as dream interpreters and soothsayers (1.107). An integral part of the activities of the magi was comprised of their ritual functions connected with astrology and magic (hence the Greek term *mageía* [μαγεία]).[166]

Given the fact that mechanical timepieces had not yet been discovered, the people of ancient times were very observant of the stars for navigation. In addition, the pagan religious association of nature with gods led to their interest in astrology. The magi were interpreters of the stars; in fact, astrology was developed in the third century BC in Hellenistic Mesopotamia. Astrology became the source of *divination*—"which is interpreting the influence of the stars and planets on earthly affairs and human destiny."[167]

From the fourth century BC onward, magi were increasingly associated with observation and the interpretation of the stars. In fact, Babylon became the center of ancient astronomy and astrology.

During the exile period, there was a strong Jewish community in Babylon. It is quite likely that the magi priests became familiar with Jewish prophecies anticipating a savior-king.[168]

So why didn't Herod and the Israelites notice the star? Molnar states, "The likely reason that no one around Herod understood the celestial event is that Chaldean astrology was not practiced among devout Jews. Further evidence that the Magi were referring to an astrological event rather than an astronomical one, is that Herod and his people did not know that a special star had existed."[169]

Characteristics of the Star

Humphreys lists three characteristics of the star:

1. It newly appeared
2. It travelled slowly through the sky against a star background
3. It stood over Bethlehem

The most theorized explanations for the star are: (1) a miraculous new star, (2) a conjunction of a star and planet, (3) a supernova, and (4) a comet.

A Miraculous New Star

The simplest explanation is to accept the literal text of Matthew 2:2, 9–10. There are eighty-three miracles recorded in the Old Testament and over eighty in the New Testament.[170] Of these, five involve celestial alterations of nature:

1. Creation of the planets and stars (Gen. 1:14–16)
2. Darkness over Egypt (Exod. 10:21)
3. The sun and moon stood still (Josh. 10:12–14)
4. Sun's shadow moves backward (2 Kings 20:9–11)
5. Midday darkness at Jesus's Crucifixion (Matt. 27:45; Luke 23:44)

No doubt the birth of the incarnate God-Christ was a celestial event, evidenced by the presence of angels (Luke 9:10–14). It would certainly have been within the power of the God who created the universe to manipulate His creation as He pleased.

Conjunction or Occultation of Stars and Planets

Humphreys reviews the possibility of a conjunction of Saturn and Jupiter as described by Kennedy and Pingree. (An astrological *conjunction* is when two or more objects appear to line up close together.) A conjunction of Jupiter and Saturn occurred in 2020. Such a conjunction is not rare, but it was the closest visible separation distance since 1623![171] Humphreys suggests that a triple conjunction of Saturn and Jupiter (with Mars) in the constellation of Pisces in 7 BC may have caused the magi to start their journey.

The astrological significance is that Pisces is associated with the Jewish people. Saturn was the star of Near Eastern deity, and Jupiter was the star of royalty. A close triple conjunction occurred in 7 BC, then a near conjunction occurred in Pisces again in 6 BC.[172]

The probable astrological significance of this event to the magi was that a divine king would be born in Israel. Such a massing occurs every eight hundred years (and very much more infrequently in Pisces), and it would have confirmed to the magi that the king to be born in Israel would be a mighty king.[173]

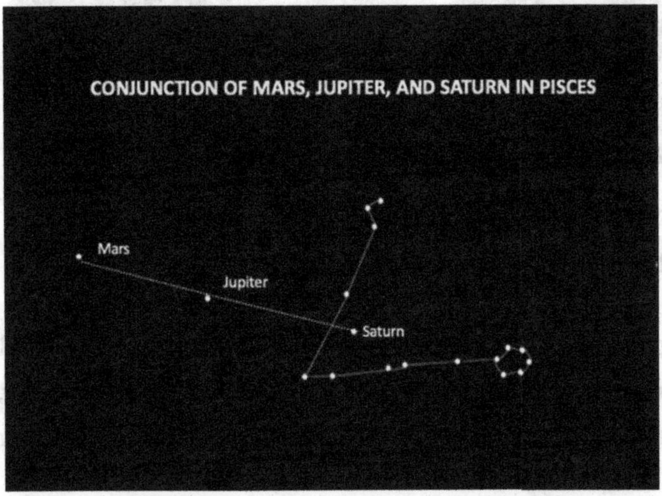

Molnar suggested the lunar occultation of Jupiter. (An *occultation* is when one object passes in front of another to obscure the former from visibility.) He reports that the zodiacal symbol of Judea was Aries. Therefore, the magi would have been watching Aries for the star. By his research, Molnar reports a lunar occultation of Jupiter to have occurred on March 20 and again on April 17 in the year 6 BC. The first occultation coincides with the birth of Christ; the second with the magi's visit to Herod.[174] Lanser agrees with Molnar's theory.[175] The documented timing of the first occultation on March 20, 6 BC, also coincides with Lanser's other research on the date of Jesus's birth. The lunar occultation of

Jupiter and the conjunction Saturn, Jupiter, and Mars appear to occur at the same time on April 17, 6 BC.[176]

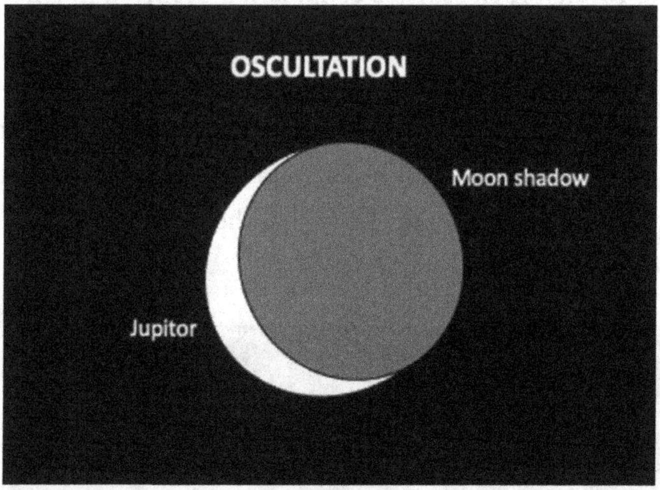

Recurring Nova

The suggestion of a recurrent nova has been fostered by Hugh Ross. Ross points out that the Greek word for star in Matthew is *aster*, which can indicate different celestial bodies—star, planet, comet, asteroid, or meteor.[177]

Ross dismissed the idea of a supernova, arguing that such a bright phenomenon would have been seen and recorded by others in the region—Egypt, Rome, Greece, and so on. Also, Ross interprets the Matthew account to indicate the star occurred at two different occasions. He proposed that recurrent eruption of a white dwarf star could have fulfilled the criteria.[178]

Comet

One of the main proponents of the comet theory is Colin Humphreys. He observes:

> The curious terminology in Matthew 2:9 is that the star "stood over" Bethlehem ... Phrases such as "stood over" and "hung over" appear to he uniquely applied in ancient literature to describe a comet, and I can find no record of such phrases being used to describe any other astronomical object.[179]

He also points out that comets move against the backdrop of stars and appear to move across the night sky because of the rotation of the earth. Finally, the tail of the comet could create the appearance of pointing toward a city.[180]

Humphreys notes the historical association of comets with new dynasties:[181]

> The identification of a comet with the star of Bethlehem goes back to Origen in the third century, and this is the earliest known theory for the star. Origen (Contra Celsum 1.58) stated "The star that was seen in the East we consider to be a new star ... partaking of the nature of those celestial bodies which appear at times such as comets ... If then the commencement of new dynasties or on the occasion of other important events there arises a comet ... why would it be a matter of wonder that the birth of Him who was to introduce a new doctrine ... a star should have risen?

The Chinese meticulously recorded the dates of major comets. There were records of comets in 12 BC and 4 BC, but these are outside the likely date of Jesus's birth. However, a comet was detected in 5 BC, which closely approximates the birth date. A sui-hsing (tailed comet) appeared in the Ch'ien niu (Capricornus) portion of the sky (the important area of five planets—Saturn, Jupiter, Mars, Venus, and Mercury) and persisted for seventy days. The seventy-day interval would allow the magi travel time of one to two months.[182]

The account of Matthew can be interpreted that the star appeared on two different occasions. Such could potentially be explained by being seen initially on its way to perihelion (the point in orbit closest to the sun) and again on exit.[183]

Humphreys believes that the combination of three astronomical events caused the magi to make their journey: (1) the triple conjunction of Saturn, Jupiter, and Mars in 7 BC; (2) the massing of the three planets in 6 BC; and (3) the appearance of the comet in Capricornus in 5 BC.[184]

The legend that the star guided them to Jerusalem is not required (and Matthew neither states nor implies this); it is suggested that the magi went to Jerusalem because their interpretation of the 7 BC conjunction and the 6 BC planetary massing was that a Messiah-king would be born in Israel, and the appearance of the 5 BC comet notified them the birth had happened.[185]

Conclusion

The presence of a new miraculous star is always a possibility that cannot be excluded. But while God chooses to violate His natural laws of physics, He also tends to use directed acts of nature to achieve His effect (rain, flood, fire, etc.). So the use of a natural phenomenon remains a possibility.

Of the theories of natural phenomena, the conclusions of Humphreys would seem to be the most feasible:

Astrology apparently developed during the intertestamental period (450 BC–1 AD) in Babylon. The Magi were Medes (Persians) priests who were interpreters of astrologic predictions. The Magi likely learned the Jewish Messianic prophecies from the Jews in captivity in Babylon. As the Magi watched the celestial movements, the formations of 7 BC and 6 BC alerted them to the upcoming birth of a king of Israel. The comet of 5 BC, documented by the Chinese, announced the birth of the king.

19

Why Was Herod Fearful of Jesus's Birth?

Herod, the king of the area of Judah, was so fearful of the birth of Jesus that he had all the male babies up to the age of two in the area of Bethlehem killed.

> Then when Herod saw that he had been tricked by the magi, he became very enraged, and sent and slew all the male children who were in Bethlehem and all its vicinity, from two years old and under, according to the time which he had determined from the magi. (Matt. 2:16 NASB)

So why was Herod so afraid of baby Jesus, who had not even reached adulthood to start his ministry?

There may have been two reasons.

Jewish Expectation of a Messianic King

Herod's grandmother was an Edomite Jewess, and his ancestors had converted to Judaism. Herod, therefore, was raised as a Jew. As such, he no doubt new of the prophecies of an expected Messiah who would restore the nation of Israel as king.

> I will raise up a prophet from among their countrymen like you, and I will put My words in his mouth, and he shall speak to them all that I command him. (Deut. 18:18 NASB)

> "When your days are complete and you lie down with your fathers, I will raise up your descendant after you, who will come forth from you, and I will establish his kingdom. He shall build a house for My name, and I will establish the throne of his kingdom forever. I will be a father to him and he will be a son to Me; when he commits iniquity, I will correct him with the rod of men and the strokes of the sons of men, but My lovingkindness shall not depart from him, as I took it away from Saul, whom I removed from before you. Your house and your kingdom shall endure before Me forever; your throne shall be established forever." (2 Sam. 7:12–16 NASB)

> So you are to know and discern *that* from the issuing of a decree to restore and rebuild Jerusalem until Messiah the Prince *there will be* seven weeks and sixty-two weeks. (Dan. 9:25 NASB)

> I kept looking in the night visions,
> And behold, with the clouds of heaven
> One like a Son of Man was coming,
> And He came up to the Ancient of Days
> And was presented before Him.
> And to Him was given dominion,

Glory and a kingdom,
That all the peoples, nations and men of every language
Might serve Him.
His dominion is an everlasting dominion
Which will not pass away;
And His kingdom is one
Which will not be destroyed. (Dan. 7:13–14 NASB)

"Behold, days are coming," declares the Lord, "when I will make a new covenant with the house of Israel and with the house of Judah." (Jer. 31:31 NASB)

"But as for you, Bethlehem Ephrathah,
Too little to be among the clans of Judah,
From you One will go forth for Me to be ruler in Israel.
His goings forth are from long ago,
From the days of eternity." (Mic. 5:2 NASB)

Political Vulnerability

Herod was not actually a Roman citizen, and his authority was achieved by virtue of serving the interests of the Roman rulers as governor of Galilee, then of Jerusalem, and finally tetrarch. In approximately 40 BC, Mark Antony convinced the Roman Senate to appoint Herod; he was appointed king of Judea.[186] To maintain his authority, Herod's responsibility was to collect taxes and to suppress Jewish rebellion against Roman rule. The latter was his biggest threat.

Having lived under foreign occupiers for seven hundred years, the Jews were a rebellious people.

The Maccabean Revolt occurred in 167–160 BC against the Seleucids. In the few years preceding Herod's death in 4 BC, Judas of Galilee led a resistance "fourth philosophy" movement. Along with Sadduc

(Zadok) the Pharisee, Judas formed the "zealots" in approximately 6 BC to protest the census, taxation, and Roman polytheism.[187] Josephus comments that "they have an inviolable attachment to liberty; and say that God is to be their only Ruler and Lord."[188] Apparently "extremists among them turned to terrorism and assassination, and became known as Sicarii (Greek *sikarioi*, "dagger men')."[189] While Judas himself was apparently killed, the zealot movement remained disruptive well into the first century AD.

Luke mentions their activity in the book of Acts:

> After him, Judas the Galilean appeared in the days of the census and led a band of people in revolt. He too was killed, and all his followers were scattered. (Acts 5:37)

The zealots were responsible for the Jewish revolt in AD 66, which culminated in the destruction of the Second Temple in AD 70.

Conclusion

It is therefore likely that Herod foresaw a Messianic king who would overthrow his Roman-friendly rule. And with the presence of the militant zealot activity, Herod may have wanted to eliminate the problem early.

But since Herod was raised in Judaism, why did he not look forward to the Messianic king who would restore the nation of Israel as a positive outcome, as did the other Jews?

Apparently, his political ambition outweighed his religious commitment.

20

Did Jesus Actually Claim to Be God?

There is no doubt that the thesis of the Gospel of John is to validate Jesus as the eternal Son of God. It is loaded with Jesus's self-references to his deity:

> If I told you earthly things and you do not believe, how will you believe if I tell you heavenly things? No one has ascended into heaven, but He who descended from heaven: the Son of Man. As Moses lifted up the serpent in the wilderness, even so must the Son of Man be lifted up; so that whoever believes will in Him have eternal life.
>
> For God so loved the world, that He gave His only begotten Son, that whoever believes in Him shall not perish, but have eternal life. For God did not send the Son into the world to judge the world, but that the world might be saved through Him. He who believes in Him is not judged; he who does not believe has been judged already, because he has not believed in the name of the only begotten Son of God. (John 3:12–18)

Therefore Jesus answered and was saying to them, "Truly, truly, I say to you, the Son can do nothing of Himself, unless it is something He sees the Father doing; for whatever the Father does, these things the Son also does in like manner. For the Father loves the Son, and shows Him all things that He Himself is doing; and the Father will show Him greater works than these, so that you will marvel. For just as the Father raises the dead and gives them life, even so the Son also gives life to whom He wishes. For not even the Father judges anyone, but He has given all judgment to the Son, so that all will honor the Son even as they honor the Father. He who does not honor the Son does not honor the Father who sent Him.

"Truly, truly, I say to you, he who hears My word, and believes Him who sent Me, has eternal life, and does not come into judgment, but has passed out of death into life." (John 5:19–24)

For just as the Father has life in Himself, even so He gave to the Son also to have life in Himself; and He gave Him authority to execute judgment, because He is the Son of Man. (John 5:26–27)

"But the testimony which I have is greater than the testimony of John; for the works which the Father has given Me to accomplish—the very works that I do—testify about Me, that the Father has sent Me." (John 5:36–37)

"For this is the will of My Father, that everyone who beholds the Son and believes in Him will have eternal life, and I Myself will raise him up on the last day." (John 6:40)

"I am He who testifies about Myself, and the Father who sent Me testifies about Me." So they were saying to Him, "Where is Your Father?" Jesus answered, "You know neither Me nor My Father; if you knew Me, you would know My Father also." (John 8:18–19)

And He was saying to them, "You are from below, I am from above; you are of this world, I am not of this world." (John 8:23)

So Jesus said, "When you lift up the Son of Man, then you will know that I am He, and I do nothing on My own initiative, but I speak these things as the Father taught Me. And He who sent Me is with Me; He has not left Me alone, for I always do the things that are pleasing to Him." (John 8:28–29)

Jesus heard that they had put him out, and finding him, He said, "Do you believe in the Son of Man?" He answered, "Who is He, Lord, that I may believe in Him?" (John 9:35–36)

"I and the Father are one." (John 10:30)

"If I do not do the works of My Father, do not believe Me; but if I do them, though you do not believe Me, believe the works, so that you may know and understand that the Father is in Me, and I in the Father." (John 10:37–38)

Jesus said to her, "I am the resurrection and the life; he who believes in Me will live even if he dies, and everyone who lives and believes in Me will never die. Do you believe this?" (John 11:25–26)

Jesus said to him, "I am the way, and the truth, and the life; no one comes to the Father but through Me. If you had known Me, you would have known My Father also; from now on you know Him, and have seen Him." (John 14:6–7)

Jesus said to him, "Have I been with you for so long a time, and yet you have not come to know Me, Philip? The one who has seen Me has seen the Father; how can you say, 'Show us the Father'?

"Do you not believe that I am in the Father, and the Father is in Me? The words that I say to you I do not speak on My own initiative, but the Father abiding in Me does His works. Believe Me that I am in the Father and the Father is in Me; otherwise believe because of the works themselves." (John 14:9–11)

"In that day you will know that I am in My Father, and you in Me, and I in you." (John 14:20)

Jesus spoke these things; and lifting up His eyes to heaven, He said, "Father, the hour has come; glorify Your Son, that the Son may glorify You, even as You gave Him authority over all flesh, that to all whom You have given Him, He may give eternal life. This is eternal life, that they may know You, the only true God, and Jesus Christ whom You have sent." (John 17:1–3)

> "And all things that are Mine are Yours, and Yours are Mine; and I have been glorified in them." (John 17:10)

> Jesus answered, "My kingdom is not of this world. If My kingdom were of this world, then My servants would be fighting so that I would not be handed over to the Jews; but as it is, My kingdom is not of this realm." (John 18:36)

References Other Than the Gospel of John

Bart Ehrman[190] claims that Jesus hardly ever refers to Himself as God, except in the Gospel of John.[191] In a 2014 NPR interview, Ehrman elaborates this claim:[192]

> EHRMAN: Well, what I argue in the book is that during his lifetime, Jesus himself didn't call himself God and didn't consider himself God and that none of his disciples had any inkling at all that he was God. The way it works is that you do find Jesus calling himself God in the Gospel of John, our last Gospel. Jesus says things like: Before Abraham was, I am, and I and the father are one, and if you've seen me, you've seen the father. These are all statements that you find only in the Gospel of John, and that's striking because we have earlier Gospels, and we have the writings of Paul, and in none of them is there any indication that Jesus said such things about him. I think it's completely implausible that Matthew, Mark, and Luke would not mention that Jesus called himself God if that's what he was declaring about himself. That would be a rather important point to make.

But that isn't true. The famous "Who do you say that I am" quotes are in Matthew 16:15–16, Mark 8:29, and Luke 9:18–20.

> He said to them, "But who do you yourselves say that I am?" Simon Peter answered, "You are the Christ, the Son of the living God." (Matt. 16:15–16)

> And He continued questioning them: "But who do you say that I am?" Peter answered and said to Him, "You are the Christ." (Mark 8:29)

> And it happened that while He was praying alone, the disciples were with Him, and He questioned them, saying, "Who do the people say that I am?" They answered and said, "John the Baptist, and others say Elijah; but others, that one of the prophets of old has risen." And He said to them, "But who do you say that I am?" And Peter answered and said, "The Christ of God." (Luke 9:18–20)

And Jesus proclaimed himself to be God:

> "All things have been handed over to Me by My Father; and no one knows the Son except the Father; nor does anyone know the Father except the Son, and anyone to whom the Son determines to reveal Him." (Matt. 11:27)

Furthermore, the apostle Paul believed Jesus was God. As reported in Acts 9:3–7, Paul directly encountered the risen Jesus on the road to Damascus. The encounter was sufficiently credible that it totally changed Paul's life mission.

Also, in his letter to the Romans, Paul makes a statement that appears to designate Jesus Christ as God. The exact translation phrasing of the verse is debated. The NET Bible most clearly states, "Christ, who is God overall."

> To them belong the patriarchs, and from them, by human descent, came the Christ who is God over all, blessed forever! Amen. (Rom. 9:5 NET)

Other versions have slightly different phrasing:

> Whose are the fathers, and from whom is the Christ according to the flesh, who is over all, God blessed forever. Amen. (Rom. 9:5 NASB)

> Theirs are the patriarchs, and from them is traced the human ancestry of the Messiah, who is God over all, forever praised! Amen. (Rom. 9:5 NIV)

Both Bart Ehrman[193] and the notes of the NIV[194] offer that the verse could be read two different ways:

Or *Messiah, who is over all. God be forever praised!*

Or *Messiah. God who is over all be forever praised!*

This debate suggesting that Paul was not referring to the Messiah (Jesus Christ) but rather to God the Father in this isolated verse seems a minor distraction of little consequence when considering all the quotations of deity in the Gospels and the dramatic conversion of Paul.

Doubting Disciples

A point can be made that even the apostles didn't understand the concept of a Son of God being crucified. No doubt their faith in Jesus fluctuated, as was recorded.

Jesus was explaining they would remember Him by the communion sacrament:

> "But there are some of you who do not believe." For Jesus knew from the beginning who they were who did not believe, and who it was that would betray Him. And He was saying, "For this reason I have said to you, that no one can come to Me unless it has been granted him from the Father." (John 6:64–66)

And at Gethsemane when Jesus was captured:

> "But all this has taken place to fulfill the Scriptures of the prophets." Then all the disciples left Him and fled. (Matt. 26:56)
>
> And they all left Him and fled. (Mark 14:50)

John, the Apostle Jesus Loved

Additional attention should be given as to why the apostle John focuses more in depth on Jesus's eternal identity as the Son of God.

It is well understood that Peter and John were the apostles closest to Jesus. However, they were very different personalities.

Peter, the impulsive one, was quick to acknowledge Jesus as God at Caesarea Philippi (Matt. 16:16; Mark 8:29; Luke 9:20). But trying not to be noticed, he stealthily followed Jesus to His trial. But he also denied knowing Jesus three times (Matt. 26:60, 72, 74; Mark 14:68, 70, 71; Luke 22:57, 58, 60; John 18:17, 25, 27). To his credit, however, he did not flee with the others at Gethsemane.

John, on the other hand, was the steady, loyal one (John 13:23). He not only accompanied Jesus to the trial but did so acknowledging his own presence. John was known to the high priest who let him inside the court (John 18:15). In fact, he facilitated allowing Peter inside (John 18:16).

John's loyalty and attentiveness to Jesus's trial is shown by the length and detail of the interrogation listed in John 18. While the trial narrative is recorded in all four Gospels, it is worth noting that Matthew was not present, having fled from Gethsemane; Peter (recorded by Mark) was present but likely not paying close attention to avoid discovery; Luke, not one of the original twelve, was not present at the trial and therefore recorded secondhand information.

Finally, it apparently was only John who was present at the Crucifixion since Jesus recognized only John and Mary in the crowd (John 19:26–27).

John's loyal accompaniment of Jesus through the trial and the Crucifixion no doubt came at great personal risk. It is therefore likely that he, more than the other apostles, realized during Jesus's life that He was, indeed, the Son of God. After the resurrection appearances, all the apostles became believers, but prior to the resurrection, it is likely that John was the sole unshakeable believer.

Conclusion

It should also be remembered that the Gospel of John was the last of the four Gospels to be written (approximately AD 90), and its content is distinctly different from the three Synoptic Gospels. Could it be that seeing the wavering of faith in the other apostles and the blossoming heretical theories on the deity/humanity of Jesus, the apostle John felt the need to emphasize and record the true deity of Jesus from the eyes of a firsthand witness?

Jesus's statement in John 10:30 is unequivocal: "I and the Father are one."

21

Did the Voice at Jesus's Baptism Adopt Him into Deity?

The Baptism References

In his book *Jesus Interrupted*, Bart Ehrman compares the accounts of Jesus's baptism and finds discrepancies among the Gospels.[195]

However, the standard western translations are remarkably consistent in thought:

> "This is My beloved Son, in whom I am well-pleased." (Matt. 3:17 NASB)

> "This is my beloved Son, in whom I am well pleased." (KJV)

> "This is my one dear Son; in him I take great delight." (NET)

> "You are My beloved Son, in You I am well-pleased." (Mark 1:11 NASB)

> "Thou art my beloved Son, in whom I am well pleased." (KJV)
>
> "You are my one dear Son; in you I take great delight." (NET)
>
> "Thou art my beloved Son; in thee I am well pleased." (Luke 3:22 KJV)
>
> "You are My beloved Son, in You I am well-pleased." (NASB)
>
> "You are my one dear Son; in you I take great delight." (NET)

Regardless of small wording differences in modern English translations, the voice of God shows approval of Jesus, His Son, to begin His earthly ministry. While the incarnate virgin birth had already established Jesus's deity, that fact likely was not recognized by the populace of Israel until His ministry began. Thus, the acknowledgment by God at the baptism certified Jesus's divine identity. As illustrated, this interpretation of the original Greek is consistent among almost all the English translations.

But Ehrman reached back to a fourth-century manuscript, the Codex Bezae Cantabrigiensis, to utilize the translation of Luke 3:22 to be "You are my son, today I have begotten you."

This wording quotes the words of Psalm 2:7 and is a contrary translation.

The Codex Bezae

So what is the Codex Bezae and is it more valid than the other translations we have? It appears that the validity of Codex Bezae Cantbrigiensis is at best controversial.

The Codex Bezae Cantbrigiensis (D-Gospel of Acts) is thought to be from the fourth or sixth centuries. It is so named because "it once belonged to Theodore Beza, who in 1581 gave it to the University of Cambridge where it is now kept ... The Greek text is quite peculiar, with many interpolations found nowhere else, a few remarkable omissions, and a capricious tendency to rephrase sentences ... In general, the Greek text is treated as an unreliable witness, and rightly so."[196]

Professor David Parker of the University of Birmingham says, "It provides a strikingly different form of text to that preserved in almost every other manuscript, and to the printed Greek text and the translations derived from it."[197]

George Edward Rice, in his doctoral thesis at Case Western Reserve University, concludes, "Pone would conclude two things about the copyist of D in Luke: (1) he was more than a copier; he was an editor; and (2) the editor of D in Luke worked with the aim of altering or strengthening Luke's tradition in compliance with his theological views."[198]

Even Metzler and Ehrman, in their book on textural criticism, acknowledge,

> No known manuscript has so many and so remarkable variations from what is usually taken to be the normal New Testament text. Codex Bezae's special characteristic is the free addition (and occasional omission) of words, sentences and even incidents.[199]

Nonetheless, Ehrman argues that even though the Codex Bezae translation stands alone versus thousands of opposing manuscripts, it somehow might be the valid one.[200]

The Motive

Such a translation suggests a perspective of one of the heresies of the first four centuries: Adoptionism (at His baptism, God adopted Jesus as a divine Son). In his book *The Orthodox Corruption of the Scripture*, Ehrman emphasizes the influence of the Ebionites of the first and second centuries.[201]

The Ebionites believed Jesus was a human who, because of His exemplary life, was adopted into divine status by God at the baptism. Ehrman argues that the "proto-orthodox" Christians came to dominate the church history and thus purged "heretical" transcription from the New Testament manuscripts. He suggests that the heretical Codex Bezae is an overlooked surviving remnant of the original Gospel of Luke.

Conclusion

So why would Ehrman reach such an extreme conclusion?

As an agnostic (atheist), and deconverted Christian, Ehrman must find continued theories to nullify the incarnated deity of Jesus. Although it is an isolated and questionably reliable translation, the eccentric Codex Bezae Cantbrigiensis document has become extraordinarily popular among textural critics like Ehrman who are anxious to invalidate the eternal deity of Jesus. In this case, relying on this codex seems too big a stretch.

22

When Did Jesus Become the Son of God?

Bart Ehrman[202] argues that there are two ways Jesus could have become divine: (1) adoption or (2) incarnation. He concludes that Mark describes Adoptionism at Jesus's baptism; Matthew and Luke seem to indicate He became God at birth (Matt. 1:18–23; Luke 1:26–33); while John describes Jesus as present from eternity (John 1:1; 1:14).

In a 2014 NPR interview, Ehrman explains his theory: [203]

> GROSS (Interviewer): There's another view of that, which is that, you know, Jesus was always divine.
>
> EHRMAN: That's right, and what I try to show in the book is that that's a later view within Christian circles, that the initial view, based on these pre-literary traditions, is that Jesus is exalted to be divine and that as Christians thought about it more and more, they tried to put it all together.

And so, the first Christians, as soon as they believe in the resurrection, they think God has taken Jesus up into heaven, he's made a divine being. Then they thought, well, it wasn't just at his resurrection, he must have been the son of God during his entire ministry. And so, Christians then started saying he must have been made the son of God at his baptism.

That's a view that you appear to get in the Gospel of Mark, which begins with Jesus being baptized and God declaring him his son at the baptism. As Christians thought about it more, they started thinking, well, he wasn't just the son of God during his ministry; he must have been the son of God during his entire life. And so, they started telling stories about how Jesus was born the son of God. And so there developed traditions about Jesus being born of a virgin.

And so, in our Gospels written after Mark, Matthew and Luke, Jesus's mother is virgin so that he's the son of God from his birth. And Christians thought about it more, they thought, well, he wasn't just the son of God during his life, he must have always been the son of God. And so, then you get to our last Gospel, the Gospel of John, where Jesus is a pre-existent divine being who becomes human.

That point of view I call not an exaltation Christology, not going from a human to being made a divine being, I call it an incarnation Christology, where you start out as a divine being and then temporarily become human. And so, these are the two fundamental kinds of Christology that you get in your earlier years, an exaltation, and an incarnation Christology.

Deity at the Baptism

The NASB, KJV, and NET translations give consistent verbiage:

> And behold, a voice from the heavens said, "This is My Beloved Son, with whom I am well pleased." (Matt. 3:17)
>
> And a voice came from the heavens: "You are My beloved Son; in You I am well pleased." (Mark 1:11)
>
> And the Holy Spirit descended upon Him in bodily form like a dove, and a voice came from heaven: "You are My beloved Son, in You I am well pleased." (Luke 3:22)

Ehrman argues that early manuscripts of Jesus's baptism in Luke 3:22 state, "You are my son, today I have begotten you."[204] While the veracity of this particular Luke reference is suspect (see *What Did the Voice at Jesus's Baptism Say?*), there are other references where Jesus is called "begotten" (John 1:14; John1:18; John 3:16; John 3:18; 1 John 4:9) (see *The Begotten Controversy*).

In this instance, Ehrman uses the "begotten" wording to infer the act of biologic descendance—in this case as adoption.

Ehrman points out that in Roman times, humans were sometimes elevated to "god" status. The example is Octavian, the son of Julius Caesar, who became known as Caesar Augustus. He argues that Mark shows that Christians merely assimilated the adoption into deity principle with Jesus.

But the Greek word here used for "begotten" is *monogenes (μονογενής),* translated "only, only—begotten; unique" (Strong).[205] It does not mean the act of conception nor adoption.

The voice of God at the baptism merely shows God's approval of Jesus, His already established eternal Son, to begin His earthly ministry.

Deity at the Incarnation (Birth)

Luke 1:35 specifically tells of the angel specifically telling Mary, "The Holy Spirit will come upon you, and the power of the Most High will overshadow you, and for that reason the holy child shall be called the Son of God."

Matthew similarly records the incarnation explained by the angel in Matthew 1:20: "The child who has been conceived in her is of the Holy Spirit."

Jesus became God at the virgin birth. Technically, what occurred is that God's eternal Son became incarnate in a newly born human who was named Jesus.

Deity at the Crucifixion

The context of Hebrews 5:5 is Jesus becoming the high priest Son of God at the time of the Crucifixion ("crying and tears to the One able to save him from death.") By employing Psalm 2, it could be interpreted that God begat Jesus as His Son at the Crucifixion "because of his piety."

Deity at the Resurrection

Acts 13:33 context is Paul (recorded by Luke) speaking about the resurrection. Paul invokes the "begotten" narrative of Psalm 2 as a typology of Jesus Christ. This could be interpreted that Jesus was given birth at the resurrection.

Deity Eternal

Clearly the apostle John's Gospel intends to point out the eternal existence of the Son of God as announced in John 1:1–3:

> In the beginning was the Word, and the Word was with God, and the Word was God. He was in the beginning with God. All things came into being through Him, and apart from Him nothing came into being that has come into being.

John further clarifies that the Word (Son) became flesh at the incarnation:

> And the Word became flesh, and dwelt among us, and we saw His glory, glory as of the only begotten from the Father, full of grace and truth. (John 1:14)

So while the apostle John makes the eternal deity of the Son unmistakably clear, he also introduces the term *begotten*. Again, the inference of the Greek term translated "begotten" is the "unique" or "only" son. It does not address at what point in time sonship was initiated. That, of course, is another question.

Conclusion

In fact, comparisons of the scriptural references do not indicate discrepancy or adoption. The eternal Son of God (Gospel of John) entered a human child (incarnation) (Gospels of Matthew and Luke) and was God from inception.

23

What Is the Begotten Controversy?

Few issues in Christianity have stirred as much controversy as the word *begotten* when associated with Jesus.

In the Hebrew Culture

To understand the issues, one must reach back into Hebrew theology.

The Israelites clearly understood there was one God who chose them as His people to represent Him on earth. This commitment between God and His people was codified in the Shema:

> "Hear, O Israel! The LORD is our God, the LORD is one!
> You shall love the LORD your God with all your heart
> and with all your soul and with all your might.
> You shall not follow other gods, any of the gods of the
> peoples who surround you." (Deut. 6:4–5, 14).

This concept of God forming a relationship with a people was then extended to the relationship God formed with David.

> I will be a father to him and he will be a son to Me; when he commits iniquity, I will correct him with the rod of men and the strokes of the sons of men. (2 Sam. 7:14)

The decree refers to the Davidic Covenant in which God declared that He would be Father to the King, and the King would be His Son. When David became king, God described their relationship as a "Father-son" relationship. The expression *son* took on the meaning of a messianic title. So how did David become God's son? Presumably through adoption.[206]

This commitment was memorialized in Psalm 2, presumably written by David (Acts 4:25).

> The kings of the earth take their stand
> And the rulers take counsel together
> Against the Lord and against His Anointed …
> "I will surely tell of the decree of the Lord:
> He said to Me, 'You are My Son,
> Today I have begotten You.
> 'Ask of Me, and I will surely give the nations as Your inheritance,
> And the very ends of the earth as Your possession."
> (Ps. 2:2, 7–8)

The Hebrew word *begotten* in Psalm 2:7 is *yə·liḏ·tî·ḵā* (מוֹ‌ִיַה יְּבָא ‌:ְדיִתְּלִי). Strong's concordance finds it used only this one time in the Old Testament. It is translated "have begotten."[207] By contrast, the typical Hebrew term for producing offspring is *yalad* (דַלָי).[208]

This psalm was thought to be read at the anointing of the successive kings of Israel. In Hebrew, the word for anointed one is *Messiah.*

The theological interpretation of the role of the Davidic king went far beyond the reality of the historical monarchy. No king of Judah (not even David) ever exercised worldwide dominion. As kings of Judah fell progressively more and more short of this ideal that was held before them, men looked into the future for the fulfilment of the divine promise to David (2 Sam. 7:8–16, cf. Isa. 9:7; 11:1–5; Jer. 23:5). After the fall of Jerusalem in 587 BC and the end of the monarchy, psalms like this came to be understood in a prophetic and messianic way. The NT writers (and Christians generally) see the fulfilment of this psalm in the kingship of Jesus the Messiah (Acts 4:25–28; 13:13; Heb. 1:5, 5:5; cf. Matt. 3:17; Rom. 1:4; Rev. 2:26f, 12:5, 19:15).[209]

The king of Israel, beginning with David, became "begotten" of God. Since David was already in existence at the time he was begotten, the process was assumed to be by adoption.

Thus, in the Old Testament, several concepts were established:

1. Beginning with the kingship of David, the king was officially "anointed." The English term for "anointed one" is Messiah.
2. The Messiah of Israel was destined to become the political leader who would lead a restored Israel to world dominance.
3. The kings of Israel, the anointed one (Messiah), acquired sonship with God, presumably by adoption.

In the New Testament

The concept of God adopting the Messiah was then carried into the New Testament. But just like in Hebrew, the English translation "begotten" contains several Greek terms. Strong recognizes the presence of the English term *begotten* twenty-four times in the Bible.[210] Of those, fifteen are in the New Testament, with five of them referring to Jesus as the begotten Son of God

When used in the classic verses describing the relationship of Jesus to God the Father, the Greek term used is *monogenes* (μονογενής, ές,). The specific English translation is "only; only—begotten; unique."[211]

John 1:14	"an only begotten"	monogenous	μονογενοῦς
John 1:18	"[the] only begotten"	monogenēs	μονογενὴς
John 3:16	"only begotten"	monogenē	μονογενῆ
John 3:18	"only begotten"	monogenous	μονογενοῦς
1 John 4:9	"one and only"	monogenē	μονογενῆ

The term *monogenes* is also used other than in relation to Jesus, referring to the "only son or daughter" (Luke 7:12; Luke 8:42; Luke 9:38; Heb. 11:17). Note that the term *monogenes* does not specifically indicate how the parent-sibling relationship was established (biologic birth, adoption, or preexisting).

In fact, when *begotten* is used in the New Testament to indicate biologic birthing, the verb *gennao* (γεννάω) is used[212] (Matt. 1:16; Matt. 1:20, Luke 1:35).

Matthew 1:16	"begat"	egennēsen	ἐγέννησεν
Matthew 1:20	"having been conceived"	gennēthen	γεννηθὲν
Luke 1:35	"being born"	gennōmenon	γεννώμενον

As we know, the NT apostles reconsidered the Old Testament to have future messianic significance, a process called typology. A good definition of typology follows:[213] typology (or typological symbolism) is a Christian form of biblical interpretation that proceeds on the assumption that God placed anticipations of Christ in the laws, events, and people of the Old Testament.

This typological literary maneuver is utilized by Paul where the Psalm 2 "begotten" term is repeatedly used in reference to Jesus (Acts 13:33). It is also utilized in the book of Hebrews. Hebrews was likely actually written by Barnabas,[214] who was Paul's companion on the first missionary journey. As such, he likely recorded the theology of Paul (Heb. 1:5; Heb. 5:5).

> That God has fulfilled this promise to our children in that He raised up Jesus, as it is also written in the second Psalm, "You are My Son; today I have begotten You." (Acts 13:33)

> For to which of the angels did He ever say,
> "You are My Son,
> Today I have begotten You"?
> And again,
> "I will be a Father to Him
> And He shall be a Son to Me"? (Heb. 1:5)

> So also Christ did not glorify Himself so as to become a high priest, but He who said to Him,
> "You are My Son,
> Today I have begotten You." (Heb. 5:5)

But these uses of Psalm 2 create two problems. First, Paul (and Barnabas?) uses the Greek verb *gennao* (γεννάω) when quoting Psalm 2. This changes the meaning from "only" or "unique" to a direct conceived descendant. Plus, Acts and Hebrews seem to indicate different time frames at which God begat the Son.

1. The Acts 13:33 context is Paul (recorded by Luke) speaking about the resurrection. This could be interpreted that Jesus was given birth at the resurrection.
2. The context of the Hebrews 1:5 infers that God gave birth to Jesus in eternity past, along with the angels.
3. The context of Hebrews 5:5 is Jesus becoming the high priest Son of God at the time of the Crucifixion ("crying and tears to

the One able to save him from death.") It could be interpreted that God begat Jesus as His Son at the Crucifixion "because of his piety."

Conclusion

The variation in Hebrew and Greek terminology translated as "begotten" in English poses problems as to the identity of Jesus as the "Son" of God.

The Old Testament Psalm 2 suggests adoption into sonhood of the previously living individual (David?).

Paul's typological use of Psalm 2 could be interpreted in two variations: (1) Jesus, the "Son," was birth subordinate to God, and (2) the birthing of the Jesus deity could have occurred either in eternity past (Heb. 1:5), at the time of the Crucifixion (Heb. 5:5), or at the resurrection (Acts 13:33).

By contrast, the apostle John consistently uses the term *monogenes* in the classic New Testament references to Jesus's deity (John 1:14; John 1:18; John 3:16; John 3:18; John 4:9). Could there be a reason for the terminology difference between Paul and John?

Paul's writings were in broad circulation in the late AD 50s. Acts and Hebrews were probably written in the 60s—least before AD 70—but John did not write his Gospel until AD 90, at least twenty years after the previous two books were circulated. It was during that period that confusion over the true identity of Jesus led to competing heresies: *Ebionism* (Jesus was merely a good human who died); *Docetism* (Jesus was really fully divine, and His humanism was an illusion); *Adoptionism* (God adopted Jesus into divinity, either at baptism, resurrection, or ascension, due to Jesus's piety); and *Arianism* (Jesus was divine but created in the past, subordinate to the Father).

It could be that John's emphasis on the eternal deity of Jesus, including restriction of His sonship to "unique' or "only"—versus adoption or subordinate birthed descendant—was a direct attempt to clarify the competing heresies.

24

Why Did a Sinless Jesus Need to Be Baptized?

One of the major controversies of the first century AD was why Jesus needed to be baptized by John the Baptist. Jesus was sinless, so why would He need baptismal cleansing of sin?

Jesus's baptism is recorded in three of the four Gospels.

In Matthew, John the Baptist protests his unworthiness to baptize his superior, but Jesus commands him to do so, "for in this way it is fitting for us to fulfill righteousness" (Matt. 3:15b NASB). Interestingly, Jesus does not elaborate on when or where in the Old Testament God made the requirement for the sinless Jesus to need baptizing. Mark (1:4–11) offers no explanation. Luke (3:19–22) deflects the issue by reporting John the Baptist's imprisonment by Herod and then doesn't say who baptized Jesus. John's Gospel (John 1:29–34) infers that John the Baptist baptized Jesus without knowing who He was until seeing the dove representing the Spirit descend upon Jesus.

John P. Meier comments, "Quite plainly, the early church was stuck with an event in Jesus's life that it found increasingly embarrassing, that it tried to explain away by various means, and that John the Evangelist finally erased from his gospel."[215]

To try to understand baptism, we must go back to the Old Testament rituals.

Washing before entering the presence of the Lord was instituted as early as when God spoke to Moses on Mount Sinai during the desert sojourn after the Exodus (Exod. 19:10–11). Then, at the institution of burnt offerings, Moses had Aaron and his sons wash themselves with water before entering the tent of meeting (tabernacle, the portable earthly dwelling of God as the Israelites moved from the Egypt exodus to Canaan) where the sacrificial alter was located (Lev. 8:6). Finally, the process of cleansing a leper from disease included washing his clothes (Lev. 14:8) before the priest could present him "before the LORD at the doorway of the tent of the meeting" (Lev. 14:11).

"Old Testament washings were almost always for those of the already believing community. They symbolized cleansing from sin and guilt. Whereas sacrifices were to atone for acts of sin, washing or bathing seems generally associated with cleansing from a sinful or otherwise unholy condition."[216]

The association of washing with water to do more than physical cleaning was well established in Old Testament times.

The New Testament command to be baptized initially came from John the Baptist. His command is important in the way it was stated. "Repent, for the kingdom of heaven is at hand" (Matt. 3:2). Matthew then goes on to observe, "And they were being baptized by him in the Jordan River, as they confessed their sins" (Matt. 3:6). Mark reports, "John the Baptist appeared in the wilderness preaching a baptism of repentance for the forgiveness of sins. … they were being baptized by him in the Jordan River, confessing their sins" (Mark 1:4–5). Luke similarly reports John the Baptist "preaching a baptism of repentance for the forgiveness of sins" (Luke 3:3).

So was the act of baptizing with water what cleansed people of sin, as it did symbolically in the Old Testament? That would seem to be the case at that time. People were to acknowledge their sin and then be cleansed by water. But why the sudden need for all people to be cleansed of sin by water, even though they were not entering the presence of God?

The answer most likely is John the Baptist's proclamation, the "the kingdom of heaven is near" (Matt. 3:2). He was announcing the coming of Jesus, the incarnate Son of God, who was bringing the kingdom of heaven to earth. Given the fact that the holiness of God will not allow sin in His presence, a person would need to be cleansed of sin to enter the kingdom.

This leads to the question, what and where is the kingdom of heaven? The Pharisees were expecting a military-political Messiah who would overthrow the Roman domination and reestablish the earthly Davidic kingdom. But in respect to this baptism discussion, the kingdom of heaven (the kingdom of God) is the metaphysical realm of God interacting with His chosen people while they are on earth, and later in heaven eternally.

Jesus proclaimed, "The Kingdom of God is not coming with signs to be observed; nor will they say, 'Look, here it is!' Or 'There it is!' For behold, the kingdom of God is in your midst" (Luke 17:20b–21).

There are three popular interpretations of Jesus's words in Luke 17:21 that the kingdom of God is within you (or among you): 1) the kingdom of God is essentially inward, within man's heart; 2) the kingdom is within your reach if you make the right choices; and 3) the kingdom of God is in your midst in the person and presence of Jesus. The best of these interpretations, it seems, is the third: Jesus was inaugurating the kingdom as He changed the hearts of men, one at a time.[217]

John the Baptist realized that Jesus was instituting a whole new relationship between man and God. "As for me, I baptize you with water for repentance, but he who is coming after me is mightier than I, … He will baptize you with the Holy Spirit and fire" (Matt. 3:11; cf. Mark 1:8; Luke 3:16; John 1:33b). This was forecasting the introduction of the Holy Spirit into interaction with humankind (Matt. 28:19).

But this raises several subsequent questions. Was it the confession of sins or the water immersion that cleansed? Given that sin was not ultimately forgiven until the Crucifixion, how did believers enter the kingdom of heaven before the cross? And what and where is the kingdom of heaven?

First, it is important to look specifically at John the Baptist's admonition. The first step was "repent" (Matt. 3:2). The definition of repentance is "a change of mind, with sorrow for something done, and a wish that it was undone."[218] That establishes that the key step is the change of attitude and commitment. The immersion was just a public demonstration of the prior step of repentance.

So how did repentance cleanse sin? Apparently, this step is similar to the faith of Abraham, that his faith in God "credited him with righteousness" (Gen. 15:6; Rom. 4:9; Rom. 4:22; Gal. 3:6; James 2:23). Abraham's steadfast faith achieved *credit* for forgiveness of his sin, which would be formally atoned at the time of the cross.

That leads us back to, why did Jesus feel He needed to be baptized when He had never sinned (2 Cor. 5:21; Heb. 4:15; 7:26; 1 John 3:5)? Walvoord and Zuck's *New Testament Commentary* offers the following explanation:[219]

> John's message was a message of repentance, and those experiencing it were looking forward to a coming Messiah who would be righteous and who would bring in righteousness. If Messiah were to provide righteousness for sinners, He must be identified with sinners.

It could also be considered that at the moment of His baptism, Jesus took on the responsibility of the sins of his followers. He assumed the debt to be paid in full later by his death on the cross.

A second element of Jesus's baptism needs identifying. John the Baptist proclaimed that the coming Messiah would baptize with the

Holy Spirit and fire (Matt. 3:11b; Mark1:8; Luke 3:16b; John 1:33b). Bailey and Constable point out the following:[220]

> The baptism of Jesus identified him with the righteous remnant, inaugurated His public ministry, and enabled the Holy Spirit to be identified with him. The presence and descent of the Spirit, along with the statement of the Father from heaven, link Psalm 2:7 and Isaiah 42:1. This to shows that Jesus is both the Son of God and the promised Messiah, who came from God the Father with the anointed power of the Holy Spirit.

All of which leads to the following conclusions:

1. Water cleansing was associated with cleansing of sin from Old Testament times
2. The baptism immersion was merely a visible demonstration of repentance and commitment to God
3. Jesus chose to be baptized—not because he had sinned—but in order to identify with and accept responsibility for the sins of those who believe in Him, to confirm his Sonship with God, and to demonstrate His association with the Spirit

25

What Was the Chronology of Jesus's Ministry?

Since the story of Jesus is spread throughout the Gospels, it is difficult to compose the big picture of His ministry. The following is a summary taken mainly from the excellent chronicle in the BibleJourney.com.[221]

In early AD 26, after spending his youth in Nazareth, thirty-two-year-old Jesus ventures south to Bethany beyond the Jordan River. There He joins the ministry of John the Baptist and is baptized (Mark 1:9). At Jesus's baptism, God affirms Jesus's deity (Matt. 3:17; Mark 1:11; Luke 3:32).

It is not clear at exactly what point Jesus is tempted by Satan in the wilderness and in Jerusalem (Matt. 4:1–11; Luke 4:1–13), but it was likely just after His baptism.

It is likely Jesus initially joins the ministry of John the Baptist, who acknowledges Jesus as the "Lamb of God"—the Messiah (John 1:29; 34). Two of the Baptist's followers, Andrew and another not named, are introduced to Jesus. Andrew then recruits Simon (Peter) to follow Jesus, the Messiah (John 1:41). At that point, Jesus changes Simon's name to Peter (John 1:42).

Leaving the area of Judea, Jesus returns to the area of Galilee to *begin his public ministry.* There He encounters Nathaniel and Philip (John 1:43–45).

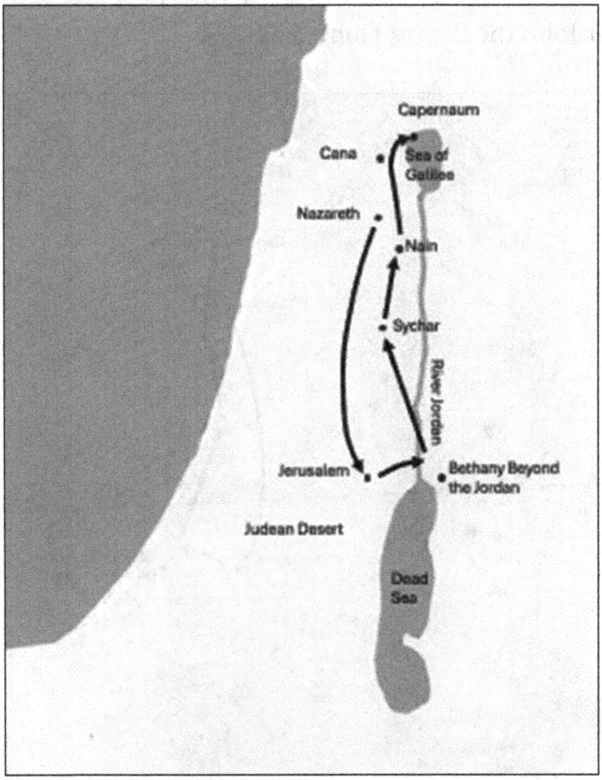

In the autumn of AD 26 AD, Jesus performs his first miracle at Cana, where he turns water into wine (John 2:1–11). Returning to Nazareth, Jesus (reads Isa. 61:1–2) teaches in the local synagogue (Luke 4:17–22). The people are filled with rage (Luke 4:28–30) and try to throw Jesus off a cliff, but He escapes and moves to Capernaum (Luke 4:31).

In Capernaum, Jesus heals a man possessed by demon (Mark 1:23–26; Luke 4:33–35) as well as Simon's mother-in-law (Mark 1:30–31; Luke 4:39).

After spending time in Capernaum, Jesus attends the Passover festival in Jerusalem in the spring of AD 27. This was the first time He drives merchants from the Temple (John 2:13–15). While in Jerusalem, Jesus encounters Nicodemus, whom He tells that one must be "born again" to enter the kingdom of God (John 3:3).

In the summer of AD 27, Jesus baptizes people along the River Jordan near John the Baptist (John 3:22–23).

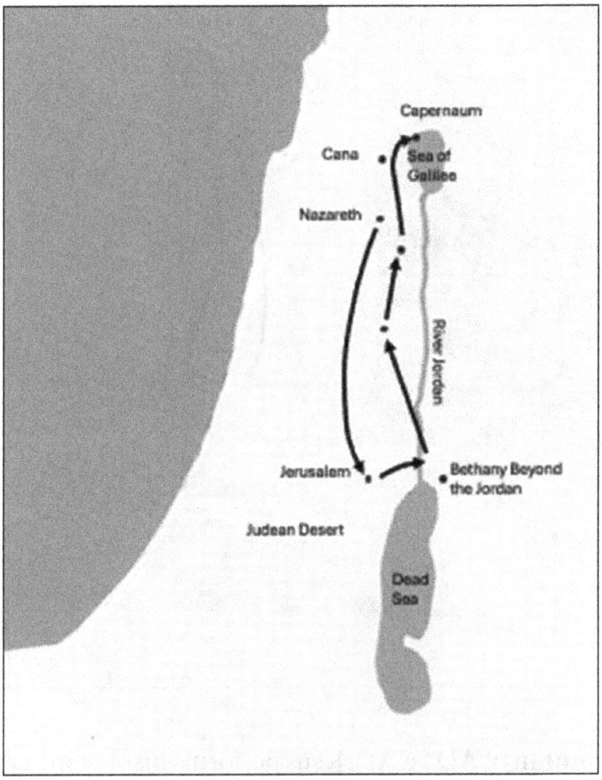

Shortly after, John the Baptist is arrested by Herod and later beheaded (Matt. 14:1–12). Jesus returns to Galilee, passing through Sychar where he speaks with the Samaritan woman regarding "living water" (John 4:14). He tells her that the time is coming when people will not need to go to the temple to worship, and that He is the Messiah (John 4:26).

In autumn of AD 27, Jesus arrives back in Galilee, where He heals the dying son of the official (John 4:46–54) and raises the son of a widow from Nain (Luke 7:11–17).

It is in Capernaum, after the death of John the Baptist, that Jesus definitively calls the twelve to follow Him (Matt. 4:18–22; Mark 1:16–20; Luke 5:1–11). Having been followers of the Baptist, the twelve move to follow Jesus, whom John has designated as the Messiah (John 1:36–37)

During the winter of AD 27/28, Jesus preaches in the villages around Galilee, including healing the leper (Mark 1:40-41).

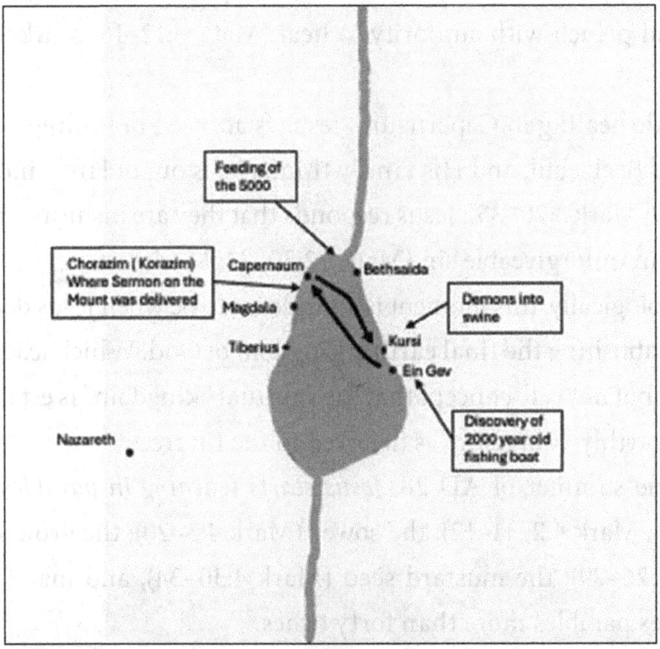

In spring of AD 28, Jesus delivers the Sermon on the Mount on the hillside east of the Sea of Galilee (Matt. 5:1–12). The eight "blessings" have become known as the Beatitudes (Matt. 6:20–45). He also preaches the "salt of the earth" (Matt. 5:13) and the "light of the world" (Matt. 5:14–16). During this period, Jesus also instructs the Lord's Prayer (Matt. 6:1–18; Luke 11:1–4); not to worry about the future and store up treasures on earth (Matt. 6:19–34); not to judge others (Matt. 7:1–23); and to build your house (faith) on solid ground (Matt. 24:27).

Returning to Capernaum, Jesus heals the paralytic lowered through the roof of His house (Mark 2:1–12). He also calls Matthew (Levi the tax collector) to discipleship (Mark 2:13–28). The Pharisees get angry about Jesus's disciples harvesting wheat on the Sabbath, to which Jesus responds that the Sabbath was made for man—not man for the Sabbath (Matt. 6:1–5; Mark 2:27). Jesus also heals the man with the withered hand in the synagogue on a Sabbath, to the rage of the Pharisees (Matt. 6:6–11).

Jesus appoints the twelve followers as apostles (messengers) to go forth and preach with authority to heal (Matt. 6:12–16; Mark 3:13–18; Luke 9:1–6).

While healing in Capernaum, Jesus is accused of healing from the power of Beelzebul, and His family thinks he is out of His mind (Matt. 12:22–29; Mark 3:20–35). Jesus responds that they are insulting the Holy Spirit—an unforgiveable sin (Matt. 12:30–32; Mark 3:39).

Theologically, this moment is considered to be when Jesus decides to defer establishing the final earthly kingdom of God. Which leads to the "already but not yet" concept that the spiritual "kingdom" is established, but the earthly "kingdom" is deferred to the future.[222]

In the summer of AD 28, *Jesus starts teaching in parables* (Matt. 13:10–13; Mark 4:2; 11–12): the sower (Mark 4:3–20); the growing seed (Mark 4:26–29); the mustard seed (Mark 4:30–34), and many others. Jesus uses parables more than forty times.[223]

In autumn of AD 28, Jesus is asleep on the fishing boat on the Sea of Galilee when a storm arises. Jesus calms the storm (Mark 4:37–41). Arriving on the eastern shore of the lake, Jesus casts out the demons from the Gerasene demoniac into the herd of pigs (Mark 5:1–17).

After sailing back across the Sea of Galilee to Capernaum, Jesus heals Jairus's daughter and an "unclean" woman who touches His coat (Mark 5:21–43).

In winter of AD 28, Jesus, along with the disciples, walks to Nazareth, where He is rejected in the synagogue as just a "local boy" (Mark 6:3). Jesus leaves Nazareth to teach along the Galilean villages and sends His apostles to preach elsewhere in the region (Mark 6:7–13).

At this point, Jesus's ministry, which has largely been confined to the Jewish settlements in the area around the Sea of Galilee, expands to broader areas of the Gentiles.

Jesus goes to Jerusalem to attend one of the required festivals, during which time He heals the invalid at the Pool of Bethesda (John 5:1–18).

Back in Capernaum in the spring of AD 29, Jesus escapes the crowds by sailing into the Sea of Galilee, but the crowd runs ahead and is waiting for Him on the eastern shore. Here Jesus feeds the five thousand with two loaves and five fishes (Matt. 14:13–21; Mark 6:33–44).

Jesus then sends His disciples ahead by boat to Bethsaida, while He goes to pray. A squall comes up, and the disciples struggle to stay afloat. Jesus walks across the water and calms the storm (Mark 6:47–52).

Pharisees come from Jerusalem to Galilee and criticize Jesus because His disciples do not follow the Jewish laws of ritual washing before eating. Jesus responds that it's what is on the inside, not the outside, that makes a person unclean (Mark 7:20).

Jesus travels north to Tyre and to Sidon, after which He returns to Decapolis on the eastern shore of the Sea of Galilee. There He heals a deaf man (Mark 7:32–27) and feeds four thousand (Mark 8:1–21).

In summer of AD 29, now two years into His ministry, Jesus visits Bethsaida, where He heals a blind man by placing His hands on the man's eyes (Mark 8:22).

From Bethsaida, Jesus and His disciples travel north to Caesarea Philippi, where Jesus asks His disciples who they think He is. Peter says he believes Jesus to be the Messiah (Matt. 16:13–16; Mark 8:27–29).

This episode represents a turning point in Jesus's ministry. From this point on, Jesus begins to teach that over the nine remaining months of His ministry, He will be rejected and killed but that He will rise from the dead three days later (Matt. 20:17–19; Mark 8:31–38; John 20:27–36).

Peter argues that Jesus should not allow Himself to die, to which Jesus replies, "Get behind me Satan; for you are not setting your mind on God's interests, but man's" (Mark 8:33).

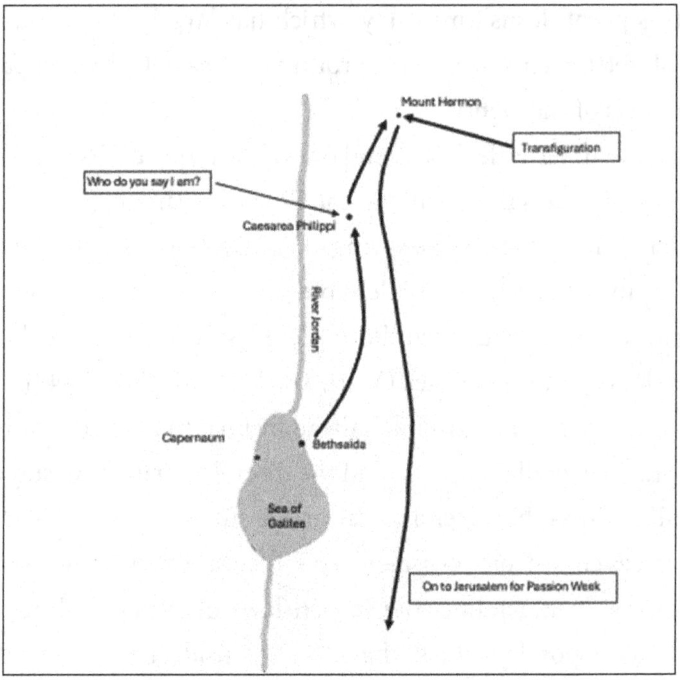

Six days after the confession at Caesarea Philippi, Jesus takes His three closest disciples—Peter, James, and John—to Mount Hermon, where He is transfigured in the presence of Elijah and Moses (Mark 9:2–13). God's voice speaks, "This is my beloved Son. Listen to Him!" (Mark 9:7).

Jesus returns to Capernaum, where Jesus continues to teach about His impending death and resurrection (Mark 9:30). He confronts His disciples on their personal rivalry over who is the greatest (Mark 9:34–35). At Capernaum, Jesus pays the Temple tax by the miracle of the shekel in the fish's mouth (Matt. 17:27).

In autumn of AD 29, He sends out seventy-two apostles to spread His message (Luke 10:1–27).

In October of AD 29, Jesus attends the Feast of the Tabernacles in Jerusalem secretly, because He knows the Pharisees are already plotting to kill Him (John 7:1–13). On the last day of the festival, Jesus talks about the indwelling power of the Holy Spirit that believers will receive after

His death and resurrection (John 7:38). The Pharisees want to arrest Him, but Nicodemus intervenes (John 7:50–53).

Jesus continues to teach around Jerusalem, challenging the Pharisees and claiming to be the "light of the world" (John 8:24). Jesus washes the blind man's eyes at the Pool of Siloam on the Sabbath (John 9:1–7), which further infuriates the Pharisees.

Jesus tells the parable of the Good Samaritan (Luke 10:25–37); the kingdom of God being with them (Luke 17:20–21); and the Good Shepherd (John 10:1–16).

In December, AD 29, Jesus attends the festival of Hanukkah (Feast of Dedication). He is asked if He is the Messiah. He responds that He has already told them, "The Father and I are one" (John 10:25–30). The Pharisees try to stone Him for blasphemy, so He escapes past Jericho across to Bethany, east of the Jordan River (John 10:40–42).

At the beginning of AD 30, Jesus is summoned to Bethany near Jerusalem (different from the Bethany across the Jordan) because Lazarus, the brother of Mary and Martha, is dying. Jesus raises Lazarus from the dead (John 11:43). The chief priests hear of the raising of Lazarus and want to kill Jesus. Jesus escapes to the village of Ephraim (John 11:54).

In the spring of AD 30, at the time of Passover, Jesus and His followers pass through Jericho on the way to Jerusalem. In Jericho, Jesus meets Zacchaeus, a wealthy Jewish official who climbs a tree to see Jesus pass by (Luke 19:1–10).

Jesus then makes His triumphal entry into Jerusalem from the east and sends two disciples to secure a donkey (Mark 11:1–7). Jesus enters the city (Mark 11:8–11) on what has come to be called Palm Sunday.

After a brief visit to the Temple courtyards, Jesus and His twelve disciples retire to Bethany, just east of Jerusalem.

The next morning, Jesus returns to Jerusalem. On the way, He curses a barren fig tree (Mark 11:12–14). The next day, Jesus enters the Temple and again drives out merchants (Mark 11:15–19). He teaches of "sheep and goats" (Matt. 25:31–460); tenets of the vineyard (Mark 12:1–12); taxes to Caesar (Mark12:13–17); loving your neighbor (Mark 12:28–32); and about giving (Mark 12:41–44).

Jesus laments that Jerusalem was unwilling to allow Him to "gather your children together" (Matt. 23:37–39), referring to His wish to have established the earthly kingdom.

Jesus leaves the Temple and goes up to the Mount of Olives, where He delivers the Olivet Discourse (Matt. 41:1–25:46; Mark 13:1–37; Luke 21:5–36) on the future of the nation of Israel.

The timing of activities of Passion Week has been up for debate for centuries, and it is discussed in chapter 36. Therefore, it will not be covered in detail here. Knowing of His impending betrayal and death, Jesus …

- gathered the disciples in the upper room for the Last Supper (Matt. 26:26–35; Mark 14:22–31; Luke 22:14; John:13:1–17:26)
- was betrayed by Judas Iscariot (Matt. 26:14–25; Mark 14:10; Luke 22:47–48; John 13:21; John 18:2–3)
- was arrested in the Garden of Gethsemane (Matt. 26:47–56; Mark 14:14:43–49; Luke 22:47–53)
- was tried before Pilate (Matt. 27:11–26; Mark 15:1–15; Luke 23:1–25; John 18:28–40)
- was denied three times by Peter (Matt. 26:70, 72, 74; Mark 14:66, 70, 71; Luke 22:57, 58, 60; John 18:17, 25, 27)
- was crucified (Matt. 27:33–54; Mark 15:22–39; Luke 23:33–47; John 19:16–18)
- was buried (Matt. 27:57–66; Mark 15:42–47; Luke 23:50–53; John 19:38–42)

26

Who Were the Women Who Supported Jesus's Ministry?

Women played an important role in Jesus's ministry. They can be grouped in two categories: Mary, the mother of Jesus, and the group of women who accompanied the ministry.

Mary, the Mother of Jesus

Mary, the mother of Jesus, is mentioned almost exclusively in the birth stories of Matthew and Luke.

She summoned Jesus to perform his first miracle at Cana:

> When the wine was gone, Jesus's mother said to him, "They have no more wine."
> "Woman, why do you involve me?" Jesus replied. "My hour has not yet come."
> His mother said to the servants, "Do whatever he tells you." (John 2:3–5)

Did Mary expect Jesus to perform the miracle of water to wine, or was she just expecting Him to go procure additional wine?

Despite hearing directly from the angel Gabriel that she would bear a son who would be the "son of God" (Luke 1:35), and having an immaculate pregnancy, it is not clear whether Mary truly believed in Jesus's deity prior to the resurrection. Even after Jesus performed the water-to-wine miracle in front of her, there is no evidence that she believed. Jesus also had four half brothers and an unnamed number of sisters (Mark 6:3). But when Jesus began performing healing miracles, His family thought He was out of His mind:

> When his family heard about this, they went to take charge of him, for they said, "He is out of his mind." (Mark 3:21)

In response, Jesus rejected Mary and His brothers (Mark 3:31–35).

Consistent with doubt, Mary is not listed among the several women who supported Jesus in His ministry. Perhaps it was because she had other younger children to parent.

Mary finally showed up at the Crucifixion cross, where Jesus committed John to care for her (John 19:26–27). Interestingly, Mary (Jesus's mother) is not listed among those who visited the tomb, either at Jesus's burial or the morning of the discovery of the empty tomb.

It seems that Mary, like Jesus's siblings, was not convinced of Jesus's deity until He appeared after the resurrection. It is also interesting that while Jesus appeared to the supporting women, the twelve, and over five hundred other followers, there is no record that Jesus appeared to His mother or siblings.

However, it appears that Mary, like Jesus's brothers, became a convert after the resurrection appearances. Mary is reported as participating in the post-ascension meeting of the apostles in the upper room (Acts 1:14).

> They all joined together constantly in prayer, along with the women and Mary the mother of Jesus, and with his brothers. (Acts 1:14)

Tradition states that Mary lived under the apostle John's care until her death, but nothing is noted of her active participation in the church ministry.

The Supporting Women

Luke describes the women who followed Jesus and supported His ministry.

> And also some women who had been cured of evil spirits and diseases: Mary (called Magdalene) from whom seven demons had come out; Joanna the wife of Chuza, the manager of Herod's household; Susanna; and many others. These women were helping to support them out of their own means. (Luke 8:2–3)

It is not clear exactly what the women did to provide support, but they somehow managed to provide food and financial support for the twelve. Since Jesus and the twelve disciples had sold all their worldly possessions and lived an ascetic lifestyle, their requirements were minimal.

It is also relevant that the vast majority of Jesus's ministry, as opposed to that of Paul, took place in a small area around the Sea of Galilee. Jesus only occasionally went north as far as Sidon and south to the area around Jerusalem, a range of no more than fifty miles in either direction from His base in Capernaum. Only in His terminal visit to Jerusalem was Jesus gone from Capernaum more than a few days. Therefore, it is likely His provisions were provided from Capernaum.

Mary Magdalene

Mary Magdalene, as she was addressed in the Gospels, was actually Mary from Magdala. Magdala was a prosperous fishing village on the Sea of Galilee. Little is known about her personal history, except the brief pericope of Luke 8:2 indicating that Jesus cured her of "seven demons." Likely, the "seven demons" indicate a physical ailment. The spurious rumor that she was a repentant prostitute was theorized due to the juxtaposition of the story of the adulteress immediately preceding the reference to Mary in John 8. In fact, the story of the adulteress is not in the early manuscripts at all. Her availability to follow Jesus in His ministry likely indicates that she was unmarried. Since she was from a wealthy fishing industry city, it may be that she had independent financial means.

Mary Magdalene was Jesus's closest supporter among the women who provided for His itinerant ministry.

Mary Magdalene was present at the Crucifixion cross (Mark 15:40; John 19:25). She followed Joseph of Arimathea to the tomb at Jesus's burial (Matt. 27:61; Mark 15:47), and she was the apparently leader of the group of women who went to the tomb to anoint Jesus's body (Matt. 28:1; Mark16:1). It was Mary Magdalene who was the first to encounter the risen Jesus outside the tomb (John 20:16–17); the corresponding reference in Mark 16:9 is not present in the earliest manuscripts. And it was Mary Magdalene who reported the resurrection to the disciples (Luke 24:10).

After reporting Jesus's resurrection to the disciples, Mary Magdalene is not heard from again in the New Testament.

Mary Clopas

A fourth Mary in the Bible is identified as Mary, the mother of James the younger and Joseph and the wife of Clopas (also called Alphaeus in Luke 6:15). She is mentioned in Mark 15:40, Matthew 27:56, and John 19:25 as watching the Crucifixion of Christ. She is mentioned again in Mark 15:47 as seeing the place where Jesus was buried. And this Mary appears again in Mark 16:1 and Matthew 28:1 (where she is called "the other Mary") in connection with the empty tomb, as she was one of the women who brought spices for Jesus's body and met an angel instead.

Clopas is thought to be the same person as Alphaeus, the father of the disciple James (the lesser) (Matt. 10:3; Mark 3:18; Luke 6:15). He is again mentioned as Cleopas, one of the two disciples to whom the risen Jesus appears on the road to Emmaus (Luke 24:18). There apparently is variation in the English translation of the Greek name Κλ[ε]οπᾶς, such that the KJV renders Clopas as Cleopas.[224] Interestingly, Mark 2:14 names the father of Levi (Matthew) as Alphaeus, which may have been a common Hebrew name. Clopas also appears in early Christian writings, such as the second-century writers Papias and Hegesippus, as a brother of Joseph, the husband of Mary, mother of Jesus.[225] In such a case, Mary of Clopas would have been the sister of Jesus's mother, Mary, and be married to Joseph's brother, in which case James of Alphaeus would have been another cousin of Jesus.

Mary of Clopas apparently is the same person Matthew and Mark address as "Mary the mother of James and Joses" (Matt. 27:56; Mark 15:40; Mark 15:47; Mark 16:1) as well as the "other Mary" (Matt. 27:61; Matt. 28:1) at the tomb. John addresses her as "Mary the wife of Clopas."

"According to many biblical scholars, and in early Christian tradition from the time of Papias of Hierapolis (c. AD 70–163), this Mary was the sister of Mary the mother of Jesus and the wife of Alphaeus, as we apparently see in John 19:25: 'Near the cross of Jesus stood his mother, his mother's sister, Mary the wife of Clopas, and Mary Magdalene.' So, the 'other Mary' may well have been Jesus's aunt (and her husband, Clopas, his uncle)."[226]

Mary of Clopas was present at the Crucifixion (John 19:25); at the tomb as "the mother of Joseph' (Mark 15:47); at the resurrection tomb as "Mary the mother of James and Joseph "(Mark 15:47; and was among the women who go to tell the disciples Jesus is risen (Luke 24:10).

Salome

There are two Salomes in the New Testament. The "unrighteous" one was Herodias's daughter through Philip, the half brother of Herod Antipas,[227] who requested the beheading of John the Baptist (Mark 6:21–28).

The Salome mentioned as a follower of Jesus was the wife of Zebedee, the father of the disciples James and John. Salome is mentioned by name only in the Gospel of Mark. She was present at the Crucifixion (Matt. 27:56; Mark 15:40; John 19:27) and at the attempt to anoint the body of Jesus (Mark 16:1). It's not clear whether Salome is the "mother of James" who goes with the women to tell the disciples Jesus is risen (Luke 24:10), but it is likely so, since James, the brother of John, was considered of more importance than James, the brother of Joses. In John's Gospel, "his mother's sister" (John 19:27) must refer to Salome, since Mary of Clopas is mentioned separately.

"Papias, the scholar of John *(ex Cod . MS. Bib. Bodl.* 2397), … stated that both Mary, the wife of Cleophas, and Mary Salome, were aunts of our Lord, and consequently sisters of the Virgin Mary."[228]

Joanna

Joanna was the wife of Chuza, the manager of Herod Antipas's household estate. As such, she was a woman of influence and likely financial means. She is mentioned only in the Gospel of Luke. Apparently, Jesus also healed her of some malady, after which she apparently left her social position to become a follower.

She was among the women who went to anoint Jesus's body (Luke 23:55–56) and ran with the others from the empty tomb to tell the apostles (Luke 24:10).

Suzanna

Suzanna was one the women followers of Jesus mentioned only in Luke 8:3. She is not specifically mentioned subsequently in the New Testament. She is not to be confused with the Suzanna of Daniel 13.

Conclusion

Several interesting points arise from this survey.

While the Virgin Mary, mother of Jesus, has been sainted by Catholicism, she was of very little support to Jesus's ministry. In fact, even with her angelic encounter and immaculate pregnancy, she apparently was not convinced of Jesus's deity until after the resurrection appearances.

There may well have been family ties among the followers. Jesus's mother, Mary, Mary of Clopas, and Salome may have been sisters. And conceivably, Clopas and Joseph, Jesus's father, may have been brothers. If that is true, several of the disciples would have been cousins of Jesus. The family connections could explain their willingness to follow and support Jesus's ministry.

Which leaves one to wonder why Mary, the mother of Jesus, who had the most objective experience of Jesus's deity, was one of the least supportive of His ministry.

27

Calling of the Twelve: Why Did They Respond?

Have you ever wondered why the twelve disciples just suddenly, if not impulsively, dropped their entire worldly jobs and family to follow Jesus when He called them? Most conspicuous is the calling of the four fishermen who were apparently partners in a successful commercial fishing business: Simon (Peter), Andrew, James, and John (the sons of Zebedee).

The four Gospel references (Mark's are split into two) to the calling of the twelve are as follows:

> Now as Jesus was walking by the Sea of Galilee, He saw two brothers, Simon who was called Peter, and Andrew his brother, casting a net into the sea; for they were fishermen. And He said to them, "Follow Me, and I will make you fishers of men." Immediately they left their nets and followed Him. Going on from there He saw two other brothers, James the son of Zebedee, and John his brother, in the boat with Zebedee their father, mending their nets; and He called them. Immediately

they left the boat and their father, and followed Him. (Matt. 4:18–22 NASB)

As He passed by, He saw Levi the son of Alphaeus sitting in the tax booth, and He said to him, "Follow Me!" And he got up and followed Him. (Mark 2:14 NASB)

And He went up on the mountain and summoned those whom He Himself wanted, and they came to Him. And He appointed twelve, so that they would be with Him and that He could send them out to preach, and to have authority to cast out the demons. And He appointed the twelve: Simon (to whom He gave the name Peter), and James, the son of Zebedee, and John the brother of James (to them He gave the name Boanerges, which means, "Sons of Thunder"); and Andrew, and Philip, and Bartholomew, and Matthew, and Thomas, and James the son of Alphaeus, and Thaddaeus, and Simon the Zealot; and Judas Iscariot, who betrayed Him. (Mark 3:13–19 NASB)

Now it happened that while the crowd was pressing around Him and listening to the word of God, He was standing by the lake of Gennesaret; and He saw two boats lying at the edge of the lake; but the fishermen had gotten out of them and were washing their nets. And He got into one of the boats, which was Simon's, and asked him to put out a little way from the land. And He sat down and began teaching the people from the boat. When He had finished speaking, He said to Simon, "Put out into the deep water and let down your nets for a catch." Simon answered and said, "Master, we worked hard all night and caught nothing, but I will do as You say and let down the nets." When they had done this, they enclosed a great quantity of fish, and their nets began to break; so they signaled to their partners in the other boat for them to come and help them. And they came and filled both of the boats, so that they began to sink. But when Simon Peter saw that, he fell down at Jesus's feet, saying, "Go away from me Lord, for I am a sinful man!" For amazement had seized him and all his companions because of the catch of fish which they had taken; and so also were James and John, sons of Zebedee, who were partners with Simon. And Jesus said to Simon, "Do not fear, from now on you will be catching men." When they had brought their boats to land, they left everything and followed Him. (Luke 5:1–11 NASB)

Again the next day John was standing with two of his disciples, and he looked at Jesus as He walked, and said, "Behold, the Lamb of God!" The two disciples heard him speak, and they followed Jesus. And Jesus turned and saw them following, and said to them, "What do you seek?" They said to Him, "Rabbi (which translated means Teacher), where are You staying?" He said to them, "Come, and you will see." So they came and saw where He was staying; and they stayed with Him that day, for it was about the tenth hour. One of the two who heard John speak and followed Him, was Andrew, Simon Peter's brother. He found first his own brother Simon and said to him, "We have found the Messiah" (which translated means Christ). He brought him to Jesus. Jesus looked at him and said, "You are Simon the son of John; you shall be called Cephas" (which is translated Peter).

> The next day He purposed to go into Galilee, and He found Philip. And Jesus said to him, "Follow Me." Now Philip was from Bethsaida, of the city of Andrew and Peter. Philip found Nathanael and said to him, "We have found Him of whom Moses in the Law and also the Prophets wrote—Jesus of Nazareth, the son of Joseph." Nathanael said to him, "Can any good thing come out of Nazareth?" Philip said to him, "Come and see." Jesus saw Nathanael coming to Him, and said of him, "Behold, an Israelite indeed, in whom there is no deceit!" Nathanael said to Him, "How do You know me?" Jesus answered and said to him, "Before Philip called you, when you were under the fig tree, I saw you." Nathanael answered Him, "Rabbi, You are the Son of God; You are the King of Israel." Jesus answered and said to him, "Because I said to you that I saw you under the fig tree, do you believe? You will see greater things than these." (John 1:35–50 NASB)

One possibility to explain the responsiveness of the disciples lies in their relationship to John the Baptist.

John the Baptist, who happens to be Jesus's cousin (Luke 1:36), had apparently been baptizing Jewish followers into repentance for some time when Jesus began His ministry. In approximately AD 28, Jesus left Nazareth to travel over sixty miles from His hometown of Nazareth to the Jordan River valley to find John and be baptized.

John P. Meier hypothesizes a discipleship evolution. While the historicity of the Gospel of John is debated by textural critics, John's account yields a clue. Meier questions, "After his baptism, did Jesus stay with John for a period of time, joining an inner circle of the baptized who followed John on his baptizing tours up and down the Jordan valley (cf John 1:28, 35–37 ; 3:23), assisted John in his preaching and baptizing (3:25), received more detailed teaching from him about his message (3:26–30), and shared his ascetic spirituality of fasting (Mark 2:18), prayer (Luke 11:1), and perhaps (at least temporarily) celibacy?"[229]

By the time Jesus came to be baptized, John the Baptist's ministry was well established, and crowds followed him everywhere (Matt. 3:5–6). John 1:35–49 comments that the day following Jesus's baptism, the Baptist was standing with "two of his disciples" in Bethany, where he had just baptized Jesus. The inference is that there were more disciples following him. One of the two disciples who stayed the day with Jesus was Andrew. The other disciple is not identified. Andrew then recruited his brother Simon. And as indicated in John 1:35–36, they were directed to Jesus by John the Baptist while he (the Baptist) was still alive. The next day, Jesus found Philip, who was from Simon's hometown of Bethsaida. Philip then recruited Nathanael. These encounters tend to validate Meier's conclusion that for a time Jesus followed the ministry of John the Baptist. As such, Jesus became acquainted with the Baptist's disciples.

After the Baptist was imprisoned, Jesus's ministry grew, and great crowds began to follow Him (Mark 1:28; 2:13; Luke 4:37; Matt. 4:24–25; John 6:2).

Since Simon Peter and Andrew were fishing partners with James and John, they had no doubt related that they had met Jesus, the Messiah, in Bethany. After Jesus moved to Capernaum, and He encountered Simon (Peter), Andrew, James, and John (the sons of Zebedee) while they were fishing in Galilee (Matt. 4:18–20), He called them to intensify their discipleship (Matt. 4:18–22; Mark 1:17). So when the four fisherman reencountered Jesus along the Sea of Galilee, they didn't just drop everything to follow an unknown itinerant preacher walking along the beach. He was already known to them.

Even though Andrew, Peter, James, and John were followers of John the Baptist and subsequently Jesus, they continued their fishing occupations. It was common for first-century Hebrews to be part-time followers of their rabbi while continuing their occupations.

Jesus's encounter with the fishermen in Luke 5:11 is different from the encounter of walking along the beach of the Sea of Galilee (Matt. 4:18–22; Mark 1:16–20) while the disciples were in their boats or washing their nets. In the Luke encounter, the boats were empty, and Jesus got in Peter's boat while addressing a crowd of followers. After performing the miracle of the fish catch, Jesus called the disciples to full-time discipleship, "From now on you will be catching men" (Luke 5:10). They had known Jesus from before, but after watching Jesus's miracle of filling the fish nets, they were honored to be asked to follow Him. At that time, they left everything and followed Him (Luke 5:11).[230]

The remaining seven disciples apparently responded to Jesus's early ministry. Levi (Matthew), the tax collector, responded after Jesus healed the paralytic in Nazareth (Matt. 9:9; Luke 5:27–28). Later, Jesus went up on a mountain with His many followers. From them, He selected the original four, Philip, Matthew, and an additional six (Bartholomew, Thomas, James, son of Alpheus, Thaddeus, Simon the zealot, and Judas Iscariot) to be His core twelve whom He would send to preach and heal (Mark 3:13–19).

Jesus's final call came to the group of disciples gathered at the Sea of Galilee after the Crucifixion. Even though Jesus had appeared to Peter specifically (Luke 24:34; 1 Cor. 15:5) and the group collectively (Luke 24:36; John 20:19; John 20:26), there was still confusion (John 21:4) and doubt (Matt. 28:17; Luke 24:37–38). Peter had returned to fishing, and Jesus had to challenge him once again over his commitment. Was he returning for fishing for fish or fishing for men in the Great Commission (Matt. 28:19)? So Jesus reminded Peter, "Tend my sheep" (John 20:17).

Conclusion

In conclusion, while it was within the power of the Creator God of the universe to draw men to whatever purpose He chose, it appears that Jesus's followers came to follow Him by previous contact. The first five following John the Baptist's ministry with Jesus, and the remaining seven following Jesus's independent early ministry.

28

Why Did Jesus Command People Not to Tell Who He Was?

It has always been a mystery why Jesus, whose goal was evangelism, would tell people not to talk about His miracles, especially early in His ministry. But His secrecy was expressed in four different situations:

A. Three times, he was rebuking demons, not allowing them to announce him

1. In Galilee (Mark 1:34)
2. The crowd at the Sea of Galilee (Mark 3:12)
3. After healing Simon's mother-in-law (Luke 4:41)

B. Seven times after healing
First Galilean tour

1. After cleansing the leper (Matt. 8:4, Mark 1:44, Luke 5:14)
2. After healing the man with the withered hand (Matt.12:16)

Second Galilean tour

3. After healing the deaf and dumb man (Mark 7:36)
4. After healing the official's (Jarius's) daughter (Matt. 9:30, Mark 5:43, Luke 8:56)

Third Galilean tour

5. After feeding the four thousand (Mark 8:26)
6. Before casting the demon out of the girl at Tyre (Mark 7:24)
7. After healing the blind man of Bethsaida (Mark 8:26)

C. Four times with encounters with the disciples

1. After Peter's acknowledgment that He was the Christ at Caesarea Philippi (Matt. 16:20, Mark 8:30)
2. At the feeding of the five thousand, Peter acknowledges Christ (Luke 9:21)
3. After the transfiguration (Matt. 17:9, Mark 9:9, Luke 9:36)
4. As He ministered in Galilee foretelling His Crucifixion (Mark 9:30)

D. And when he entered the temple during passion week

1. He refused to tell the Pharisees His authority was from God (Matt. 21:27, Mark 11:33, Luke 20:8)

Although Jesus's motivation remains a mystery, there are possible explanations.

First, Jesus felt crowds inhibited His movement to spread his ministry.

This explanation is suggested by Mark 1:45, where it is reported that when the leper healed by Jesus went out and talked freely about his cure, he "spread the news around, to such an extent that Jesus could no longer publicly enter a city, but stayed out in unpopulated areas."

The counter to this explanation is illustrated by Mark 5:19, where Jesus tells the man freed from demon possession at Gearasenes, "Go home to your people and report to them what great things the Lord had done for you, and how He has had mercy on You."

Second, Jesus didn't want to be known purely as a healer by miracles.

In first-century Middle East, faith healers were common (Acts 18:19). History also records the life of Apollonius of Tyana, who reportedly was a miracle healer and paralleled the ministry of Jesus.[231]

In fact, Jesus never explained His strategy.

29

Who Was John the Disciple?

John, the second most influential disciple, is mentioned thirty-five times in the New Testament.[232]

Biography

Tradition states that John was born in AD 6, the son of Zebedee and Salome. He was likely the younger brother of James and the youngest of the disciples. It has been suggested that Salome, the mother of James and John, was actually the sister of Mary, the mother of Jesus. If so, John would have been Jesus's cousin.[233]

He was apparently known to the high priest Caiaphas,[234] a relationship that would prove useful at the Crucifixion trial (John18:16). It is not clear how John would have known Caiaphas. Perhaps their families were acquainted.

John and James were fisherman along with their father, Zebedee, in Capernaum. The two sons were dubbed "Boanerges" (sons of Thunder) by Jesus (Mark 3:17), perhaps because of their impulsive temper at attempting to call fire on those who opposed Jesus (Mark 9:38; Luke 9:54).[235]

Clearly John, along with his brother James, and Peter were in Jesus's inner circle, as evidenced by the fact that it was the three of them who were chosen to accompany Jesus at the transfiguration (Matt. 17:1; Mark 9:2; Luke 9:28). It is not clear why James is included in the group, given his minimal future role, unless he was, indeed Jesus's cousin.

If the Crucifixion took place in AD 30, John would have been twenty-four years old.[236]

John's Writings

Interestingly, John's actual name never appears in the Gospel that bears his name, or his three letters. The only attestation in the Gospel of John is when the sons of Zebedee are mentioned as present when the risen Jesus appears at the Sea of Galilee (John 21:2). He is, however, mentioned by name in Matthew, Mark, Luke, Acts, Galatians, and Revelation.

While John's short letters (1 John, 2 John, 3 John) as well as the Revelation are written in the first person, the Gospel of John is written in the third person. This has led many scholars to doubt that the apostle John is, indeed, the author. However, there is another explanation. John was not literate (Acts 4:13), so like many in the first century, an amanuensis (scribe) was likely used to record his verbal recount. Surprisingly, John does not mention the transfiguration in his Gospel.

John's Gospel may well reveal two personal characteristics: modesty and competition with Peter.

Although John never mentions himself by name in his Gospel, he describes himself as "the disciple whom Jesus loved" five times (John 13:23; 19:26; 20:2; 21:7; 21:20). The validity of this self-assessment is demonstrated in two situations. At the Last Supper, it is John who is reclining closest to Jesus (John 13:20). And on the cross, it is John to whom Jesus entrusts the future care of his mother, Mary (John

19:26–27). It is also likely that John is referring to himself as the other disciple in John 1:37–40 and as "another disciple" who facilitated Peter's entrance into the court of the high priest at Jesus's trial (John 18:16).

Somewhat out of character, their mother, Salome (Matt. 20:20–21), as well as James and John themselves, ask Jesus for special treatment in the afterlife (Mark 10:35–37).

John's competition with Peter comes out when they race to the empty tomb (John 20:4) and John, as "the other disciple ran ahead faster than Peter and came to the tomb first" (John 20:4). It is also interesting to observe that when he (John) and Peter entered the empty tomb, John comments that "the other disciple who had first come to the tomb then also entered, and he saw and believed" (John 20:8). His subsequent verse (John 20:9) suggests that Peter did not yet believe Jesus had been resurrected. Finally, when the resurrected Jesus appeared to the two in Galilee, it was John who identified Jesus to Peter (John 21:7).

Not too surprisingly, Peter also apparently felt the competition since he questioned Jesus's loyalty to John (John 21:20–21).

John's Post-Resurrection Ministry

John's ministry was largely as a support to Peter, who took a leadership role (Acts 1:15) after Jesus's ascension (Acts 1:9). John was present in the upper room at Pentecost (Acts 2:1–4); was present when Peter healed the lame beggar (Acts 3:7); was arrested with Peter twice (Acts 4:3; 5:18); and accompanied Peter to preach in Samaria (Acts 8:14).

While Peter continued his ministry outward toward Rome, John initially remained around Jerusalem where he and James, the brother of Jesus, became leaders of the church. John was present at the Council of Jerusalem, which recalled Paul (Galatians 2:9).

The interval fate of John is not recorded in the Bible until he reports his presence on the island of Patmos.

John reportedly cared for Mary, Jesus's mother, until the time she died. The date of Mary's death has been speculated between AD 43[237] and AD 54.[238]

It is not clear exactly when John fled to Ephesus. It could have been when King Herod Agrippa I attacked the Christians (Acts 12:1–17) between AD 41 and 44.[239] Perhaps more likely is that he fled after the Jewish revolt in Jerusalem in AD 66, which culminated in the destruction of the Second Temple and the Jewish diaspora (Luke 21:20–21).[240] The churches in Anatolia had been planted by Paul during his three missionary journeys and were likely also overseen by Peter during his ministry in Asia Minor. Both Paul and Peter were martyred in Rome around AD 64, so there was a leadership void in Asia Minor. Apparently, John filled that role[241] for thirty years, during which he is said to have written his Gospel and three letters.

The Roman Emperor Domitian considered himself a god and built a temple to himself in Ephesus in AD 86.[242] Domitian was a cruel ruler who persecuted Christians and exiled John to the small island of Patmos in AD 95.[243] While on Patmos (Rev. 1:9), John experienced the visions leading to his book of Revelation, addressed to the seven churches in Anatolia (now western Turkey).

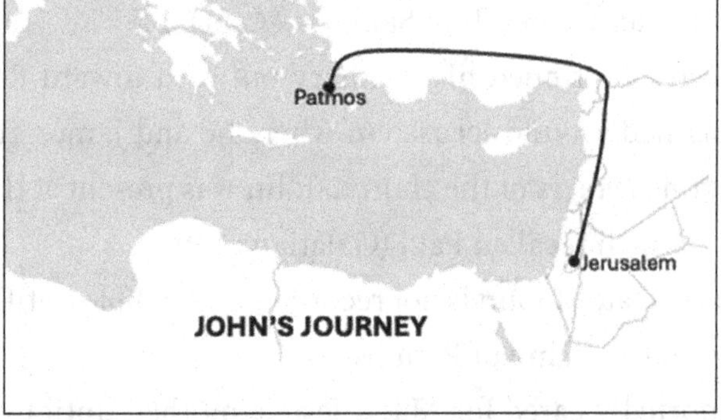

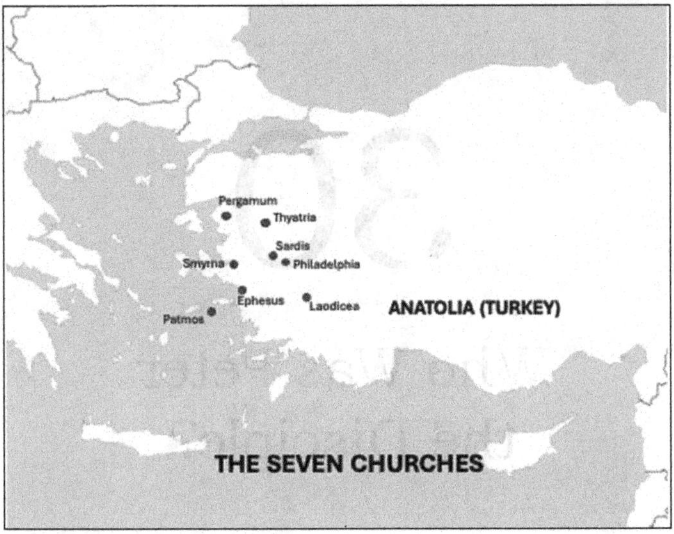

John's Revelation was apparently written around AD 95.[244] It is addressed to the seven churches to encourage their resistance to the emperor-god worship demanded by Domitian. The order of the churches addressed in the Revelation "follows a route that a messenger would naturally follow in visiting the cities."[245]

It is not clear whether John died on Patmos or returned to Ephesus, but most scholars accept that he died of natural causes rather than being executed like many of the other apostles. If John was born in AD 6, he would have been over ninety years old at his death.

The *Encyclopedia Britannica* summarizes,[246]

> At the end of the 2nd century, Polycrates, bishop of Ephesus, claims that John's tomb is at Ephesus, … That John died in Ephesus is also stated by St. Irenaeus, bishop of Lyon circa 180 CE, who says John wrote his Gospel and letters at Ephesus and Revelation at Pátmos. During the 3rd century two rival sites at Ephesus claimed the honor of being the apostle's grave. One eventually achieved official recognition, becoming a shrine in the 4th century.

30

Who Was Peter the Disciple?

Prominence in the New Testament

Peter is mentioned more than any other character except Jesus. Strong's New Expanded Exhausted Concordance of the Bible lists Peter (148); Simon Peter (forty-four); and Cephas (six). By Contrast, Jesus is mentioned over 971 times.[247]

Peter's Origin

John (John 1:44) records that Simon (Peter) originally was from Bethsaida, located on the northeast shore of the Sea of Galilee. He was the son of Jonah (Matt. 16:17; John 1:42) and had a brother, Andrew. Simon moved to Capernaum to start his fishing business. Peter also owned his own boat (Luke 5:3) and was partners in a fishing operation with Andrew (his brother) as well as the sons of Zebedee, James, and John (Luke 5:10).

Peter was apparently the only one of the original disciples who was married, although Paul suggests that other "apostles" may have been married as well (1 Cor. 9:5). Peter had his own house in Capernaum, as evidenced by Jesus's healing Peter's mother-in-law at the house (Matt. 8:14–15, Mark 1:29–31, and Luke 4:38–39). Peter's home is likely where Jesus stayed during His ministry in Capernaum, and the house later became the site of one of the first post-resurrection synagogues.[248]

The *Catholic Encyclopedia* reports that Clement of Alexandria (Stromata, III, vi, ed. Dindorf, II, 276) testified that Peter had children. The same writer relates the tradition that Peter's wife suffered martyrdom (ibid., VII, xi ed. cit., III, 306).[249]

He was considered a simple layman by the Sanhedrin because he did not receive a formal scriptural training (Acts 4:13).

Peter's Age

Peter's age is not historically documented. Old Testament law dictated that the Hebrews should procreate to populate the earth (Gen. 1:28). It must be conjectured from local customs, but there are differing conclusions of first-century marriage age.

"It was thus considered the duty of every Israelite to marry as early in life as possible. Eighteen years is the age set by the Rabbis (Ab. V.24) and anyone remaining unmarried after his twentieth year is said to be cursed by God Himself (Kid. 29b)."[250]

To the contrary, Satlow concludes that in Palestine, men tended to wait until their thirties to marry women fifteen years their younger.[251]

Catholic tradition states that the apostle St. Peter was born about the year AD 1.[252] If the Crucifixion was in AD 30, and if Peter was born in the year AD 1, that would make Peter twenty-nine years old at the time of the Crucifixion.[253]

If Peter was approximately twenty-nine at the time of Crucifixion, and if Jesus's ministry took place over three years, then Peter would have been no more than twenty-six at the time he joined the ministry. This would seem to be consistent with him marrying around eighteen years of age and having several children, developing a successful enough fishing business with boat(s), and obtaining his own house over the next few years.

Peter's Name Change

Peter was originally called the Hebrew term *Simeon* (Acts 15:14; 2 Peter 1:1 [depending upon the English translation]) or the Greek term *Simon* until Jesus changed his apostolic name to *Kephas,* from the Aramaic *Kipha* (rock). The Greek translation is *Cephas*; the Latin is *Petrus.*[254]

It is not clear at what point Jesus changed Simon's name. John 1:42 reports that the name change was shortly after Andrew brought Simon to Jesus at the initial calling. But Matthew reports the name change not to be until the end of His ministry at Caesarea Philippi (Matt. 16:17–18). The two are not necessarily mutually exclusive, since in the latter occurrence, Jesus committed to build His future church with Peter as the leader. But if so, it's not clear why Jesus changed Simon's name to the "rock" at his initial encounter, as reported by John's Gospel. Since the Gospels were not written until decades later, they all included Simon's name as Peter.

Peter's Calling

Andrew and likely Simon (Peter) were probably followers of John the Baptist, whose ministry was well established (Matt. 3:5–6). After baptism by John the Baptist, Jesus apparently worked in parallel with the Baptist's ministry for some time (John 3:22–26; 4:1). John sanctioned Jesus as the Messiah, which convinced Andrew and Simon (Peter) to follow Jesus (John 1:35–42). It may well be that Andrew, Peter, James, and John were part-time followers of John the Baptist. It was not uncommon for spiritual followers of the Baptist to continue with their businesses.[255]

However, once John the Baptist was imprisoned and then killed, the disciples switched to Jesus as the Messiah and heeded His full-time call.

Peter's Leadership

The perplexing question, given Peter's later denial of Jesus at the Crucifixion trial, is why did Jesus trust Peter with a leadership role? While there is no definitive answer to the question, several points are to be considered.

Peter was likely the oldest of the twelve, which may have contributed to his role as leader.

Peter was perhaps the first to fully believe in Jesus's deity as the Messiah. When Jesus gave His "bread of life" analogy, many of His followers withdrew (John 6:66). When Jesus challenged the loyalty of the twelve, it was Peter who spoke up of their continued commitment:

> Simon Peter answered him, "Lord, to whom shall we go? You have the words of eternal life. We have come to believe and to know that you are the Holy One of God." (John 6:68–69)

At Caesarea Philippi, when Jesus again asked who they thought He was, it was Peter who spoke up:

> When Jesus came to the region of Caesarea Philippi, he asked his disciples, "Who do people say the Son of Man is?"
> They replied, "Some say John the Baptist; others say Elijah; and still others, Jeremiah or one of the prophets."
> "But what about you?" he asked. "Who do you say I am?"
> Simon Peter answered, "You are the Messiah, the Son of the living God." (Matt. 16:13–16)

> "But what about you?" he asked. "Who do you say I am?"
> Peter answered, "You are the Messiah." (Mark 8:29)

At the transfiguration, Jesus took Peter, along with James and John, up the mountain (Matt. 17:1–8; Mark 9:2–8; Luke 9:28–36). Jesus's selection of the three likely indicates importance.

Peter was impulsive and capable of rash anger, such as cutting off the priest's slave's ear at Gethsemane (John 18:10). But this same boldness would be necessary to withstand the future persecution of Christians.

Perhaps most memorable are the three times Peter denied being a follower of Jesus. During the Crucifixion trial, the supposedly committed Peter succumbed under political pressure and denied Jesus (Matt. 26:31–35; Mark 14:27–31; Luke 22:31–38; John 13:31–38). As an aside, it is interesting to observe that when Jesus was arrested in Gethsemane, all but three followers abandoned Him and fled, presumably to Bethany. The three remaining were Peter, John, and probably John Mark. Yet their leader, Peter, was the one who betrayed Jesus. After realizing that Jesus's prophecies of his denials came true, he wept with remorse (Matt. 26:75; Mark 14:72).

It was Peter who is described as first rushing to the empty tomb (Luke 24:12) and being present with John at the tomb (John 20:3–6). Mark describes the "young man sitting in the empty tomb" as saying to go tell the disciples and Peter specifically (Mark 16:7). Post-resurrection accounts emphasize that Peter was the first disciple to whom the risen Jesus appeared (Luke 24:33–34; 1 Cor. 15:5).

In His post-resurrection appearance at the Sea of Galilee, it is Simon Peter whom Jesus reinstates after Peter's denials at the Crucifixion:

> When they had finished eating, Jesus said to Simon Peter, "Simon son of John, do you love me more than these?"

"Yes, Lord," he said, "you know that I love you."
Jesus said, "Feed my lambs."
Again Jesus said, "Simon son of John, do you love me?"
He answered, "Yes, Lord, you know that I love you."
Jesus said, "Take care of my sheep."
The third time he said to him, "Simon son of John, do you love me?"
Peter was hurt because Jesus asked him the third time, "Do you love me?" He said, "Lord, you know all things; you know that I love you."
Jesus said, "Feed my sheep." (John 21:15–17)

Peter's Post-Resurrection Ministry

It was after Jesus's ascension that Peter asserted his leadership. The timeline of his ministry is detailed by the BibleJourney.org.[256] It is summarized as follows:

In AD 30, Peter presides over the filling of a replacement for Judas Iscariot (Acts1:15). He also presided over speaking in various languages at Pentecost (Acts 1:14). His sermon to the men of Israel (Acts 1:22–41) culminated in three thousand converts.

He healed the lame man in the Temple (Acts 3:6). Peter, along with John, was temporarily arrested for preaching Jesus as the Messiah (Acts 4:3). As leader of the Jerusalem church, Peter confronted Ananias and Sapphira (Acts 5:1–10). Even as the other disciples abandoned them, Peter and John continued to add converts (Acts 5:13–14). Once again, Peter and John were arrested, after which an angel freed them (Acts 5:19).

Apparently, Peter's initial ministry remained around Judea and Samaria (Acts 8), with his headquarters remaining in Jerusalem. His initial focus was converting his fellow Jews to Christianity. Peter, along with James (the brother of Jesus), was the leader of the Christian movement in Jerusalem. As such, he was a mentor to Paul, who visited him twice (Gal. 1:18; 2:1).

In about AD 35, while traveling in the region of Lydda, Peter healed the paralytic Aeneas (Acts 9:34) and brought Tabitha back to life (Acts 9:40).

By AD 44, Peter was spreading the message to the Gentiles by preaching to Cornelius the centurion (Acts 10:34). Peter was again imprisoned, this time by Herod Agrippa I, and again freed by an angel (Acts 12:7).

Peter was next heard from at the Council of Jerusalem, in about AD 49–50, to which Paul is called after his first missionary journey. Paul is accused of not requiring circumcision for conversion, and Peter eloquently defends him (Acts 15:7–11).

In AD 50, Peter showed up in Antioch. Besides Jerusalem, Antioch was the second most important church of the new Christian movement. It was the headquarters church from which Paul's missionary journeys were commissioned. At Antioch, Peter was chastised for professing that Gentiles did not have to adopt Jewish laws for conversion yet succumbing to pressure from the "Judaizers" sent by James from Jerusalem, who reverted to Jewish law pressure (Gal. 2:14–16).

The Bible is sparse in reporting Peter's later ministry. Perhaps stimulated by his Gentile ministry experience with Cornelius, Peter apparently began to venture into Asia Minor and into Greece, perhaps either facilitating or supporting Paul's church plants. There is a suggestion in 1 Corinthians 1:12, written by Paul in AD 56, that factions in Corinth were followers of Peter.

The introduction to his first letter of Peter, probably dated about AD 66 from Rome, addresses those "scattered throughout Pontus, Galatia, Cappadocia, Asia, and Bithynia (1 Pet. 1:1). It is a 2,500–mile journey from Jerusalem to Rome, a trip that apparently occupied over twenty years of Peter's ministry.

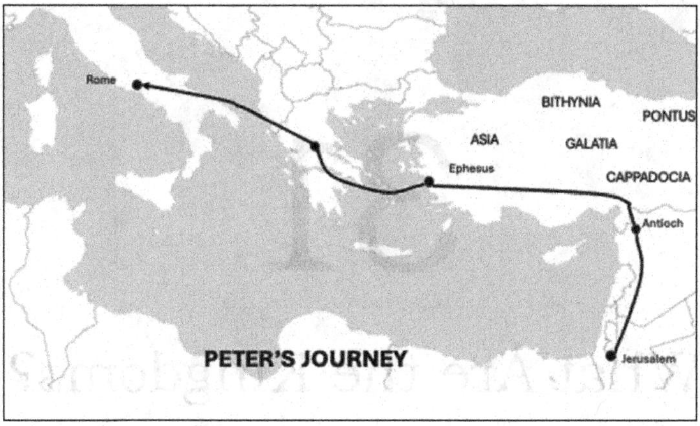

It is not clear exactly how long Peter had been in Rome, but history records that he was imprisoned along with Paul. Peter's second letter foretells his execution (2 Pet. 1:14–15).

Tradition is that he was crucified upside down at his request, due to not feeling worthy to be crucified the same as Jesus. This could be interpreted as fulfilling Jesus's prophecy in John 21:18. It is likely that his Crucifixion was between AD 64 and 67. If it is true that Peter was born in 1 AD, he would have been sixty-four to sixty-seven years old at his death.

31

What Are the Kingdoms?

Introduction

Strong's Concordance lists 342 incidences of the word *kingdom* in the Bible—187 times in the Old Testament and 155 times in the New Testament.[257]

The Greek word for "kingdom" is *Basileia* (βασιλεία, ας, ἡ).[258] A kingdom has two requisites: (1) a ruling king and (2) the territory or people subject to reign of the king.

The *territorial definition* can be applied to the Jewish prophecy of eventual reconstitution of the nation of Israel by the Messiah (Ezek. 11:17; Zech. 8:7–8; Rom. 11:26). Jewish people refer to God's four unconditional covenants promising them a future: (1) Abrahamic Covenant of seed, land, and blessing (Gen. 12:1–3; 15:18); (2) Palestinian Covenant of blessing with obedience (Deut. 28:1–2); (3) Davidic Covenant of house and kingdom (2 Sam. 7:8–16); and (4) New Covenant restoration of Israel (Jer. 31:31–37; Ezek. 36:22–37).

But the concept of sovereign God's interaction with subject people through Christ is the topic of the kingdom references in the New Testament.

The Kingdoms

The word *kingdom* is associated with several phrases:

1. Kingdom of heaven
2. Kingdom of God
3. Kingdom
4. Kingdom of Christ and God

The "Kingdom of Heaven" is present thirty-one times in the New Testament. All are exclusively in the Gospel of Matthew. A similar phrase, "heavenly kingdom," appears in 2 Timothy 4:18. It is difficult to classify the earthly realm of Jesus's kingdom from God's eternal kingdom in the Matthew references. The Sermon on the Mount and the parables could be applied to either, but multiple references to the "kingdom of heaven" in Jesus's parables recorded in Matthew 13 are interpreted as referring to the "present" or "mystery" kingdom rather than to the commonly understood eternal heaven.[259] It is this "present" form of the earthly kingdom that seems to have a wide range of interpretation among theologians.[260, 261, 262]

The "Kingdom of God" occurs sixty-five times in the New Testament: Matthew (five); Mark (fourteen); Luke (thirty); John (two); Acts (five); Romans (one); 1 Corinthians (four); Galatians (one); Colossians (one); 2 Thessalonians (one); and Revelation (one). All but possibly two verses (Luke 13:28–29) clearly refer to the earthly reign of Jesus.

"The precise phrase, 'kingdom of God' does not appear as such in the Hebrew Old Testament."[263] It is conjectured that since Matthew was writing to a Jewish audience, he honored the Jewish tradition not to mention God's name. The four exceptions are Matthew 12:28; 19:24; 21:31; 21:43. All are direct quotes from Jesus.

"Kingdom" alone appears fifty-five times in the New Testament: Matthew (twenty); Mark (four); Luke (eighteen); John (one); Acts (ten);

Colossians (one); 1 Thessalonians (one); 2 Timothy (two); Hebrews (two); James (one); 2 Peter (one); Revelation (four). The realm of reference depends upon the context of the text. Although there could be some variation in interpretation, the rough breakdown is restoration of the nation of Israel (five); worldly kingdoms (five); Christ's earthly kingdom (twenty-seven); and heaven (sixteen).

"Kingdom of Christ and God" occurs in Ephesians 5:5. The "Kingdom of our Father David" occurs in Mark 11:10.

The "Present" Kingdom

So how do we differentiate the meanings of these kingdoms?

Pentecost[264] identifies three different kingdoms: (1) the future earthly Davidic kingdom, (2) the future eternal kingdom, and (3) present form of the kingdom. Pentecost states, "At times it [Kingdom of God] is used in reference to the coming Davidic kingdom, sometimes in reference to the eternal kingdom, but most frequently it is used in reference to the new form of theocracy predicted by Christ in Matthew 13."[265] This apparent contradiction makes the different kingdoms difficult to identify. The identities of the future eternal kingdom and the future earthly Davidic kingdom are clear. It is the present form of the earthly kingdom and its relation to the "church" that is ambiguous. Pentecost goes on to state, "The term kingdom of God is equated with salvation, and it must refer to participation in or exclusion from the present form of the kingdom."[266] Typical references include 1 Thessalonians 2:12, James 2:5, and 2 Peter 1:11.

While the Old Testament focused on worldly kingdoms and God's eternal kingdom, the preponderance of kingdom references in the New Testament describe the earthly kingdom of Jesus—what Pentecost calls the "present form of the kingdom."

Jesus declared his establishment of the kingdom:

> Truly I say to you, among those born of women there has not arisen anyone greater than John the Baptist! Yet the one who is least in the kingdom of heaven is greater than he. (Matt. 11:11; Luke 7:28 NASB)

> And saying, "The time is fulfilled, and the kingdom of God is at hand; repent and believe in the gospel." (Mark 1:15 NASB)

> "Even the dust of your town we wipe from our feet as a warning to you. Yet be sure of this: The kingdom of God has come near." (Luke 10:11)

> But if I cast out demons by the finger of God, then the kingdom of God has come upon you. (Luke 11:20; Matt. 12:28 NASB)

> Now having been questioned by the Pharisees as to when the kingdom of God was coming, He answered them and said, "The kingdom of God is not coming with signs to be observed; nor will they say, 'Look, here it is!' or, 'There it is!' For behold, the kingdom of God is in your midst." (Luke 17:20–21 NASB)

Already but Not Yet

So how do these two kingdoms—the earthly and the eternal—integrate?

This topic is called kingdom theology, and it defines the process as "inaugurated eschatology." Gerhadus Vos, a Princeton theologian in the early twentieth century, proffered that there are two ages: the "now" and the "age to come." He then coined the term "already, but not yet."

The concept was further elaborated by George Eldon Ladd of Fuller Seminary in the 1950s.[267]

The concept is that Jesus's incarnation initiated the first eschatological step in establishment of the eternal kingdom of God by establishing a kingdom on earth. Even though the earthly realm is dominated by satanic rule, Christian believers can spiritually enter the kingdom realm through belief in Jesus. Salvation into the future eternal kingdom is assured at this "new birth." This is the "already" portion of "inaugurated eschatology."

At the end of this age, with the second coming of Jesus, satanic rule will be quashed. At that time, Christians will not only spiritually but also physically enter the eternal kingdom of God in heaven for eternity. This is the "not yet" conclusion step being awaited currently.

So Jesus was dealing with two separate but simultaneous movements: (1) the expected messianic reestablishment of the Temple and the nation of Israel and (2) the establishment of the kingdom of God on earth.

Against this backdrop of revolutionary expectation, Jesus established God's kingdom on earth. At the incarnation, God sent His Son as Jesus to begin to establish direct interaction with believers. Beginning with the virgin birth, Jesus's ministry introduced the earthly kingdom.

The Crucifixion accomplished atonement for sin. Then Jesus ascended back to heaven while bringing the Holy Spirit to continue guiding the believers (the church). This period will continue until the return of Christ (the Parousia), the rapture, the final judgment, and the thousand years of God's reign on earth.

Conclusion

In the Old Testament, God dealt with humankind from a distance. While God occasioned to intercede in earthly affairs, the kingdom of God was separate and distant. According to Jewish doctrine, entrance into the kingdom was to take place only at the end of the earth age when the Messiah reestablished the nation of Israel and the Temple. At that time, the deceased saints and those living at that time were gathered to enter the eternal kingdom with God.

With the incarnation of Jesus, the kingdom of God extended to earth. The present ("already, not yet") kingdom became the point of entry into spiritual salvation. Having entered the present kingdom by faith in Jesus, the Christian secured eternal life, both spiritually and bodily. After Jesus's ascension back into the heavenly kingdom, the Holy Spirit became the substitute for Jesus in the present earthly kingdom of God. The mechanism for salvation remains to be faith in Jesus as Savior.

32

Why Did Jesus Start Speaking in Parables?

Webster defines "parable" as "a usually short fictitious story that illustrates a moral attitude or a religious principle."[268] As opposed to an allegory, which usually uses inanimate objects, a parable is a story using human actions to make a moral or religious point.[269] A simile is defined as a comparison between two things, often using the term "like "or "as." Finally, a metaphor is a "figure of speech in which a word or a phrase that ordinarily designates one thing is used to designate another. Whereas a simile states that A is *like* B, a metaphor states that A *is* B or substitutes B for A."[270] These literary definitions are relevant when attempting to define Jesus's use of illustrations.

Over forty parables are listed in the New Testament.[271] All are found in the first three Gospels:

PARABLES	MATTHEW	MARK	LUKE
Salt of the Earth	Matthew 5:13	Mark 9:50	
Lamp Under a Bowl	Matthew 5:14-16	Mark 4:21-22	Luke 8:16, 11:33
Wise and Foolish Builders	Matthew 7:24-27		Luke 6:47-49
New Cloth on an Old Coat	Matthew 9:16	Mark 2:21	Luke 5:36
New Wine in Old Wineskins	Matthew 9:17	Mark 2:22	Luke 5:37-39
The Two Debtors			Luke 7:40-43
The Sower	Matthew 13:1-23	Mark 4:1-20	Luke 8:4-15
The Good Samaritan			Luke 10:25-37
The Friend at Midnight			Luke 11:5-13
Growing Seed		Mark 4:26-29	
The Rich Fool			Luke 12:13-21
The Watchful Servants		Mark 13:35-37	Luke 12:35-40
Unfruitful Fig Tree			Luke 13:6-9
The Weeds	Matthew 13:24-30, 36-43		
The Seed	Matthew 13:31-32	Mark 4:26-30	Luke 13:18-19
Yeast	Matthew 13:33		Luke 13:20-21
The Concealed Treasure	Matthew 13:44		
The Pearl	Matthew 13:45-46		
The Casting of the Net into the Sea	Matthew 13:47-50		
Owner of a House	Matthew 13:52		
The Lost Sheep	Matthew 18:12-14		Luke 15:3-7
The Unforgiving Servant	Matthew 18:23-35		
The Vineyard Workers	Matthew 20:1-16		
Lowest Seat at the Feast			Luke 14:7-14
The Great Feast			Luke 14:16-24
Cost of Discipleship			Luke 14:28-33
The Lost Coin			Luke 15:8-10
The Prodigal Son			Luke 15:11-32
The Shrewd Manager			Luke 16:1-13
The Rich Man and Lazarus			Luke 16:19-31
Master and His Servant			Luke 17:7-10
Persistent Widow			Luke 18:1-8
The Two Sons	Matthew 21:28-32		
The Vineyard Owner	Matthew 21:33-44	Mark 12:1-11	Luke 20:9-18
The Marriage Feast	Matthew 22:1-14		
Fig Tree	Matthew 24:32-35	Mark 13:28-31	Luke 21:29-33
Faithful and Wise Servant	Matthew 24:45-51		Luke 12:42-48
The Pharisee and the Tax Collector			Luke 18:9-14
Ten Virgins	Matthew 25:1-13		
The Talent	Matthew 25:14-30		Luke 19:11-27
The Sheep and the Goats	Matthew 25:31-46		

Not that it matters in content, but the categorization of parables is somewhat loose grammatically. The illustrations Jesus uses are a mixture of metaphor, allegory, simile, and true parable. The NASB version of the New Testament labels twenty-four illustrations as parables, even though at least nine of these are actually similes (mainly in Matthew's Gospel). One of the best known of Jesus's parables is that of the Good Samaritan. It is not labeled as a parable by Luke in 10:25–37.

Interestingly, John the apostle does not include the term *parable* in his Gospel. Rather he portrays Jesus as making use of figures of speech, for example, the image of the sheepfold (John 10:1–6), the door of the sheepfold (John 10:7–10), the good shepherd (John 10:11–18), and the vine and the branches (John 15:1–8).[272]

The burning question is why Jesus, whose ministry was aimed at repentance and conversion, would intentionally conceal the mysteries of the kingdom from those to whom he preached?

Perhaps the point in time of Jesus's ministry that He began using parables is significant. During the first part of His ministry, Jesus taught with clear declarative instruction, with occasional allegory and metaphor. But His method suddenly changed. Matthew reports that Jesus's transition to parables was at the midpoint in His ministry (approximately summer of AD 28). While healing in Capernaum, Jesus was accused of healing from the power of Beelzebul, and His family thought He was out of His mind (Matt. 12:22–29; Mark 3:20–35). Jesus responded that they were insulting the Holy Spirit—an unforgiveable sin (Matt. 12:30–32; Mark 3:39). This was the breaking point in Jesus's ministry when He apparently deferred instituting the earthly kingdom. Jesus announced, "He who is not with me is against me" (Matt. 12:30) and rejected His family (Matt. 12:48–50; Mark 3:31–35).

At this point, Jesus's ministry appeared to become more aggressive. He announced that He had come to create division on earth, even within families (Luke12:51–53). He tended to utter the parables in public (Matt.

13:34), particularly in the presence of Pharisees, then explain them to His followers in private (Matt. 13:34; Mark 4:33–34; 4:10; 7:16–17; 10:10).

Viljoen observes that Jesus used parables to separate communication between the "insiders" of his followers and the "outsiders" who were nonbelievers.[273] Apparently, Jesus's goal was to communicate the "mysteries" of the kingdom (Matt. 13:11; Matt. 13:35; Mark 4:11; Luke 8:10), which had been hidden since creation (Matt. 13:35), to His followers. Jesus uses Psalm 78:2 to illustrate how God had previously excluded unbelievers from understanding:

> So was fulfilled what was spoken through the prophet:
> "I will open my mouth in parables,
> I will utter things hidden since the creation of the world." (Matt. 13:35)

Jesus's explanation for using parables immediately follows the parable of the sower in the first three Gospels (Matt. 13:1–9; Mark 4:1–9; Luke 8:4–8). The parable of the sower can be regarded as the parable about the parables,[274] since it illustrates that the determining factor in the parable is the soil, rather than the seed itself. Jesus used this parable to indicate that not all people will be able to interpret his parables.

> Then Jesus said to them, "Don't you understand this parable? How then will you understand any parable?" (Mark 4:13 NIV)

The disciples were confused by Jesus's change in communication and asked him, "Why do you speak to the people in parables?" (Matt. 13:10; Mark 4:10). Jesus invoked Isaiah 6:9 in hiding understanding of the mysteries from unbelievers (Matt. 13:10–17; Mark 4:11–12; Luke 8:10).

> He told them, "The secret of the kingdom of God has been given to you But to those on the outside everything is said in parables so that,
> 'they may be ever seeing but never perceiving,
> and ever hearing but never understanding;
> otherwise they might turn and be forgiven!'" (Mark 4:11–12)

Jesus also made it clear that the ability to comprehend His parables was a gift of grace from God (Luke 8:9) to those who accepted Him.

Conclusion

It seems clear that Jesus's abrupt transition from declarative instruction to the masses to parables coincided with his rejection in Matthew 12. From that point on, Jesus became less focused on converting unbelievers—particularly the scribes and Pharisees—and more focused on nurturing His committed followers.

33

When Was Jesus's Last Supper?

The Question

Ehrman writes, "In Mark, Jesus eats the Passover meal (Thursday night) and is crucified the following morning. In John, Jesus does not eat the Passover meal but is crucified on the day before the Passover meal was to be eaten."[275]

But first, Ehrman is incorrect to say that John does not describe Jesus eating the Passover meal. John 13:1 begins the description of the Passover meal when Jesus washes the disciples' feet and gives a long discourse on His leaving them to be replaced by the Holy Spirit:

> It was just before the Passover Feast. Jesus knew that the hour had come for him to leave this world and go to the Father. Having loved his own who were in the world, he loved them to the end.
>
> The evening meal was in progress, and the devil had already prompted Judas, the son of Simon Iscariot, to betray Jesus. Jesus knew that the Father had put all

> things under his power, and that he had come from God and was returning to God; so he got up from the meal, took off his outer clothing, and wrapped a towel around his waist. After that, he poured water into a basin and began to wash his disciples' feet, drying them with the towel that was wrapped around him. (John 13:1–5 NIV)

Similarly, Mark details Jesus eating the Last Supper with His disciples on the first day of the Unleavened Bread (the same as Passover):

> On the first day of the Festival of Unleavened Bread, when it was customary to sacrifice the Passover lamb, Jesus's disciples asked him, "Where do you want us to go and make preparations for you to eat the Passover?" So he sent two of his disciples, telling them, "Go into the city, and a man carrying a jar of water will meet you. Follow him. Say to the owner of the house he enters, 'The Teacher asks: Where is my guest room, where I may eat the Passover with my disciples?' He will show you a large room upstairs, furnished and ready. Make preparations for us there." The disciples left, went into the city and found things just as Jesus had told them. So they prepared the Passover. (Mark 14:12 NIV)

Both Gospels, then, report Jesus having the Passover meal with His disciples the evening after the day of preparation for the next Sabbath.

The issue of the time-of-day conflict is discussed in chapter 37. Basically, John lived in a Roman-dominated culture at the time of writing of his Gospel. Thus, the "sixth hour" was six in the morning rather than noon, as inserted by modern translators.

Finally, Ehrman falsely assumes the preparation day to be Thursday before a Friday Crucifixion. As is discussed in detail in the "What

Day Did Jesus Die" chapter 36, the preparation day was Wednesday, preparation for the additional High Sabbath on Thursday.

Jesus ate the Passover meal on the evening beginning of the day of preparation, was captured at Gethsemane that night, was in Pilate's court at six in the morning, and was crucified during the day before the start of Passover that evening. The apparent conflict Ehrman sees does not exist.

The detailed timing of Passion Week and the Crucifixion is discussed in detail in chapter 36.

34

Did Jesus Really Sweat Blood at Gethsemane?

On the night of Jesus's arrest, he withdrew from the disciples to pray, asking God,

> "Father, if You are willing, remove this cup from Me; yet not My will, but Yours be done." (Luke 22:42 NASB)

And while Jesus was praying, Luke records that He sweated blood:

> And being in agony He was praying very fervently; and His sweat became like drops of blood, falling down upon the ground. (Luke 22:44 NASB)

God is certainly capable of any miraculous event, but was this a miracle or an illusion? A miracle is an event that either enhances natural processes (healing the infirmed) or suspends the laws of nature (resurrection of Lazarus). But all miracles had a purpose to glorify God. Why would God perform a miraculous event with Jesus sweating blood?

Or could it not have been a miracle but rather a known medical condition?

As it turns out, there is a known, rare condition called *hematohidrosis* in which sweating of blood occurs. Over seventy cases have been reported in the medical literature.[276, 277, 278, 279, 280, 281]

The mechanism appears to be rupture of the capillaries feeding the sweat glands with resultant bleeding into the glands. Discharge of sweat from the gland contains blood. The cause of the capillary rupture is extreme stress, either physical exertion or severe emotional distress.

Certainly, Jesus, knowing the fate that awaited him, had reason to feel extreme emotional stress.

35

Why Did Jesus Have to Die?

The purpose of Jesus's Crucifixion has been debated in church history for centuries. To explore this controversial topic, some "in the weeds" theological definitions are necessary.

- *expiation*: the removal of sin
- *propitiation*: the appeasement of wrath
- *sanctification*: purification
- *atonement*: the process of removing accountability for sin to achieve reconciliation with God
- *redemption*: regaining something in exchange for paymnt

What is the problem in the first place?

The issue of the need for reconciliation with God is seated in a dilemma. God is holy and cannot allow sin in His presence. Man became inherently sinful with the original sin of Adam. To enter God's presence in the afterlife, humans must somehow have their sins removed (expiation).

So Why Does God Bother?

Gruden makes an interesting observation, noting that "it was not necessary for God to save people at all … 'God did not spare angels when they sinned, but cast them into hell and committed them to chains of gloomy darkness to be kept until judgement.'"[282] Genesis 5:6 reveals that seeing the wickedness of humankind, he was "grieved that He had made man on earth" and was prepared to "wipe out mankind who I have created from the face of the earth" (Gen. 5:7). Fortunately, He found Noah to be worth saving. Gruden points out that the answer is that while God requires righteousness, He also loves His humankind creation (John 3:16).

Why Does God Require Atonement?

Since God created the universe and has sovereign authority over it, why didn't He just declare humankind's sin forgiven rather than requiring blood sacrifice to achieve it? While no one can understand the mind of God, several theories have been offered.

Atonement Theories

The Ransom Theory

This theory is suggested by Jesus's own words:

> "Just as the Son of Man did not come to be served, but to serve, and to give his life as a ransom for many." (Matt. 20:28)
>
> "For even the Son of Man did not come to be served, but to serve, and to give his life as a ransom for many." (Mark 10:45)

The ransom concept is additionally referenced in 1 Peter 1:18–19 and 1 Timothy 2:5–6.

It is also thought to be suggested by the redemption passages (Rom. 3:24; 8:23; Gal. 3:13–14; 1 Cor. 1:30, 6:20; Eph. 1:7; Col. 1:14; Titus 2:14; Heb. 9:12; 1 Pet. 1:18).[283]

This view, attributed to Origen (AD 185–254) and Gustaf Aulen (1879–1978), was popular in the eastern early church. According to this theory, Christ paid His life as a ransom to free believers from Satan's kingdom, in which we all reside as sinners. But while scripture says we are held accountable to God for our sins, nowhere does it say we are accountable to Satan. And a corollary to this theory is that that, if true, God deceived Satan by resurrecting Jesus. Therefore, this theory has little credibility.

The Exemplary or Moral Justice Theory

"This theory maintains that God's love displayed on the cross overwhelms sinners' resistance and persuades them to repent and be reconciled to God."[284] Its inception is attributed to Peter Abelard (1079–1142). This theory is attributed to Faustus Socinus (1539–1604), an Italian theologian. The exemplary theory, while acknowledging Jesus's teaching on following His example (Luke 9:23), fails to account for the scriptures that focus on Jesus's death as payment for sins, as listed in the redemption passages previously.

The Governmental Theory

This somewhat obtuse theory is summarized by Grudem:

> It was God's demonstration of the fact that his laws had been broken, that He is the moral lawgiver and governor of the universe, and that some kind of penalty would be required whenever his laws were broken. Thus, Christ

> did not exactly pay the penalty for the actual sins of any people, but simply suffered to show that when God's laws are broken there must be some penalty paid. [285]

"On this basis, God is able to extend forgiveness while maintaining order in the universe."[286] A part of this theory is universal atonement.

The governmental theory was forwarded by Hugo Grotius, a Dutch jurist (1583–1645). The theory has the same weakness as the exemplary (moral justice) theory in that it avoids the multiple scriptures holding sinners accountable.

The Satisfaction Theory

This theory suggests that Christ's death was to satisfy God's honor, which had been wounded by humanity's sin.

The theory was advanced by St. Anselm (1033–1109). Anselm proposed that "human beings owe God a debt of honor, and sin is failure to give God his due ... This debt creates a moral rupture in the universe that God cannot allow to continue indefinitely." In Anselm's view, the only possible way of repaying the debt was for a being of infinite greatness to live as a person on behalf of human beings and to repay the debt of honor that was owed to God.[287]

As with the two previous theories, the responsibility of man to pay for his sin is ignored.

The Universal Reconciliation Theory

As proposed by Karl Barth in 1968, this theory proposes that "by his incarnation and death Christ, our representative, united humanity (humanum) with his divine nature".[288] This theory states that God pardons sinners not because of punishment for sin but of His own desire to forgive sin. Again, this theory suggests universal atonement.

The Christus Victor Theory

This view, offered by theory, recounts the eternal cosmic battle between God and Satan. Jesus is the God form that finalizes victory over Satan. This theory was suggested in Paul's writings (1 Cor. 15:54–57). Although the theory emphasizes Christ's victory over death and evil, it does not explain exactly how the cross accomplishes victory, nor does it explain how Christ's victory over Satan achieves atonement for the sins of humankind.

The Penal Substitution Theory

This theory defines that sin separates humankind from God who is holy. To achieve reconciliation, humankind must be cleansed of sin (*expiation* leading to *sanctification*). This was the view of John Calvin (1509–1564) and the Reformers.

Beginning in Leviticus, God instituted a system in which the sins of man were transferred to an innocent animal, who was then slain as a substitute for the sinful individual. Before the animal was slain, the cofferer would lay his hands on the sacrificial animal as a symbol of transference ("vicarious substitution") of sin to the victim animal (Lev. 4:15). The shedding of blood of the sacrificed animal symbolized removal of sin (Lev. 17:11; 16:21; Num. 8:12) This ritual began as sacrifice of the Passover lamb, whose blood was smeared above the doors in Egypt so that the Lord spared the Hebrew firstborn sons (Exod. 12:13). Of course, the animal sacrifice was symbolic. The sins of the patriarchs were credited forward to the true sacrifice of Jesus (Rom. 4:1; Heb. 11:5).

Removal of sin was then associated with the shedding of blood at sacrificial death.

As the ultimate sacrifice, God sent His Son to live sinlessly in human form so that He could have the sins of humanity transferred onto Him.

Jesus became the "lamb of God" (John 1:29; Rev. 6:16; 12:11; 17:14; 21:27; 22:3). Thus, the mechanism of shedding of Jesus's blood fulfilled the sacrificial removal of sin (Rom. 3:25; Eph. 2:13; 9:12, 14; 1 Pet. 1:2; 1 John 5:6). This theory is usually associated with atonement limited to those who accept Christ as Savior.

Conclusion

The purpose of Jesus's life has been debated in church history for centuries. Ryrie summarizes:[289]

> All these viewpoints may perhaps be catalogued under three basic categories: (1) views that related the death of Christ to Satan (Origen, Aulen) (2) views that consider His death as a powerful example to influence people (Abelard, Socinus, Grotius, Barth). (3) Views that emphasize punishment due to the justice of God and substitution (perhaps Anselm -though deficient—and the Reformers.) Although there may be truth in views that do not include penal substitution, it is important to remember that such truth, if there be some, cannot save eternally. Only the substitutionary death of Christ can provide that which God's justice demands and thereby become the basis for the gift of eternal life to those who believe.
>
> This is the dominant view of the gospels, the teachings of Paul, and most evangelical Christians.

36

What Day Did Jesus Die?

The Question

What day of the week did Jesus actually die? Unfortunately, there is not a straightforward answer, so we will have to get into the weeds a little to sort it out.

We first must determine when a day started and ended in first-century Jerusalem. To this day, the point is not settled.

J. Amanda McGuire has written a very detailed analysis of whether the Jewish culture used a morning-evening or an evening-morning motif. Her conclusion is that the evening-morning pattern is most likely, based primarily upon the sequence of Genesis 1:2–5.[290]

"Conceptually, the Evening-morning motif ties in with Gen. 1:2–5, which demonstrates that the world was covered first in darkness and chaos, but then light was created. Each subsequent day is a reenactment of that sequence of events that moves from darkness (chaos) to light (order)."

This point of a new "day" beginning at dusk at the end of daylight seems to be consistent with the timing in Mark's Gospel but at odds with John's Gospel, which apparently adopts Roman time.

The Jewish calendar was tied to the moon and follows lunar cycles.

A Jewish year has twelve months, and because it is based on the circling of the moon (Num. 28:14; 1 Sam. 20:5, 18; Isa. 66:23), a Jewish year has 354 days, with twenty-nine or thirty days in each month.

The Roman republican calendar was also based on lunar cycles, but in 46 BC, Julius Caesar modified the republican calendar, converting it to fixed length for months, creating the Julian calendar with 365.25 days per year. The Roman Julian calendar was finally revised into the Gregorian calendar by Pope Gregory XIII in 1852. It is the calendar in use in the western world today. Both the Roman Julian calendar and the Gregorian calendar start a day at midnight, as opposed to twilight (approximately 6:00 p.m.) in the Hebrew calendar used in most of the Bible.

The main difference between Julian and Gregorian calendars is that an average year in Julian calendar is 365.25 days, while an average year in Gregorian calendar is 365.2425 days.[291]

The Jewish Calendar

The Old and New Testament references to days and time are somewhat confusing because while most of the time/day references are in Jewish time, there apparently is an occasional notation in Roman Julian time (the day starts at midnight), as illustrated in John 19:14.

The first month in the Jewish calendar is Nissan (also spelled Nisan) and occurs during the months of March through April in the Roman calendar. Nissan is the month that the Passover is observed.

> The Lord said to Moses and Aaron in Egypt, "This month is to be for you the first month, the first month of your year." (Exod. 12:1–3)

The month on the Gregorian calendar we now use is difficult to specifically correlate with the onset of Nissan, again because of the difference between the lunar and solar cycles.

"As Passover is a spring festival, it should fall on a full moon day around, and normally just after, the vernal (northward) equinox."[292]

"The March equinox or Northward equinox is the equinox on the Earth when the subsolar point appears to leave the Southern Hemisphere and cross the celestial equator, heading northward as seen from Earth. The March equinox is known as the vernal equinox in the Northern Hemisphere and as the autumnal equinox in the Southern. ... The March equinox may be taken to mark the beginning of spring and the end of winter in the Northern Hemisphere but marks the beginning of autumn and the end of summer in the Southern Hemisphere."[293]

There has been controversy over exactly which day Nissan starts.

> The Creation calendar defines the commencement of a month with the conjunction of a new moon. (Numbers 28:14; 1 Samuel 20; Isaiah 66:23). But the ancient Babylonian calendar, later adopted by the Jews, defines the commencement of a month with sighting the first crescent of a new moon.

After the Babylonian exile, the Jews were divided on the date of the observance of Passover. Some Jews insisted on following Creation's calendar, that is, Nisan 1 began on the day of a new moon. Jewish leaders, however, insisted on using the Babylonian method for determining the first day of each month. The High Priest waited until the first crescent of the new moon was sighted before declaring the commencement of Nisan 1.

Because the conjunction of a new moon and the sighting of the first crescent of a new moon in Jerusalem is typically 16 to 40 hours later, the celebration of two Passovers on two different days in Israel was not uncommon. In fact, the national Passover usually occurred two days later than the Passover observed by conservative Jews.[294]

As Christians reading the Bible in the twenty-first century, we try to convert the Gospel accounts to our days of the week. This likely leads to confusion.

Jewish Week

One of the greater mysteries in terms of telling time is the seven-day week.

> Most of the other increments make sense based on the cycles of the moon and the sun. But there seems to be no obvious reference in the natural order to explain a week being seven days. Surely the book of Genesis is the theological source for this practice. God worked for six days and creating the heavens and the earth and rested on the seventh. [Gen 2:3] Thus man, made in God's image, did the same [Ex20:11]. And yet it seems clear that most cultures throughout human history seem to "reset the clock" every seven days. Where exactly this comes from naturally is not clear. It is possible that the influence of the Jewish scriptures had some role. Yet the seven-day cycle seems common even where Jewish faith could not have had much influence. Perhaps there is some inner circadian rhythm in the human person; it's not clear. But for the Jews of Jesus' time, it is clear enough that God had set this forth and thus it was to be followed. Weeks lasted from one sabbath to the next; there is no evidence that the Jews named each day.
>
> Of course, the Sabbath was named, and the day before the Sabbath was called Preparation Day (e.g., Mk 15:42). However other days were simply called the first day of the week (e.g., Mk 16:2), the second day of the week, and so forth. Romans and Greeks named each

day off after a god or a planet, but there is no evidence that the Jews did this.[295]

Thus, assigning days of the week to the Nissan calendar is questionable. We merely assume that the week of creation started with Sunday and that Saturday was the seventh "day of rest."

"Although God's rest on the seventh day (Gen. 2:3) did foreshadow a future Sabbath law, there is no biblical record of the Sabbath before the children of Israel left the land of Egypt ... God's intent for giving the Sabbath to Israel was not that they would remember creation but that they would remember their Egyptian slavery and the Lord's deliverance."[296]

"According to the Hebrew calendars and traditional Christian calendars, Sunday is the first day of the week. ... The weekdays start with Sunday (day 1, or Yom Rishon) and proceed to Saturday (day 7), Shabbat. Since some calculations use division, a remainder of zero signifies Saturday."

Shavua (שבוע) is a weekly cycle of seven days, mirroring the seven-day period of the book of Genesis in which the world is created. The names for the days of the week, like those in the creation account, are simply the day number within the week, with Shabbat being the seventh day. Each day of the week runs from sunset to the following sunset and is figured locally.

The Hebrew calendar follows a seven-day weekly cycle, which runs concurrently with but independently of the monthly and annual cycles. The names for the days of the week are simply the day number within the week. In Hebrew, these names may be abbreviated using the numerical value of the Hebrew letters, for example יום א' (day 1, or Yom Rishon (יום ראשון)):[297]

1. Yom Rishon: יום ראשון (abbreviated יום א'), meaning "first day" [corresponds to Sunday] (starting at preceding sunset of Saturday)

2. Yom Sheni: יום שני (abbr. יום ב') meaning "second day" [corresponds to Monday]
3. Yom Shlishi: יום שלישי (abbr. יום ג') meaning "third day" [corresponds to Tuesday]
4. Yom Revi'i: יום רביעי (abbr. יום ד') meaning "fourth day" [corresponds to Wednesday]
5. Yom Chamishi: יום חמישי (abbr. יום ה') meaning "fifth day" [corresponds to Thursday]
6. Yom Shishi: יום ששי (abbr. יום ו') meaning "sixth day" [corresponds to Friday]
7. Yom Shabbat: יום שבת (abbr. יום ש'), or more usually, simply Shabbat—שבת meaning "rest day" [corresponds to Saturday]

The seven-day week was not adopted by Romans until Constantine declared it so in 324 CE. [298]

Sabbath Saturday or Sunday?

The early Christians were Jews, and thus, they worshiped in the synagogues on Saturday.

> A change happened several decades after Jesus's death and resurrection because Jesus's apostles, who were all Jewish and were accustomed to attending synagogue services on Saturdays, were trying to assimilate their new beliefs in Jesus as the Son of God with their developing practice of celebrating the Eucharist. (More accurately these early followers of Jesus after his resurrection are known as Jewish-Christians.)
>
> Eventually it became incompatible for Jewish-Christians to continue worshipping in the synagogue with Jews who didn't profess Jesus as their savior. The

> Jewish-Christians then began celebrating the Sabbath on Sundays (the first day of the week) as a testament to the day that Jesus rose from the dead. Over time, Christians have almost all adopted Sunday as their day of weekly worship, the "sabbath" day, with the exception of some like Seventh Day Adventists who still celebrate the sabbath on Saturday.[299]

In AD 321, Roman Emperor Constantine the Great enacted the first civil law regarding Sunday observance. The law did not mention the Sabbath by name but referred to a day of rest on "the venerable day of the sun."[300]

High Sabbaths

In addition to the standard weekly Saturday Sabbaths, the Jews of the first century celebrated seven other "high Sabbaths" or "special Sabbaths." Three of the high Sabbaths are in the spring of the year, one of them (the first day of Unleavened Bread) fell on Thursday of Passion Week. It began at sunset on Wednesday night.

The Jewish Passover

Few Christians know that the Jewish Passover is currently a seven-day period in Israel and eight days for the Jews who live outside of Israel. At the time of Christ, the Jews had two names for the same festival; it was called the Feast of the Passover or the Feast of the Unleavened Bread. The Greek word is Pascha (ἡμέρας τὸ πάσχα γίνεται καὶ).

The establishment of Jewish Passover was to commemorate God's provision of the Exodus from Egypt and is referenced in Exodus 12:14–20.

> "This is a day you are to commemorate; for the generations to come you shall celebrate it as a festival to the Lord—a lasting ordinance. For seven days you are to eat bread made without yeast. On the first day remove the yeast from your houses, for whoever eats anything with yeast in it from the first day through the seventh must be cut off from Israel. On the first day hold a sacred assembly, and another one on the seventh day. Do no work at all on these days, except to prepare food for everyone to eat; that is all you may do. Celebrate the Festival of Unleavened Bread, because it was on this very day that I brought your divisions out of Egypt. Celebrate this day as a lasting ordinance for the generations to come. In the first month you are to eat bread made without yeast, from the evening of the fourteenth day until the evening of the twenty-first day. For seven days no yeast is to be found in your houses. And anyone, whether foreigner or native-born, who eats anything with yeast in it must be cut off from the community of Israel. Eat nothing made with yeast. Wherever you live, you must eat unleavened bread." (Exod. 12:14–20)

In addition, two pericopes in Exodus 12 are particularly relevant.

> The Lord said to Moses and Aaron in Egypt, "This month is to be for you the first month, the first month of your year. Tell the whole community of Israel that on the tenth day of this month each man is to take a lamb for his family, one for each household." (Exod. 12:1–3)
>
> The animals you choose must be year-old males without defect, and you may take them from the sheep or the

> goats. Take care of them until the fourteenth day of the month, when all the members of the community of Israel must slaughter them at twilight. (Exod. 12:5–6)

Given that Jewish months averaged twenty-nine days (with an additional month thrown in to catch up from time to time), the days of the week did not annually coincide with the lengths of the lunar months (i.e., twenty-eight weekdays versus twenty-nine lunar cycle days). As a result, the fourteenth day of Nissan could have fallen on different days of the week in different years.

Year of Jesus's Death

While we have a basis for the Nissan days of Passion Week, the Gregorian weekdays' correspondence to the Nissan days is less clear. If we knew for certain the Gregorian year of Jesus's death, we could look up the synchrony with days of the week and Nissan days. But the exact years of Jesus's birth and death are in dispute. It is thought that Jesus was born between 6 and 4 BC.

> We arrive at this date based on the death of Herod the Great, who was procurator of Judaea from 47 BC until he died in 4 BC. It was "after Herod died" that Joseph and Mary with the infant Jesus were told to return to Israel from Egypt (Matthew 2:19).
>
> Several factors allow us to pinpoint the year of the death of Jesus. We calculate that John the Baptist commenced his ministry c. AD 26, based on the historical note in Luke 3:1 that John started preaching in the fifteenth year of Tiberius's reign. Tiberius was named emperor in AD 14, but he started reigning two years prior to that, AD 12,

> as co-regent with Augustus Caesar. Using the earlier date, John's ministry began c. AD 26–27. Jesus probably began His ministry soon after John began his and ministered for the next three and a half years, approximately. So, the end of Jesus' ministry would have been c. AD 29–30.
>
> Pontius Pilate is known to have ruled Judea from AD 26–36. The crucifixion took place during a Passover (Mark 14:12), and that fact, plus astronomical data (the Jewish calendar was lunar-based), narrows the field to two dates—April 7, AD 30, and April 3, AD 33. There are scholarly arguments supporting both dates; the later date (AD 33) would require Jesus to have had a longer ministry and to have begun it later. The earlier date (AD 30) would seem more in keeping with what we deduce about the start of Jesus' ministry from Luke 3:1.[301]

It appears the year AD 30 is likely, although the exact day date is more controversial.

It would be possible to synchronize the days of the week with Nissan days if we knew the exact year of Jesus's death. As mentioned, opinions vary between AD 30 and 33. The most scientific analysis I can find uses the US Navy Astronomical Department calculations. By that analysis, the only date the author finds that matches the New Testament references is AD 30. By this calculation, Nissan 15 was Thursday (Julian April 6). That would make Wednesday, Nissan 14, to be Julian April 5.[302]

A second scientific calculation to identify Nissan 14 in AD 30 is provided by Aristeo Canlas Fernando, who used the online Hebrew calculator[303] to determine the day of the week in AD that Nissan 14 would fall upon. By his calculation, Nissan 14 was a Wednesday; therefore, Nissan 15 was a Thursday.[304]

Finally, the online Calendar Converter and Translator converts Julian Wednesday, April 5, AD 30, to be Gregorian April 3, AD 30.[305]

Passion Week Timeline

From them, we can establish the Gregorian days of Passion Week. Remember that we are naming the days with daylight hours—the Jewish day started at 6:00 the evening before, so we are really referring to the last twelve hours (daylight hours) of each day.

On the fourteenth day of the first month at twilight is Yahweh's Passover. And on the fifteenth day of the same month is the Feast of Unleavened Bread to Yahweh. Passover then is on the fourteenth day from the commencement of the new year and is eaten after twilight on that day, before the start of the fifteenth day and the first high Sabbath of the week of Unleavened Bread.

Just as with the weekly Sabbath, the day before any high Sabbath is a preparation day. This means that the fourteenth was the preparation day for the Pascha (ἡμέρας τὸ πάσχα γίνεται καὶ), and Feast of the Passover (Feast of the Unleavened Bread) was on Nissan 15. It is relevant to remember that the Jews often used the terms Passover Week and Festival of Unleavened Bread interchangeably.

With the weekdays established, it remains controversial exactly which day Jesus was crucified and placed in the tomb. There are vigorous proponents of the traditional Friday[306, 307, 308, 309] as well as Wednesday[310, 311, 312, 313] and Thursday.[314]

The Gospel references to the day of the Last Supper indicate it was on the first day of the Unleavened Bread festival, which was the day of eating of the Passover lamb.

> Then came the day of Unleavened Bread on which the Passover lamb had to be sacrificed. Jesus sent Peter and John, saying, "Go and make preparations for us to eat the Passover." (Luke 22:7–8)

> On the first day of the Festival of Unleavened Bread, when it was customary to sacrifice the Passover lamb, Jesus's disciples asked him, "Where do you want us to go and make preparations for you to eat the Passover?" (Mark 14:12)

> Then came the day of Unleavened Bread on which the Passover lamb had to be sacrificed. Jesus sent Peter and John, saying, "Go and make preparations for us to eat the Passover." (Luke 22:7–8 NIV)

The designation of the first day of the Unleavened Bread festival indicates the day before the high holiday. We have already identified the high holiday of Passion Week to be on Nissan 15, Thursday. That indicates the Passover Last Supper to be early the evening of the beginning of Wednesday, Nissan 14.

The Gospel of John further indicates Jesus to be on trial on the day of preparation for the Feast of Passover (Feast of the Unleavened Bread) at noon. Again, the day of preparation for the Thursday high Sabbath was Wednesday.

> It was the day of Preparation of the Passover; it was about noon. (John 19:14)

In addition, closer reading of John 19:14 (NIV) says, "It was the Day of Preparation of Passover *Week*, about the sixth hour." This does not say preparation for the day of Passover. Remember that the Jews often used the terms Passover Week and Festival of Unleavened Bread interchangeably. There was no preparation day for the eating of the Passover lamb. In fact, the Wednesday of Passover in AD 30 was the day before a high Sabbath. John 19:31 references that the Jews "did not want the bodies left on the crosses during Sabbath." This would be compatible with the Thursday high Sabbath rather than the traditional Saturday Sabbath.

It would, therefore, seem to reconcile Mark's account with John's if Jesus's Crucifixion occurred on Wednesday (Nissan14) before the high Sabbath on Thursday (Nissan 15).

This timing is also compatible with Jesus's comment regarding His timing before resurrection (Matt. 12:38–40):

> Then certain of the scribes and of the Pharisees answered, saying, Master, we would see a sign from thee. But he answered and said unto them, An evil and adulterous generation seeketh after a sign; and there shall no sign be given to it, but the sign of the prophet Jonas: For as Jonas was three days and three nights in the whale's belly; so shall the Son of man be three days and three nights in the heart of the earth.

If Jesus was placed in the grave before sunset Wednesday, as John 19:31 reports, his first night would have been Thursday (starting sunset after Wednesday daylight hours). He would then have been in the grave dark Thursday, dark Friday, dark Saturday, and arisen after dusk on Saturday (weekly Sabbath) so that the tomb was empty Sunday morning.

This sequence is well summarized:

> If Jesus rose exactly three days and three nights after His burial (just before sunset; see Matthew 27:46; Mark 15:34), the only candidate for His resurrection is the very end of the Sabbath at sunset. Counting back three full days, then, Jesus must have died on the previous Wednesday, which would have been the day of the Passover (Jesus and His disciples had observed the Passover the evening before). The first day of Unleavened

Bread began just minutes after Joseph of Arimathea and Nicodemus sealed His tomb.

The gospel account says that, after this, His disciples and the women kept the holy day on Thursday (Mark 16:1). On Friday, the preparation day for the weekly Sabbath, the women prepared spices for His embalming (this was a normal workday; see Luke 23:56), then kept the weekly Sabbath. When they came to the tomb early Sunday morning, He had already risen some time before. He rose exactly three days and three nights from His interment (a full 72 hours) at sunset as the weekly Sabbath ended. This shows that there were two Sabbaths—a high day and a weekly Sabbath—during the time of His burial, not one![315]

Placed in chart form, the Wednesday Crucifixion sequence follows:

11 Nissan	12 Nissan	13 Nissan	14 Nissan	15 Nissan	16 Nissan	17 Nissan	18 Nissan
Sunday	Monday	Tuesday	**Wednesday**	Thursday	Friday	Saturday	Sunday
Palm Sunday Bethany that night	Jesus clears temple Bethany that night	Withered fig tree Olivet Discourse	Passover Day of Preparation for High Sabbath Last Supper **Trial and Crucifixion**	High Sabbath & Feast of Unleavened Bread	"Morrow Day" Cutting barley sheaves	Regular Sabbath	**Resurrection** Feast of First Fruits

Coulter reports church history:[316]

Knowledge of a Wednesday Crucifixion was passed down for at least three centuries after the founding of the apostolic church. The *Didascalia* which dates from the third century, offers historical evidence that belief in a Friday Crucifixion was a change from the original teaching. The following description of the day of Jesus's Crucifixion appears in Book V of the *Apostolic Constitutions*, which contains the original words of the *Didascalia*:

"For they began to hold a council against the Lord on the second day of the week, in the first month, which is Xanthicus; and the deliberation continued on the third day of the week; but on the fourth day [Wednesday] they determined to take away His life by crucifixion" (*Apostolic Constitutions—Didascalia Apostolorum*, book V, section I, paragraph xiv). A church historian explains the significance of this record in the *Didascalia*: " …the only reason can have been that Jesus's passion began on a Wednesday, i.e., the day when He was arrested [and crucified]" (Lietzmann, A History of the Early Church, p 69).

Friday (Traditional) Crucifixion sequence:

A Friday Crucifixion would not have allowed enough "nights in the tomb." Friday night would be the start of Saturday, the Saturday night would be the start of Sunday when Jesus arose from the grave. This difficulty is discussed in more detail in Chapter 39.

Conclusion

While the dating remains controversial, it appears that the most credible date for Jesus's Crucifixion is Wednesday (Nissan 14), which in on the modern Gregorian calendar would have been April 5, AD 30.

Our traditional Christian timing of Jesus's Crucifixion on Friday (Good Friday) and resurrection on Sunday morning appears to be incorrect. The Wednesday Crucifixion date also explains the fact that the traditional timing cannot explain what happened on Wednesday.

37

What Was the Time of Jesus's Crucifixion?

Noon or Sixth Hour?

In *Jesus Interrupted*, Bart D. Ehrman suggests a time discrepancy between the Gospels of Mark and John regarding the trial and Crucifixion of Jesus.[317] Mark reports that Jesus was put on the cross at approximately 9:00 a.m., but John describes Jesus still being interrogated in Pilate's court at noon. So how could that be?

First, let's examine the biblical references. Note that the wording is different in different translations, and even in different editions of the same translation.

Mark's version:

> It was nine in the morning when they crucified him. (Mark 15:25 NIV 2011)

> It was nine o'clock in the morning when they crucified Jesus. (Mark 15:25 NCV)

> It was the third hour when they crucified him. (Mark 15:25 NIV Zondervan 2008)

> And it was the third hour when they crucified him. (Mark 15:25 ESV)

> And it was the third hour, and they crucified him. (Mark 15:25 KJV)

John's version:

> It was the day of Preparation of the Passover; it was about noon.
> "Here is your king," Pilate said to the Jews. (John 19:14 NIV 2011)

> It was about noon on Preparation Day of Passover week. Pilate said to the crowd, "Here is your king!" (John 19:14 NCV)

> It was the day of Preparation of Passover Week, about the sixth hour. (John 19:14 NIV Zondervan 2008)

> Now it was the day of Preparation of the Passover. It was about the sixth hour. He said to the Jews, "Behold your King!" (John 19:14 ESV)

> "And it was the preparation of the passover, and about the sixth hour: and he saith unto the Jews, Behold your King!" (John 19:14 KJV)

What we see is different translations of the time of day—not only the time but the phrasing: "nine o'clock in the morning" versus "third hour," and "noon" versus "sixth hour." Even more confusing is that the same translation, the New International Version, states it two different ways, depending upon the time of printing of the translation. The 2008 edition of the NIV by Zondervan uses the terms "third hour" and "sixth hour"; whereas the later 2011 edition of the NIV by Biblica uses the terms "nine in the morning" and "noon." So what's going on here?

BibleGateway explains the translation of the NIV Bible:[318]

> A self-governing body of fifteen biblical scholars, the Committee on Bible Translation (CBT) was formed and charged with responsibility for the version, and in 1968 the New York Bible Society (which subsequently became the International Bible Society and then Biblica) generously undertook the financial sponsorship of the project.
>
> From the very start, the NIV sought to bring modern Bible readers as close as possible to the experience of the very first Bible readers: providing the best possible blend of transparency to the original documents and comprehension of the original meaning in every verse. With this clarity of focus, however, came the realization that the work of translating the NIV would never be truly complete. As new discoveries were made about the biblical world and its languages, and as the norms of English usage developed and changed over time, the NIV would also need to change to hold true to its original vision.
>
> And so in the original NIV charter, provision was made not just to issue periodic updates to the text but also to create a mechanism for constant monitoring of changes in biblical scholarship and English usage. The CBT was charged to meet every year to review, maintain, and strengthen the NIV's ability to accurately

> and faithfully render God's unchanging Word in modern English.
>
> The 2011 update to the NIV is the latest fruit of this process. By working with input from pastors and Bible scholars, by grappling with the latest discoveries about biblical languages and the biblical world, and by using cutting-edge … research on English usage, the Committee on Bible Translation has updated the text …

The actual Greek term in Mark 15:25 is ὥρα τρίτη, strictly translated "third hour"—not "nine in the morning." The actual Greek term in John 19:14 is ὥρα ἦν ὡς ἕκτη, strictly translated "hour was about sixth"—not "noon."[319, 320]

So how did this confusion arise? Well, it apparently has to do with the method of keeping time.

Although experts debate the metrics,[321] it appears that there were two different systems of timekeeping in the first-century Mediterranean. Actually, the day lengths, and thus key reference points, varied with the seasons. But for practical purposes, there were two patterns.

For most Jews, the day and night were separate time scales. Daylight was measured in hours, starting at sunrise (6:00 a.m.) and ending at sunset (approximately what we would call 6:00 p.m.). The "end of the day" was dark when agriculture and commerce stopped. The nighttime, however, was divided into three-hour watches; 6:00 p.m. to 9:00 p.m. was the first watch, 9:00 p.m. to 12:00 a.m. was the second watch, and so on. Presumably, these sections of time in the dark had fewer activities and therefore required fewer time divisions.[322] Remember, light was a premium in the dark hours—oil lamps and torches were the only source.

The Romans, however, started their day at midnight (12:00 a.m.), and the day ran to the next midnight. We keep Roman time.[323]

It is apparent that the translators of the 2011 Biblica version of the NIV and the New Century Version of the Bible translated both passages assuming Jewish time (a Jewish clock starting at 6:00 a.m.). This assumption works fine for the Mark verses, but in John's Gospel, using "noon" as the translation of "sixth hour" creates conflict between Mark's and John's accounts. Modern translators created an apparent discrepancy in the Gospels!

If, on the other hand, as translated in the Zondervan (2008) New International Version (NIV), the English Standard Version (ESV), and the King James Versions (KJV), the "sixth hour" is the accurate Greek-English translation, the conversion to Roman time in John resolves the issue.

This difference in time referencing is not surprising. Mark, whose Gospel was the first written, lived in the dominant Jewish communities of Jerusalem, then Alexandria, Egypt. The Jewish timetable was likely dominant there. John, on the other hand, wrote his Gospel last, presumably either from Ephesus or exile in Patmos. With the rise of Roman influence, the area where John resided likely used the Roman timetable.

Conclusion

Therefore, using the Roman clock of the day starting at midnight in John's Gospel, the "sixth hour" would be 6:00 a.m. when Jesus was in Pilate's court. This is consistent with Mark's account that Jesus was on the cross at the "third hour," at "nine o'clock in the morning" using Jewish time.[324, 325, 326]

38

How Many Ascensions?

Jesus's ascension is described in three references. Outsides the tomb, Jesus addressed Mary:

Jesus said to her, "Mary!" She turned and said to Him in Hebrew, "Rabboni!" (which means, Teacher). Jesus said to her, "Stop clinging to Me, for I have not yet ascended to the Father; but go to My brethren and say to them, 'I ascend to My Father and your Father, and My God and your God.'" (John 20:16)

After appearing to the disciples on "that very day" (presumably the Sunday of the resurrection—the first day of the week of verse 24:1), "they got up that very hour and returned to Jerusalem" to join eleven disciples (v. 33). Jesus then led them to Bethany, where "He parted from them and was carried to heaven (Luke 24:51).

And after He had said these things, He was lifted up while they were looking on, and a cloud received him out of their site. (Acts 1:9)

The account of Mary with Jesus at the empty tomb is only recorded in the Gospel of John (John 20:16). Some interpret Jesus's statement in John to indicate His ascension was imminent, but that is debatable.

More suggestive of an early ascension occurs in the twenty-fourth chapter of Luke. Luke 24:1 states Mary came to the tomb on the "first day of the week," presumably the Sunday of the resurrection. Verse 13 states that the Emmaus road encounter occurred "that very day." After encountering Jesus, Cleopas and his companion "got up that very hour and returned to Jerusalem to tell the eleven disciples of their encounter."

In apparent temporal continuation, Jesus appeared, then led them to Bethany, from which he "parted from them and was carried to heaven" (v. 51).

There is, however, controversy regarding the Luke 24 narrative.

First, the last phrase, "he was carried up [brought up] to heaven" is not present in several of the earliest manuscripts—notably Codex Sinaiticus (fifth century), Codex Cantabrigiensis (fifth century).[327] It is, however, found in Codex Vaticanus (fourth century), and Papyrus 75 (early 200s).[328] This is the only reference to the ascension in the Gospels.

While the temporal sequence would seem to indicate an ascension at the end of resurrection day Sunday, the Gospel writers were not precise about historical sequencing; rather they tended to write in topical ordering. It is quite likely that the segue from Luke 24:35 to verse 36 was not immediate but reported an episode from a later time.

Regardless, the presence of Luke 24:51 is not critical, since it occurs at the termination of the book of Luke. The book of Acts is actually the second book of Luke, and an ascension narrative occurs eleven verses later in Acts 1:9. The writer of Luke may have decided to omit duplication of the same event in such proximity in the text.

Acts 1:9

It is quite likely that the ascension of Luke 24:51 is the same as the Acts 1:9 episode, even though Acts 1:3 indicates an interval of forty days. In both cases, Jesus tells the disciples to stay in Jerusalem (Luke 24:49; Acts 1:4) until "they are clothed with power from on high" (Luke 24:49) and "wait for what the Father had promised" (v. 4) … "you will receive power when the Holy Spirit has come upon you" (v. 8).

This sequencing is made even more likely by the pattern of Jesus's post-resurrection instructions. Shortly after His resurrection, Jesus instructed the disciples to go to Galilee (Matt. 28:10; John 21:1), where He appeared to the disciples as well as to "more than five hundred. Then at near the end of the forty-day period, Jesus gathered the disciples back in Jerusalem, where they were to stay until the ascension and Pentecost.

Conclusion

The John 20:16–17 reference does not indicate a specific imminent ascension but rather that it is to occur. The Luke 24:51 and Acts 1:9 references are probably duplicate reports of the same event. Presumably, this occurred after forty days of post-resurrection appearances (Acts 1:3).

Therefore, there was only one ascension of Jesus.

39

Was Jesus in the Grave for Three Days?

Why was Jesus in the tomb for three days? Why not one or two days?

The interval "three days" is utilized twenty-seven times in the Old Testament.[329]

In scripture the number three is one of the so-called perfect numbers. The other perfect numbers are seven, ten, and twelve. In scripture, the number three signifies completeness or perfection and points to what is solid, real, and substantial. As a number that indicates completeness, the number three always identifies some important event in salvation history.[330]

Dead for Three Days

There is a body of evidence indicating the need for three full days.

> Resurrection after three days of death proved to Jesus' opponents that He truly rose from the dead. Why? According to Jewish tradition, a person's soul/spirit

remained with his/her dead body for three days. After three days, the soul/spirit departed. If Jesus' resurrection had occurred on the same day or even the next day, it would have been easier for His enemies to argue He had never truly died. Significantly, Jesus waited several days after Lazarus had died before He came to resurrect Lazarus so that no one could deny the miracle (John 11:38–44):[331]

> Jesus, once more deeply moved, came to the tomb. It was a cave with a stone laid across the entrance. "Take away the stone," he said.
> "But, Lord," said Martha, the sister of the dead man, "by this time there is a bad odor, for he has been there four days."

According to the Talmud (Gen. Kabbah 100:7), the soul hovers over the body for three days after death. The human soul is somewhat lost and confused between death and before burial, and it stays in the general vicinity of the body, until the body is interred. The shomrim sit and read aloud comforting psalms during the time that they are watching the body. This serves as a comfort for both the spirit of the departed who is in transition and the shomer or shomeret.[332]

Three Full Days and Nights

The question of how long Jesus was in the tomb has been controversial. It brings up the question of whether Jesus's Crucifixion was on Wednesday or on the traditional Friday date. Jesus's own statements seem to suggest a full three days and three nights.

> Then some of the scribes and Pharisees answered, saying, "Teacher, we want to see a sign from You." But He answered and said to them, "An evil and adulterous generation seeks after a sign, and no sign will be given to it except the sign of the prophet Jonah. For as Jonah was three days and three nights in the belly of the great fish, so will the Son of Man be three days and three nights in the heart of the earth." (Matt. 12:38–40)

> On the next day, which followed the Day of Preparation, the chief priests and Pharisees gathered together to Pilate, saying, "Sir, we remember, while He was still alive, how that deceiver said, 'After three days I will rise.'" (Matt. 27:62–66)

> Jesus answered and said to them, "Destroy this temple, and in three days I will raise it up." Then the Jews said, "It has taken forty-six years to build this temple, and will You raise it up in three days?" But He was speaking of the temple of His body. (John 2:19–21)

With a Wednesday Crucifixion, Jesus would have been placed in the grave just before dusk on Wednesday, so that the night/day sequence began Thursday night:

> Thursday night/day
> Friday night/day
> Saturday night/day

Then Jesus would have been resurrected after the end of Saturday dusk, which would be "after three days and nights."

There is no mathematical way for a Friday Crucifixion to accomplish three days and three nights.

Partial Days

Several biblical references suggest "on the third day" rather than "after" a complete three days. And two of those references are direct quotes from Jesus:

- Matthew 16:21 ... raised up on the third day
- Luke 9:22 ... *raised up on the third day*
- Luke 18:33 ... *the third day he will rise again*
- Acts 10:40 ... but God raised him on the third day and allowed him to appear
- 1 Corinthians 15:4 ... and that he was raised on the third day

To reconcile the timing, it has been postulated that any part of a day counts as a full day. Fourth-century scholar/priest St. Jerome explains in his "Commentary on Jonah," written between AD 390 and 406.[333] Jerome postulates "partial days" to explain Jesus's "three days and three nights" in the "belly of the earth":

> *And Jonah was in the belly of the fish three days and three nights.* LXX: "and Jonah was in the belly of the whale for three days and three nights." The Lord shows in the Gospel the symbolism of this passage, and it is superfluous to say in the same terms or even in other terms what he who has suffered has already said. But we ask ourselves this: how was he three days and three nights in the belly of the earth. Some scholars take the view according to *paraskeuen*, because of the solar eclipse from the sixth to the ninth hour when night followed day, this would be two days and nights, and adding the Sabbath, believe that we should count this as three days and three nights. But I prefer to understand this by reason of synecdoche, seeing the whole as a part: where

> he is dead in *paraskeuen*, let us count one day and one night; two with the Sabbath; the third night which arises from the day of the Lord, let us take that as the beginning of the next day, for, in Genesis the night is not of the preceding day, but of the following day, that is to say the beginning of the next day, not the end of the previous. To understand this better I will say it more simply: if a man leaves his house at nine and the next day, he arrives at his other house at three. And if I say that he has been two days in travelling, I will not be reprimanded as a liar, because he has not used all the hours of two days, but only a part for his journey. Nonetheless this seems to me to be the interpretation. If someone does not agree with this, and he can explain the meaning in a clearer way, then we should follow his interpretation.

In his sermon from his Church Postil in 1538, Martin Luther proposed a similar "partial day" theory when describing Jesus in the tomb:[334]

> 2. The question now arises: How can we say that he rose on the third day, since he lay in the grave only one day and two nights? According to the Jewish calculation it was only a day and a half; how shall we then persist in believing there were three days? To this we reply that he was in the state of death for at least a part of all three days. For he died at about two o'clock on Friday and consequently was dead for about two hours on the first day. After that night he lay in the grave all day, which is the true Sabbath. On the third day, which we commemorate now, he rose from the dead and so remained in the state of death a part of this day, just as if we say that something occurred

> on Easter-day, although it happens in the evening, only a portion of the day. In this sense Paul and the Evangelists say that he rose on the third day.
>
> 3. For this period and no longer Christ was to lie in the grave, so that we might suppose that his body remained naturally uncorrupted and that decomposition had not yet set in. He came forth from the grave so soon that we might presume that corruption had not yet taken place according to the course of nature; for a corpse can lie no longer than three days before it begins to decompose. Therefore, Christ was to rise on the third day, before he saw corruption.

So how does the partial day explanation facilitate the traditional Friday Crucifixion? It assumes the brief period of Friday dusk counted as first day:

> Friday day
> Saturday night/day
> Sunday night/day

This would make Sunday the third day, as is traditionally thought. It would fit with the partial day concept, since it includes only two nights

Conclusion

Controversy arises over whether one interprets "partial days," "on the third day" or after "three days and nights." If one accepts the specific reference of Jesus of "three days and three nights" in Matthew 12:38–40, it is more likely that Jesus was crucified on Wednesday and arose Saturday evening at dusk and was seen before daylight on Sunday morning.

40

Where Is Paradise?

On the cross, Jesus spoke to the penitent criminal:

> Jesus answered him, "Truly I tell you, today you will be with me in paradise." (Luke 23:43)

Paradise is mentioned two other times in the New Testament:

> Was caught up to paradise and heard inexpressible things, things that no one is permitted to tell. (2 Cor. 12:4)

> Whoever has ears, let them hear what the Spirit says to the churches. To the one who is victorious, I will give the right to eat from the tree of life, which is in the paradise of God. (Rev. 2:7)

There seems to be consensus that after physical death, while our bodies remain in the ground, our souls go to an intermediate location awaiting the final judgment.

This is referenced in the following passages:

> Multitudes who sleep in the dust of the earth will awake: some to everlasting life, others to shame and everlasting contempt. (Dan. 12:2)

> "Do not be amazed at this, for a time is coming when all who are in their graves will hear his voice and come out—those who have done what is good will rise to live, and those who have done what is evil will rise to be condemned." (John 5:28–29)

> We are confident, I say, and would prefer to be away from the body and at home with the Lord. (2 Cor. 5:8)

So where is paradise?

There seem to be two suggestions: (1) an intermediate area of heaven or (2) a partition of Hades (Sheol).

An Intermediate Heaven

As explained by Alcorn,[335]

> When we die, believers in Christ will not go to the heaven where we'll live forever. Instead, we'll go to an intermediate Heaven. In that Heaven—where those who died covered by Christ's blood are now—we'll await the time of Christ's return the earth, our bodily resurrection, the final judgement, and the creation of the new heavens and New Earth.

> Strong's online concordance lists the Greek word for paradise as *paradeisos* (παράδεισος, ου, ὁ) meaning "a park, a garden, paradise." It is referenced three times: Luke 23:43; 2 Cor 12:4; Rev. 2:7.[336]

> An upper region of heaven: the abode of God and heavenly beings, to which true Christians will be taken after death, ... According to the opinion of many of the church Fathers, the paradise in which our first parents dwelt before the fall still exists, neither on earth nor in the heavens, but above and beyond the world.[337]

Alcorn, quoting Alister McGrath, explains,[338]

> "In the Septuagint, the Greek translation of the Old Testament, the Greek word for paradise is used to describe the Garden of Eden (e.g. Genesis 2:8; Ezekiel 28:13). Later, because of the Jewish belief that God would restore Eden, paradise became the word to describe the eternal state of the righteous, and to a lesser extent, the present Heaven."

A Partition of Hades

Sheol is mentioned sixty-six times throughout the Hebrew Bible, first appearing in the book of Genesis.[339]

While the Hebrew Bible appears to describe Sheol as the permanent place of the dead, in the Second Temple period (roughly 500 BCE–70 CE) a more diverse set of ideas developed. In some texts, Sheol is the home of both the righteous and the wicked, separated into respective compartments. When the Hebrew scriptures were translated into Greek in ancient Alexandria around 200 BCE, the word *Hades* (the Greek underworld) was substituted for Sheol, owing to its similarities to the underworld of Greek mythology.[340]

Thayer's Greek Lexicon[341] also explains *paradeisos* (paradise) related to Hades: "that part of Hades which was thought by the later Jews to be the abode of the souls of the pious until the resurrection."

That location seems to be defined in Luke 16:23–26:

> In Hades, where he was in torment, he looked up and saw Abraham far away, with Lazarus by his side. So he called to him, "Father Abraham, have pity on me and send Lazarus to dip the tip of his finger in water and cool my tongue, because I am in agony in this fire."
>
> But Abraham replied, "Son, remember that in your lifetime you received your good things, while Lazarus received bad things, but now he is comforted here and you are in agony. And besides all this, between us and you a great chasm has been set in place, so that those who want to go from here to you cannot, nor can anyone cross over from there to us."

When Did Jesus Go to Paradise?

All English translations list the phrase Jesus spoke to the penitent criminal on the cross, "Truly I tell you, today you will be with me in paradise."

The classic reading of the verse is that Jesus went to paradise from the cross. Certainly, he could have done so. But a controversy arises due to the comment Jesus made to Mary at the tomb on the morning of resurrection:

> Jesus said, "Do not hold on to me, for I have not yet ascended to the Father. Go instead to my brothers and tell them, 'I am ascending to my Father and your Father, to my God and your God.'" (John 20:17)

This verse could imply that Jesus has not yet gone to paradise. A proposed solution to the dilemma is that the punctuation of Luke 23:43 is incorrect in modern English translations. The argument goes that since writing in Greek does not use punctuation, the comma is misplaced.[342]

"Truly I tell you, today you will be with me in paradise." It is proposed that the verse should be translated as "Truly I tell you today, you will be with me in paradise."

On the other hand, in the John 20:17 verse, Jesus may have been referencing that He had not yet gone to permanent heaven rather than to the intermediate heaven paradise.

Why Did Jesus Go to Paradise?

First Peter 3:18 indicates that Jesus felt the need to visit those souls waiting in paradise.

The best explanation seems to be that when Jesus gave up His spirit, His spirit joined Abraham and the other believers on the comfortable side of Sheol, which He called "Paradise." While He was there awaiting His resurrection, Jesus preached to the souls of the disobedient (1 Pet. 3:19–20a) who were immersed in the flames on the other side. And when Jesus rose from the dead, "He led captivity captive" by taking the souls of the godly with Him (Eph. 4:8).

Conclusion

To sum it up, before the resurrection of Jesus, everyone went down to Sheol (the realm of the dead), awaiting the death, burial, and resurrection of God's Son. The lost went to Hades, where they will continue being tormented until the Great White Throne judgment (Rev. 20:11–14). The saved went to a place of comfort called paradise (also known as

Abraham's bosom). They could not go straight to heaven, into the presence of God, until the blood of Jesus had been shed to pay for and cover their sin. Thus, Jesus Christ is the "first-fruits" of the dead (1 Cor. 15:20).[343]

41

Did Jesus Really Go to Hell?

Harrowing of Hell

The harrowing of hell is the Old English and Middle English term for the triumphant descent of Christ into hell between the time of His crucifixion and His resurrection when He brought salvation to all of the righteous who had died since the beginning of the world. After His death, the soul of Jesus descended into the realm of the dead, which the Apostles' Creed calls "hell" in the old English usage. In some Christian theologies, it is believed that Jesus's soul remained united to the divinity during this time. The realm into which Jesus descended is called Sheol by some Christian theologians to distinguish it from the hell of the damned. This nearly extinct term in Christian theology is referenced in the Apostles' Creed and the Athanasian Creed, which state that Jesus Christ "descended into hell." However, there are no explicit New Testament references to Christ having descended to the underworld. Its near absence in scripture has given rise to controversy and differing interpretations. It is unclear how it became part of the Apostles' Creed.[344]

The expression "Apostles' Creed" is first mentioned in a letter from the Synod of Milan dated AD 390, referring to a belief at the time that each of the twelve apostles contributed an article to the twelve articles of the creed. The version used in the Presbyterian Church of America reads as follows:[345]

> I believe in God the Father Almighty,
> Maker of heaven and earth.
> I believe in Jesus Christ, his only Son, our Lord,
> who was conceived by the Holy Spirit,
> and born of the virgin Mary.
> He suffered under Pontius Pilate,
> was crucified, died, and was buried;
> he descended into hell.
> The third day he rose again from the dead.
> He ascended into heaven
> and is seated at the right hand of God the Father Almighty.
> From there he will come to judge the living and the dead.

The biblical references supporting Jesus descending into hell follow:

> Seeing what was to come, he spoke of the resurrection of the Messiah, that he was not abandoned to the realm of the dead, nor did his body see decay. (Acts 2:31)

> For Christ also suffered for sins once for all, the righteous for the unrighteous, in order to bring you to God. He was put to death in the flesh, but made alive in the spirit, in which also he went and made a proclamation to the spirits in prison. (1 Pet. 3:18–19)

> For this is the reason the gospel was preached even to those who are now dead, so that they might be judged according to human standards in regard to the body, but live according to God in regard to the spirit. (1 Pet. 4:6)

> What does "he ascended" mean except that he also descended to the lower, earthly regions? He who descended is the very one who ascended higher than all the heavens, in order to fill the whole universe. (Eph. 4:9–10)

Where Is Hell?

The English word "Hell" occurs fifty-three times in the Bible.[346]

Easton's Bible Dictionary lists three different variations that are translated as "Hell."[347]

> 1.Sheol

> Sheol occurs sixty-five times in the Old Testament. In thirty-one cases the word is rendered "hell," the place of disembodied spirits. The inhabitants of Sheol are "the congregation of the dead" (Proverbs 21:16). It is (a) the abode of the wicked (Numbers 16:33; Job 24:19; Psalm 9:17; 31:17, etc.); (b) of the good (Psalm 16:10; 30:3; 49:15; 86:13, etc.)
>
> Sheol is described as deep (Job 11:8), dark (10:21, 22), with bars (17:16). The dead "go down" to it (Numbers 16:30, 33; Ezek. 31:15, 16, 17)

As described by Emerson,

> So ancient peoples believed that in various ways your body was buried or disposed of and your human soul departed to the place of the dead. And Jewish persons

believed that early Christians believed that. And so, when the early Christian writers said, "he descended to hell," or "he descended to the dead," that's what they meant. They meant that Jesus experienced death like all human beings do. His body was buried, and his soul departed to the place of the dead … in general, the underworld, or the place of the dead, was not just viewed as the place where the dead reside, but also the place where the evil angels reside as well. Satan and the evil angels.[348]

2. Hades

The Greek word hades of the New Testament has the same scope of signification as Sheol of the Old Testament. It is a prison (1 Peter 3:19), with gates and bars and locks (Matthew 16:18; Revelation 1:18), and it is downward (Matthew 11:23; Luke 10:15).

The righteous and the wicked are separated. The blessed dead are in that part of hades called paradise (Luke 23:43). They are also said to be in Abraham's bosom (Luke 16:22).

3. Gehenna

Gehenna, in most of its occurrences in the Greek New Testament, designates the place of the lost (Matthew 23:33). The fearful nature of their condition there is described in various figurative expressions (Matthew 8:12; 13:42; 22:13; 25:30; Luke 16:24, etc.).

Gehenna refers to the valley of Hinnom, south of Jerusalem, where idolatrous Jews sacrificed their children. Later it became a receptacle for dead bodies of animals and criminals. The image of Glenna became a place of everlasting destruction.

In this sense it is used in Matthew 5:22, 29, 30; 10:28; 18:9; 23:15, 33; Mark 9:43, 45, 47; Luke 12:5. In these passages, and in James 3:6, the word is uniformly rendered "hell," the Revised Version placing "Gehenna" in the margin.

As described by Alcorn,[349] with the physical death of a person, the physical body is buried in the earth, while the soul goes to an "intermediate" location, awaiting the return Christ and the final judgement. The destination depends upon the faith commitment of the individual: Christian "believers" go to Paradise; the reprobate go to Hades/Sheol/Gehenna.

It would appear, from the pericope of Luke 16:19-31, that Hades/Sheol/Gehenna (the place of the reprobate) and Paradise (the place of Christian souls) are in some degree of proximity such that there could be communication between the two domains. Perhaps that is how Jesus was able to experience Hades while "making proclamation to the spirits now in prison" (1 Pet 3:19) and "the gospel was preached even to those who are now dead" (1 Pet 4:6).

Given the sequence of eschatology, the first judgement of faith occurs at the time of physical death leading to the intermediate destiny. The final judgement of deeds (Rev 20:13) and disposition to either the eternal heaven (Rev 21:3,7; 22:12) or the eternal hell fire (Rev 20:13–314; 21:8). Therefore, it would appear that the "hell" to which Jesus descended was the intermediate Hades.

Was It Necessary for Jesus to Experience Hell?

Whether Jesus actually descended into hell or whether He experienced hell on the cross has been debated for centuries.

Even though the spiritual part of Jesus was the Trinitarian Son, when He underwent incarnation, He accepted not only a human body, but also a human soul.

> Who, being in very nature God,
> did not consider equality with God something to be used to his own advantage;
> rather, he made himself nothing
> by taking the very nature of a servant,
> being made in human likeness.
> And being found in appearance as a man,
> he humbled himself
> by becoming obedient to death—
> even death on a cross! (Phil. 2:6–8)

While His body was crucified and placed in the tomb, His soul was subjected to spiritual death (temporarily), since He had assumed the guilt of all believers (penal substitution).

Many in the reformed theology camp conclude that the penal substitution payment was accomplished on the cross:[350]

> "Descended into Hell" as referring to Christ's pain and humiliation *prior* to his death, and that this humiliation had a spiritual dimension as part of God's judgement upon the sin which he bore on behalf of Christians. The doctrine of Christ's humiliation is also meant to assure believers that Christ has redeemed them from the pain and suffering of God's judgment on sin."

Jesus's words on the cross could be interpreted as experiencing hell as separation from God's presence:

> About three in the afternoon Jesus cried out in a loud voice, "Eli, Eli, lema sabachthani?" (which means "My God, my God, why have you forsaken me?"), (Matt. 27:46)

> And at three in the afternoon Jesus cried out in a loud voice, "Eloi, Eloi, lema sabachthani?" (which means "My God, my God, why have you forsaken me?"). (Mark 15:34)

This was a reference to Psalm 22:

> My God, my God, why have you forsaken me?
> Why are you so far from saving me,
> so far from my cries of anguish?
> My God, I cry out by day, but you do not answer,
> by night, but I find no rest. (Ps. 22)

John Calvin concluded that Jesus experienced hell in the form of separation from God, on the cross, before he was laid in the grave. However, he recommended keeping the phrase "descended into hell" in the Apostles' Creed. Calvin wrote,[351]

> Nothing had been done if Christ had only endured corporal death. In order to interpose between us and God's anger, and satisfy his righteous judgement, it was necessary that he feel the weight of divine vengeance. Whence also it was necessary that he should engage, as it were, at close quarters with the powers of hell and the horrors of eternal death … not only was the body of

> Christ given up as the price of redemption, but that there was a greater and more excellent price—that he bore in his soul the tortures of condemned and ruined man.

If Jesus Went to Sheol, What Did He Do There?

The verses in 1 Peter (3:29, 4:6) have created major interpretive controversy. While no consensus has been reached, one possible scenario follows. Since Luke 16 indicates that paradise and Hades were in proximity in the intermediate state, a possible scenario could be as follows:

- Jesus's soul briefly entered Hades to fulfill the price of atonement (penal substitution). But once there, He broke the bars and exited victorious, having defeated Satan and spiritual death (Christus Victor).
- Perhaps, after exiting Hades, Jesus went to paradise to bring eternal salvation to the Old Testament faithful. The Old Testament patriarchs were saved into the intermediate state by their faith in Yahweh, but their eternal salvation still had to be through Jesus Christ.

Calvin interpreted the 1 Peter 3:29 reference to "made a proclamation to the spirits in prison" as follows:

> Believers who had died before that time were partakers of the same grace with ourselves: for he celebrates the power of Christ's death, in that he penetrated even to the dead, pious souls obtaining an immediate view of that visitation for which they had anxiously awaited; while, on the other hand, the reprobate were more clearly convinced that they were completely excluded from salvation.

Contrary Interpretation

The contrary opinion is summarized by Storms:[352]

> Although the Harrowing of Hell is taught by the Lutheran, Catholic, Reformed, and Orthodox traditions, a number of Christians reject the doctrine of the "harrowing of hell," claiming that "there is scant scriptural evidence for [it], and that Jesus's own words contradict it." John Piper, for example, says "there is no textual [i.e. Biblical] basis for believing that Christ descended into hell," and, therefore, Piper does not recite the "he descended into hell" phrase when saying the Apostles' Creed. Wayne Grudem also skips the phrase when reciting the Creed; he says that the "single argument in … favor [of the "harrowing of hell" clause in the Creed] seems to be that it has been around so long. … But an old mistake is still a mistake." In his book *Raised with Christ*, Pentecostal Adrian Warnock agrees with Grudem, commenting, "Despite some translations of an ancient creed [i.e. the Apostles' Creed], which suggest that Jesus … 'descended into hell,' there is no biblical evidence to suggest that he actually did so."

Conclusion

There remains debate among evangelical theologians as to whether Jesus's soul actually went temporarily to Hades to fulfill penal substitution or whether the mere temporary separation on the cross was adequate. While the beating and physical death were cruel punishment, the necessary step of penal substitution to atone for the sins of believers was the crucial step.

42

Who Is Satan?

Origin

Where did he come from and how did he get in power?

The English word *Satan* is present fifty-two times in the Bible—eighteen times in the Old Testament and thirty-four times in the New Testament.[353] Satan is referred to as the *devil* sixty-one times in the Bible.[354] In ancient Hebrew, the word is שָׂטָן, and it is often translated as "adversary" in English translations, particularly in the Old Testament. He is variously referred to as Satan (cf. Matt. 12:26; Mark 3:23, 26; Luke 22:3), Beelzebul (2 Kings 1:2; Matt.12:24, 27). All three Abrahamic religions Satan is identified as a serpent, as exampled in Genesis 3:1–5.[355]

The story of Lucifer is sketchy in the Bible. There are three references.

Ezekiel 28 tells the story of the king of Tyre, but this pericope has been interpreted as a description of Lucifer. There are several attributes of the king of Tyre that are not representative of humans:[356]

> The king is portrayed as having a different nature from man (he is a cherub, verse 14); he had a different position from man (he was blameless and sinless, verse 15); he

> was in a different realm from man (the holy mount of God, verses 13,14); he received a different judgment from man (he was cast out of the mountain of God and thrown to the earth, verse 16); and the superlatives used to describe him don't seem to fit that of a normal human being ("full of wisdom," "perfect in beauty," and having "the seal of perfection," verse 12 NASB).

Lucifer was "full of wisdom and perfect beauty" (Ezek. 28:12) until he rebelled against God (Ezek. 28:15) and was cast out of heaven (Ezek. 28:16–17). It is interesting that the Ezekiel passage comments that Lucifer was initially in the Garden of Eden (Ezek. 28:13), a location that becomes relevant in Genesis.

Isaiah 14:12–17 has been interpreted as referring to Lucifer, who determined to make himself "like the Most High" (Isa. 14:14). In describing Lucifer's fall, Isaiah 14:12 indicates that Lucifer was "cut down to the earth." Again, this passage seems to indicate that the earth became Lucifer's realm.

Revelation 12:1–13 describes a great war in heaven between the "dragon" and his angels against Michael, the archangel, and his army of angels. The dragon was defeated and cast down to earth along with his fallen angels.

The Names

How did we get the names Lucifer and Satan when neither prophet called them by those names (Ezekiel: King of Tire; Isaiah; "shining one")?

Apparently, the ancient Hebrew word used in Isaiah 14 is *Helel* . It is variously translated "day star" or "bearer of light."[357] *Helel* (הֵילֵל) is translated by Strong as "shining one" and occurs only in Isaiah 14:12.[358] When the Hebrew was translated to Latin, the word *Helel* was converted to Lucifero, which was later Anglicized to Lucifer by the King James translators (Stewart). The word Satan was then used by Jesus to describe

Lucifer's fall (Luke 10:18) and by the apostle John in Revelation 12:9. John also included the name "Devil."

Satan's Influence

Satan's realm of influence is said to be isolated to wreaking havoc on planet Earth. It's interesting to recall that Ezekiel 28:13 indicates Satan's presence in the Garden of Eden, and Isaiah 14:12 indicates that earth is now his realm.

The most extensive episodes of Satan's earthly activities are (1) in the Garden of Eden (Genesis 3); (2) tormenting Job; and (3) tempting Jesus in the desert (Matt. 4; Luke 4).

Satan is said to command a legion of angels who rebelled with him and were, likewise, cast from heaven. These fallen angels manifest themselves on earth as demons who are emissaries of Satan to invade humans, causing maladies.

Interestingly, as prominent as the influence of Satan is in the Bible, he is recorded to have directly spoken only three times: as a serpent in the Garden of Eden (Gen. 3:1, 4–5); as Satan during the wager with God over tempting Job (Job 1:7, 9–11; 2:2, 4–5); and as the devil at the temptation of Jesus in the wilderness (Matt. 4:3, 6, 9; Luke 4:3, 6–7, 9–11).

The remainder of the times Satan, or the devil, is mentioned in the Bible are reports of his indirect influence on people's thinking or action. Most notable are the reports of Satan's deception of Judas Iscariot (Luke 22:3; John 13:27) and Peter's denials of Jesus (Matt. 26:69–74; Mark 14:68–71; John 18:25–27).

Demons

Satan's influence is frequently carried out through demons, his fallen angels. The characteristics of demons include the following:[359]

1. Demons are able to take shape, form and be visible to humans (Job 4:15).
2. Demons may be exorcised, or driven out, from a possessed person. However, this may be dangerous if not followed by stringent cleaning and discipleship. Without proper spiritual care, the person might then be open for a seven-fold infestation (Matthew 12:45).
3. Demons confuse the truth by utilizing demonic lies and half-truths (1 John 4:4).
4. Those who worship idols and pagan gods are really worshipping and sacrificing to demons. Demons live to deceive people into worshipping themselves (1 Corinthians 10:20–21).
5. The Bible teaches that demons can inhabit animals (Matthew 8:31).

There are only two clear references to demons ("shed" [שֵׁד]) in the Old Testament: Deuteronomy 32:17 and Psalm 106.37. The word *satyr* (or sa'iyr [שָׂעִיר]) is described as a "goat demon" in Leviticus 17:7 and 2 Chronicles 11:15. The remaining fifty-one descriptions of demons are in the New Testament. All the accounts of demonic activity in the New Testament are in the Gospels, except for two instances. Saul is infested by an "evil spirit" (1 Sam. 14–15), and the slave girl filled with a "spirit," which was exorcised by Paul (Acts 16:16–18).

Satan's Ultimate Fate

Prophecy foretells that at the time of Christ's second coming (Parousia) (Luke 21:25–36), Satan will be thrown into an abyss for one thousand years (Rev. 20:3), then eventually be thrown into eternal tormenting in the lake of fire (Matt. 25:42; Rev. 20:10). The fate of the fallen angels (demons) is not specifically addressed, but presumably, their fate accompanies that of Satan.

43

Was the Resurrection a Surprise?

The concept of resurrection was not well established in patristic Israel, but three references express hope that bodily resurrection from Sheol would occur:

1. Psalm 49:15: "But God will ransom my soul from the power of the underworld; for he will release me" Kaiser points out that the verb of the last clause is *laqach*, which means "take me out of Sheol."[360]
2. Psalm 16:10 confesses, "You will not abandon me to the grave, not will you let your Holy one see decay." Peter applied that verse to the resurrection of Jesus Christ in Acts 2.
3. Isaiah 26:14, 19:

   They are now dead, they live no more;
   their spirits do not rise.
   You punished them and brought them to ruin;
   you wiped out all memory of them.
   But your dead will live, Lord;

their bodies will rise—
let those who dwell in the dust
wake up and shout for joy—
your dew is like the dew of the morning;
the earth will give birth to her dead.

In reference to these verses, Cooper observes,

> Ambiguity is eliminated in Isaiah 26:19, however. Part of an apocalyptic vision of the future coming of the Lord, it reads as follows: " But your dead will live; their bodies will rise. You who dwell in the dust, wake up and shout for joy. Your dew is like the dew of the morning; the earth will give birth to her dead." That this speaks of actual resurrection and not merely national renewal is evident from verse 14: They are now dead, they live no more; those departed spirits do not rise.' But in verse 19 they do rise and live again. Highly significant for our inquiry is the fact that the term for the deceased in v 14b and v19d is *Rephaim*, the word used in Isaiah 14 and throughout the Old Testament to designate dwellers in Sheol. So here we have an unequivocal link between the future bodily resurrection and the inhabitants of the underworld realm of the dead. On the great day of the Lord, the *Rephaim* will be reunited with their bodies, reconstituted from the dust, and they will live as the Lord's people again.[361]

During the period of the exile, the concept of a resurrection from the grave (Sheol) advanced. The two major prophets, Daniel and Ezekiel, wrote their prophesies while in exile in Babylon.

Daniel (12:2) foretold "those who sleep" being awakened: "Multitudes who sleep in the dust of the earth will awake: some to everlasting life, others to shame and everlasting contempt."

> So I prophesied as I was commanded. And as I was prophesying, there was a noise, a rattling sound, and the bones came together, bone to bone. I looked, and tendons and flesh appeared on them and skin covered them, but there was no breath in them.
>
> Then he said to me, "Prophesy to the breath; prophesy, son of man, and say to it, 'This is what the Sovereign Lord says: Come, breath, from the four winds and breathe into these slain, that they may live.'" So I prophesied as he commanded me, and breath entered them; they came to life and stood up on their feet—a vast army. Then he said to me: "Son of man, these bones are the people of Israel. They say, 'Our bones are dried up and our hope is gone; we are cut off.' Therefore prophesy and say to them: 'This is what the Sovereign LORD says: My people, I am going to open your graves and bring you up from them; I will bring you back to the land of Israel. Then you, my people, will know that I am the LORD, when I open your graves and bring you up from them. I will put my Spirit in you and you will live, and I will settle you in your own land. Then you will know that I the LORD have spoken, and I have done it, declares the LORD.'" (Ezek. 37:7–11)

While the Ezekiel reference is most commonly thought to foretell the reestablishment of the nation of Israel, it clearly has resurrection tones.

During the Second Temple period, the Jews were subject to domination by the Seleucid Greeks. Among the influences by the Greeks was philosophy of the afterlife. Plato was the most influential of the Greek philosophers. He theorized that the soul was preexisting and immortal, being housed only temporarily within the "prison" of the physical body. Plato's philosophy was not widespread even among the common Greeks or Jews since literacy was only about 10 percent. On the other hand, the priests and scribes were the educated class, and it may well be that Plato influenced their religious doctrine in two ways: (1) an immortal component to the person, and (2) the destructive nature of the body (flesh). Both elements are seen in the writings of the apostle Paul.

There appears to have been a division in the eschatology between the Sadducees and the Pharisees. The aristocratic Sadducees, adhering strictly to the Torah, denied the concept of future resurrection of the body. They appear to have maintained the early patristic concept that the soul died at death of the body, and a Rephaim state in Sheol was the permanent termination.

But the doctrine of the Sadducees is that souls die with the bodies.[362]

The Pharisees appear to have been the more liberal group. They added hundreds of oral laws and perhaps were more influenced by Platonic concepts of the afterlife. They, like the even stricter Essenes, believed eternal salvation was merited by good works according to laws.

They also believed that souls have an immortal vigor in them, and that under the earth there will be rewards and punishment, according as they have lived virtuously or viciously in this life; and the latter are to be detained in everlasting prison but that the former shall have power to revive again.[363]

The Pharisaic Jews believed that at that time the deceased patriarchs would be resurrected and be rejoined to their souls. And this mass resurrection is to happen at the end of the age.

Resurrection of the dead—*t'chiyat hameitim* in Hebrew—is a core doctrine of traditional Jewish theology. Traditional Jews believe that during the Messianic Age, the temple will be rebuilt in Jerusalem, the Jewish people ingathered from the far corners of the earth, and the bodies of the dead will be brought back to life and reunited with their souls. It is not entirely clear whether only Jews or all people are expected to be resurrected at this time.[364]

During the first century AD, the Sadducees gradually disappeared, and the Pharisees continued as the dominant party. With the destruction of the central temple in AD 70, Jewish worship was dispersed into local synagogues, and the Sadducee temple priests were replaced in leadership by the Pharisee rabbis.

Thus, by the time of Jesus, Pharisaic Jewish thought foresaw a future bodily resurrection, but the concept of an immediate bodily resurrection into an imperishable body was not conceived. Enoch and Elijah did not physically die, and the resurrected Lazarus was returned to a perishable earthly body. The immediate resurrection of Jesus's body into His heavenly body was a monumental change in doctrine.

The apostle Paul was a Pharisee, schooled in doctrine by Gamaliel.

> I am a Jew, born in Tarsus of Cilicia, but brought up in this city. I studied under Gamaliel and was thoroughly trained in the law of our ancestors. I was just as zealous for God as any of you are today. (Acts 22:3)

It was then left for Paul, the Jewish Pharisee, to explain to the Jewish community and then to the pagan world the significance of Jesus's bodily resurrection.

> And if the Spirit of him who raised Jesus from the dead is living in you, he who raised Christ from the dead will also give life to your mortal bodies because of his Spirit who lives in you. (Rom. 8:11)

> But someone will say, "How are the dead raised? And with what kind of body do they come?" How foolish!

> What you sow does not come to life unless it dies. (1 Cor. 15:35–36 NASB)

> There are also heavenly bodies and there are earthly bodies; but the splendor of the heavenly bodies is one kind, and the splendor of the earthly bodies is another. (1 Cor. 15:40)

> So also is the resurrection of the dead. It is sown a perishable body, it is raised an imperishable body. (1 Cor. 15:42)

> It is sown a natural body, it is raised a spiritual body. If there is a natural body, there is also a spiritual body. (1 Cor. 15:44)

Conclusion

The concept of a bodily resurrection was not broadly accepted in first-century Judaism. And if it were to occur, the Pharisees thought it would be a mass resurrection at the end-time final judgment, when God would restore the nation of Israel to prominence. Except for Enoch and Elijah, no one had escaped permanent physical death—not Abraham, not Moses, not David. Not even Lazarus, who was returned to life, only to later die again.

Even the disciples did not understand that Jesus would actually rise from the grave (Matt. 28:17; Mark 16:11; Luke 24:8, 11, 37; John 20:9), even though He told them to expect it (Matt. 12:40, 16:21, 17:22–23; Mark 9:9, 10:32–33, 14:27; Luke 9:30–31; John 2:9, 10:14–18, 16:16–22).

44

Where Did Easter Come From?

Introduction

One of the questions about Christian holy days is what the origin of Easter is. Traditionally, the early Jewish Christians celebrated Passover, remembering the Crucifixion. Doctrinally, the Crucifixion sacrifice Jesus made for the atonement of sin was the critical occurrence. The resurrection, while important as evidence of Jesus's divinity, was the less important step.

The Name "Easter"

The *Encyclopedia Britannica* traces the origin of the name "Easter":[365]

> Easter, Latin Pascha, Greek Pascha, principal festival of the Christian church, which celebrates the Resurrection of Jesus Christ on the third day after his Crucifixion. The earliest recorded observance of an Easter celebration comes from the 2nd century, though

the commemoration of Jesus' Resurrection probably occurred earlier.

The English word Easter, which parallels the German word *Ostern*, is of uncertain origin. One view, expounded by the Venerable Bede in the 8th century, was that it derived from Eostre, or Eostrae, the Anglo-Saxon goddess of spring and fertility. This view presumes—as does the view associating the origin of Christmas on December 25 with pagan celebrations of the winter solstice—that Christians appropriated pagan names and holidays for their highest festivals. Given the determination with which Christians combated all forms of paganism (the belief in multiple deities), this appears a rather dubious presumption. There is now widespread consensus that the word derives from the Christian designation of Easter week as *in albis*, a Latin phrase that was understood as the plural of *alba* ("dawn") and became *eostarum* in Old High German, the precursor of the modern German and English term. The Latin and Greek Pascha ("Passover") provides the root for Pâques, the French word for Easter.

Change of Holidays

So how did we change from celebrating the Crucifixion sacrifice to celebrating the resurrection?

When reviewing the historical record of the Passover/Easter controversy, it is undeniable that the early New Testament church did not observe Easter. They continued observing Passover but with a new significance and understanding.[366]

The second-century *quartodeciman controversy* came between the western congregations of Rome and the eastern Asiatic congregations concerning changing celebration from Passover (Nissan 14) to Easter. The Eastern dioceses wanted to hold to the Pasch Passover, while the western churches insisted on changing to Easter Sunday. [367]

The motivation was to sever any relationship to the Jewish influence of the early Christian church due to resentment of the Jewish responsibility for Jesus's Crucifixion.[368]

Under the influence of Constantine, the transition to Easter Sunday was made official at the Council of Nicaea in AD 325. The outcome of the Council of Nicaea was not only to solidify the true divinity of Jesus as the Son of God but also to change the emphasis from the Crucifixion to the resurrection celebration on Easter Sunday.

45

Why Did Miracles Cease after the First Century?

God displayed miracles at least 120 times in the Bible—eighty in the Old Testament and forty in the New Testament.[369] Apparently, God felt the need to objectively display His presence and His power. And in the New Testament, Jesus validated His deity by performing miracles.

Apparently, Jesus felt it to be necessary to demonstrate His deity by performing miracles—not just expect people to believe what He was saying:

> So Jesus said to him, "Unless you people see signs and wonders, you simply will not believe." (John 4:48)

> "Do not believe me unless I do the works of my Father. But if I do them, though you do not believe Me, believe the works, so that you may know and understand that the Father is in Me, and I in the Father." (John 10:37–38)

> Then Jesus told him, "Because you have seen me, you have believed; blessed are those who have not seen and yet have believed."
>
> The Purpose of John's Gospel
> Jesus performed many other signs in the presence of his disciples, which are not recorded in this book. But these are written that you may believe that Jesus is the Messiah, the Son of God, and that by believing you may have life in his name. (John 20:29–31)

Then Jesus commissioned the disciples, Stephen, Paul, and the church to perform miracles:

> And these signs will accompany those who believe: In my name they will drive out demons; they will speak in new tongues; they will pick up snakes with their hands; and when they drink deadly poison, it will not hurt them at all; they will place their hands on sick people, and they will get well."
> After the Lord Jesus had spoken to them, he was taken up into heaven and he sat at the right hand of God.
> Then the disciples went out and preached everywhere, and the Lord worked with them and confirmed his word by the signs that accompanied it. (Mark 16:17–20)
>
> And Stephen, full of grace and power, was performing great wonders and signs among the people. (Acts 6:8)
> There he found a man named Aeneas, who was paralyzed and had been bedridden for eight years. "Aeneas," Peter said to him, "Jesus Christ heals you. Get up and roll up your mat." Immediately Aeneas got up. (Acts 9:33–34)

> Peter sent them all out of the room; then he got down on his knees and prayed. Turning toward the dead woman, he said, "Tabitha, get up." She opened her eyes, and seeing Peter she sat up. He took her by the hand and helped her to her feet. Then he called for the believers, especially the widows, and presented her to them alive. (Acts 9:40–41)

> In Lystra there sat a man who was lame. He had been that way from birth and had never walked. He listened to Paul as he was speaking. Paul looked directly at him, saw that he had faith to be healed and called out, "Stand up on your feet!" At that, the man jumped up and began to walk. (Acts 14:8–10)

> God did extraordinary miracles through Paul, so that even handkerchiefs and aprons that had touched him were taken to the sick, and their illnesses were cured and the evil spirits left them. (Acts 19:11–12)

> And God has appointed in the church, first apostles, second prophets, third teachers, then miracles, then gifts of healings, helps, administrations, various kinds of tongues. (1 Cor. 12:28)

But apparently, at the end of the first century, miracles ceased.

Why did God feel it to be necessary to demonstrate supernatural power from creation until the end of the first century but no longer feel it necessary after the end of the first century?

The standard answer is Jesus's comment to Thomas in John 20:29:

> Then Jesus told him, "Because you have seen me, you have believed; blessed are those who have not seen and yet have believed."

And the admonition to have faith in Hebrews 11:1: “Now faith is confidence in what we hope for and assurance about what we do not see.”

So people of the modern era need to have greater faith than people of Jesus’s time?

Conclusion

While there is no definite, factual answer to the question of why miracles appear to have ceased, there are at least two possible answers.

First, the approximate eighty miracles God performed in the Old Testament occurred over thousands of years. It is likely that God only felt the need to act supernaturally at times of major crisis. It is also possible that only the miracles of major significance were recorded in the Old Testament. Perhaps minor miracles occurred in between but were not recorded in the scriptures. Following that line of thinking, perhaps God hasn’t seen the need for a recent major miracle, even though small ones may be happening without being noticed.

Second, there were many sorcerers present in the first century, such as Simon (Acts 8:9–11). Their actions apparently were either illusionary magic or satanic miracles. Even Jesus was accused of performing satanic-powered miracles (Matt. 12:24). But there were two major events that changed it all: the bodily resurrection of Jesus and the advent of the Holy Spirit. Besides Jesus, the Bible records three resurrections in the Old Testament (1 Kings 17:17–24; 2 Kings 4:18–37; 2 Kings 13:20–21) and six in the New Testament (Luke 7:11–17; Luke 8:40–56; John 11; Matt. 27:50–53; Acts 9:36–43; Acts 20:7–12). However, the great difference is that all the previous people who rose from the dead later died. Jesus’s resurrection was the first in which the person remained alive. It is argued that these two events, Jesus’s resurrection and the advent of the Holy Spirit to guide future generations, are enough to provide a basis for faith.

46

What Was the Chronology of Jesus's Post-Resurrection Appearances?

The sequence of Jesus's post-resurrection appearances is recorded in all four Gospels, but the exact chronology is difficult to discern. It may be significant that only John was a firsthand observe at the tomb. It is likely that Mark, as the apprentice to Peter, was also present. Matthew apparently fled from the arrest in Gethsemane (Matt. 26:5; Mark14:50) and was not involved until later appearances. Luke was not one of the original disciples, and therefore, his account is secondhand.

Outside the Empty Tomb Sunday Morning

The first appearance took place outside the empty tomb on the day after the Sabbath (presumably the Saturday Sabbath), which would make it daylight Sunday morning. Mary Magdalene, remaining at the empty tomb, encountered Jesus (John 20:14) but did not recognize Him at first, "supposing him to be the gardener" (John 20:15). Mary then runs to tell the disciples (John 20:18). Mark 16:9 also reports Mary Magdalene alone to be the first person to whom Jesus appears, but the ending of Mark 19:9–20 is not in the earliest manuscripts,[370] so that report is suspect.

Matthew's account varies significantly in that Mary Magdalene, along with the "other Mary" (likely Mary of Clopas) were present at the tomb when an earthquake rolled away the stone and an angel sat upon it (Matt. 28:2). The angel instructs them to run and tell the others that Jesus has risen. On their way from the tomb to report to the disciples, Jesus encounters them (Matt. 28:9–10). The exact location is not indicated. John reports that it was Mary who informed the gathered disciples that Jesus was risen and she had seen Him (John 20:18).

Given the fact that John was the author most present (Mark's report being suspect), his account is probably the most accurate.

Luke writes that the disciples did not believe Mary's report that Jesus had, indeed, risen (Luke 24:11). Interestingly, the same disbelief is reported of the disciples other than John himself (John 20:9).

The Road to Emmaus

Only Luke records the encounter on the road to Emmaus (Luke 24:13). Luke reports that "on that very day," two disciples were traveling to the village of Emmaus when Jesus appeared to them. Jesus again is not recognized in his post-resurrection body when He approaches and joins the two. After He reminds them of His need to be crucified and resurrected, Jesus suddenly vanishes (Luke 24:31). This encounter was apparently not with the core disciples.

To the Gathered Disciples Sunday Evening

On the evening of resurrection Sunday, the disciples return from Emmaus to tell the group what had transpired. The gathered disciples, except Thomas and Judas Iscariot, were hiding in a room with shut doors. Jesus appears, apparently without needing to open the doors (John 20:19). As an aside, this characteristic of Jesus's post-resurrection body occurs repeatedly. He is apparently able to translocate through structures.

Thomas was not present at this meeting, and after being told Jesus was resurrected, he issued the famous statement, "Unless I see in His hands the imprint of the nails, and put my finger into the place of the nails, and put my hand on His side, I will not believe" (John 20:24–25).

In Galilee

At the Passover meal, Jesus told the disciples that after His resurrection, He would meet them in Galilee (Matt. 26:32; Mark 14:28). At the tomb, the "young man" (angel?) instructed the disciples to initially go to Galilee, where Jesus would meet them (Matt. 28:7; Mark 16:7). And at His encounter with the women outside the empty tomb, Jesus instructed them to tell the "brethren" to meet Him in Galilee (Matt. 28:10).

John records a meeting in Galilee with Simon Peter, Thomas, Nathanael, James, John, and two others (John 21:1–14). This may be the same meeting described in Matthew 28:16–17.

It is not clear at what point in time Jesus appeared in Galilee, but since John comments that "This is now the third time that Jesus was manifested to the disciples, after He was raised from the dead" (John 21:14), it would appear that it was between the two Jerusalem meetings.

The other encounter in Galilee was when Jesus met the disciples on "the mountain which Jesus had designated" (Matt. 28:16), where He issues the Great Commission (Matt. 28:19–20). Presumably, this meeting occurred before the disciples returned to Jerusalem.

Back in Jerusalem Eight Days Later

Eight days after the initial meeting with the disciples, except Thomas, Jesus again appears through locked doors (John 20:26; Luke 24:36). This time, He shows Thomas the scars, and Thomas believes (John 20:27–28). Jesus tells them to stay in the city until the Holy Spirit comes. Jesus instructs the disciples to remain in Jerusalem until "you are clothed with power from on high" (Luke 24:53).

Subsequent Appearances

In Acts 1:3, Luke reports that after His resurrection, Jesus appeared multiple times over a period of forty days. After, Jesus tells the disciples to remain in Jerusalem until they are to be "baptized by the Holy Spirit" (Acts 1:4–5). Since this command to stay in Jerusalem was the same as Jesus issued after the second Jerusalem meeting (above), it appears that the disciples remained in Jerusalem from this point onward.

Jesus's subsequent post-resurrection appearances are not recorded in the four Gospels, rather in Acts and in 1 Corinthians.

Paul reports that immediately after His resurrection, Jesus appeared to "Cephas (Peter) and then the twelve" (1 Cor. 15:5). This report is compatible with Mark's comment from the "young man" to "go tell his disciples and Peter" (Mark 16:7). The appearance to Peter is also compatible with the reference in Luke 24:34. It does not necessarily indicate Jesus met with Peter separately. Rather, Peter may have been told specifically by Paul because he (Peter) was the leader of the twelve. Paul goes on to state, "After that He appeared to more than five hundred brethren at one time" (1 Cor. 15:6). Given the unrest in Jerusalem around the time of the Crucifixion and the fact that Jesus often attracted large crowds in his home area of Galilee during His ministry, it is likely this encounter happened when the post-resurrection Jesus returned to Galilee.

Paul also mentions Jesus's appearance to "James, then to the other apostles" (1 Cor. 15:7). The timing of this appearance is not entirely clear. The appearance to James might have been along with the original disciples since he was one of the twelve. The reference to the "other apostles" has been suggested to have included apostles who were not among the original twelve.[371] Finally, Paul's reference to "and last of all to me" (1 Cor. 15:8) no doubt was referring to his conversion contact on the road to Damascus since Paul did not know Jesus during His ministry.

The Ascension

At the end of forty days after the resurrection, Jesus meets with the disciples and leads them to Bethany, east of Jerusalem, where He ascends into the clouds (Luke 24:51–52; Acts 1:9).

Post-Ascension Appearances

Jesus appeared to Stephen (Acts 7:55); Paul on the road to Damascus (Acts 9:3–6); Paul in the Temple (Acts 22:17–18); and John on the island of Patmos (Rev. 1:10–19).

Conclusion

The above chronology accounts slightly more than one week after the resurrection. Yet He was present for forty days before the ascension. There is no documentation of His activities for most of that period.

What is unclear is the amount of time Jesus spent in Jerusalem versus in Galilee. Though not substantiated by scripture, a few projections could be offered. First, due to the controversy in Jerusalem, He may have wanted to avoid it. It seems likely Jesus would have wanted to spend a significant amount of time returning to the people to whom He ministered during His life.

On the other hand, Jesus must have spent some time with His mother, Mary, and his brothers. While neither believed in Jesus's deity during His ministry, and Mary didn't even attend Jesus's burial, both became converted followers after the resurrection. Mary and Jesus's brothers are mentioned as present with the group of believers in the upper room at Pentecost (Acts 1:14). And His brother James became the leader of the church in Jerusalem (Gal. 1:19; Acts 15:13–19).

What is not chronologically clear is Jesus admonished the disciples to remain in Jerusalem the two different times (Luke 24:53; Acts 1:4–5), after otherwise telling them to go to Galilee (Matt. 26:32; Mark 14:28). It could be that since Luke was writing from secondhand research, he got this reference out of order, or it could be that Jesus wanted His disciples to remain safely secluded in Jerusalem, while He alone returned to his Galilean home area. The scriptures don't explain.

47

Why Did History Not Better Record the Crucifixion and the Resurrection?

Ministry

The vast majority of Jesus's early ministry occurred in the sparsely populated area around the Sea of Galilee.

Likely, Jesus visited Jerusalem quietly on multiple occasions, since Jews were commanded to visit the Temple in Jerusalem three times a year—the feasts of (1) Passover, the Feast of Unleavened bread on the fifteenth day of Nisan, the beginning of spring; (2) Pentecost, the Feast of Weeks, the wheat harvest in May–June; and (3) Tabernacle, the Feast of Ingathering, Tents, or Booths in late September–October (Exod. 23:17; Deut. 16:16) .

Luke 2:41 records, "Now his parents went to Jerusalem every year at the feast of the Passover." Luke 2:22 documents His infant dedication in the temple.

But Jesus apparently had only five eventful interactions in Jerusalem: (1) discussing Old Testament doctrine with teachers in the Temple at age twelve (Luke 2:41–47); (2) when He confronted the money changers (John 2:15); (3) when He attended a feast and healed the paralytic at the pool of Bethesda (John 5:1); (4) when He asserted His deity during the Feast of Dedication (John 10:22–23); and (5) at Passover when He was later crucified (John 12:12). It is to be noted that there may have been two episodes when Jesus expelled the moneychangers from the temple—John 2:15 and again in Luke 19:45.

It appears that all but the latter appearance involved a limited number of people—mostly the Pharisees who Jesus challenged. The final entry into Jerusalem on a colt was apparently the only mass gathering, and those likely were only His followers. As will be discussed subsequently, given the enlarged population of Jerusalem during Passover, Jesus's triumphal entry may have been witnessed by a small percentage of the inhabitants who were otherwise focused on the Passover rituals.

Population of Jerusalem

The population of Jerusalem during the time of Jesus (first half of the first century AD) is not well established. Most estimates center on the time of the First Jewish-Roman War (AD 66–73) and the destruction of the Temple (AD 70). The classic reference is Josephus quoting the Roman historian Tacitus, who suggested 600,000 people as the population.[372] But this estimate is suspect on two counts. First, the period referenced is thirty years after Jesus's Crucifixion, and second, neither historian was alive at the time of the Crucifixion.

More modern references of the time frame of the siege of Jerusalem vary from 60,000 to 80,000.[373, 374]

"According to Levine, because the new area encompassed by the Third Wall was not densely populated, assuming that it contained half the population of the rest of the city, there were between 60,000 and 70,000 people living in Jerusalem."[375]

The opposite view is expressed by Geva, who believes that earlier estimates were exaggerated and that the permanent population of Jerusalem in the first two-thirds of the first century was closer to 20,000.[376]

What is clear, however, is that during Passover, the population of Jerusalem swelled to one to two million as devout Jews responded to the command to visit the Temple (Exod. 23:17; Deut. 16:16). John 11:55 records, "And the Passover of the Jews was near, and many went from the country up to Jerusalem before the Passover to purify themselves."

Given the fact that the followers of Jesus present in Jerusalem at the time of Passion Week were likely few, it would not be surprising that their activities might go unnoticed by the massive general population focused on Passover celebration.

Crucifixion

But wasn't a crucifixion on the edge of the city a spectacle the masses (and historians?) would have found remarkable?

The history of the method of crucifixion is summarized by Retief and Cillers:[377]

> In antiquity crucifixion was considered one of the most brutal and shameful modes of death. Probably originating with the Assyrians and Babylonians, it was used systematically by the Persians in the 6th century BC. Alexander the Great brought it from there to the eastern Mediterranean countries in the 4th century BC, and the Phoenicians introduced it to Rome in the 3rd century BC. It was virtually never used in pre-Hellenic Greece. The Romans perfected crucifixion for 500 years until it was abolished by Constantine I in the 4th century AD.

During the reign of Tiberius (AD 14–37), Suetonius is quoted as claiming that there were as many as twenty crucifixions daily. White estimates the conservative total to be 9,500 per year throughout the Roman Empire.[378] If that estimate is true, the fact that there were three bodies hanging on crucifixion crosses on the edge of the town of Jerusalem during a festival involving over a million people focused on the Temple rituals might not be that remarkable. And the last thing the ruling Jewish leaders wanted was to have Jesus and His followers recognized as significant.

But wouldn't there have been at least some historians to have recorded all this besides the apostles?

Non-Christian References

The first thing to recognize is that there are almost no existing historical records from the first century AD. The only two historians present and writing during the first century AD were Tacitus and Josephus. Both are attributed to commenting on Jesus.

Tacitus (AD 56–120)

Publius Cornelius Tacitus was a Roman historian and politician who lived between AD 56 and 120. He is recognized as the most important Roman historian, but despite his talent for succinctness, he was also prone to editorializing. Relevant to our discussion is his publication, Annals, that spans Roman history from approximately AD 14 to 70, the period of Jesus. The Annals comprised thirty books, not all of which have been preserved. In book 15.44 (AD 116), Tacitus writes, "Christus, from whom the name had its origin, suffered the extreme penalty during the reign of Tiberius at the hands of one of our procurators, Pontius Pilatus."

While this reference confirms the history of the Crucifixion, Tacitus was not yet born at the time the Crucifixion occurred, and he apparently wrote his publication from Rome. But it does confirm the apparent knowledge of the Crucifixion by a non-Christian source.

Josephus (AD 37–100)

Josephus was a Jewish aristocrat who was born in AD 37, approximately four years after the Crucifixion. Josephus initially led Jewish forces in Galilee against the Romans in the first Jewish-Roman War (AD 66–67). After being dominated by the Roman legions, he retreated to a cave with forty of his troops. In the cave, Josephus convinced his followers to commit sequential suicide until only he and one other remained. Josephus then reneged on his suicide pact and negotiated his survival. Josephus convinced the Roman general Vespasian that prophecy predicted Vespasian would become emperor. Thus, through his cunning and guile, Josephus became a Roman citizen and court historian. He was considered a traitor by the residual Jews.

In AD 94, Josephus published his history of the Jewish nation: *Antiquities of the Jews*. He was not a firsthand observer since he was not born until after the Crucifixion. His *Antiquities* was written sixty years after the Crucifixion, obviously from hearsay. The original manuscripts were apparently written in Aramaic, then translated into Greek, and finally to English. The original manuscript does not exist.

Josephus mentions Jesus in two of his books: 18 and 20. The first, though brief, mention of Jesus is in *Ant* 20.9.1, where Josephus refers to Jesus's brother James. This reference is apparently consistent in all manuscripts and is attested by Origen of Alexandria (AD 184–253),[379] "the brother of Jesus, who was called Christ, whose name was James."

It is the more extensive reference in book 18 (*Jewish Antiquities*, 18.3.3 §63) that is in dispute. Meier points out that there remain in existence only three Greek manuscripts of book 18 of the *Antiquities*, the earliest of which dates from the eleventh century.[380]

Controversy surrounds the detailed validity of this reference for two reasons: (1) minor transliteration variations from Greek to English, and (2) suspected alterations by patristic reproductions.

One of the earliest translations of Josephus is that of Eusebius in approximately AD 314–318. Eusebius's *Demonstratio evangelica*,[381]

> And Jesus arises at that time, a wise man, if it is befitting to call him a man. For he was a doer of no common works, a teacher of men who reverence the truth. And he gathered many of the Jewish and many of the Greek race. This was Christus; and when Pilate condemned him to the Cross on the information of our rulers, his first followers did not cease to revere him. For he appeared to them the third day alive again, the divine prophets having foretold this, and very many other things about him. And from that time to this the tribe of the Christians has not failed.

The "standard" translation is that of Louis Feldman:[382]

> About this time there lived Jesus, a wise man, if indeed one ought to call him a man. For he was one who performed surprising deeds and was a teacher of such people as accept the truth gladly. He won over many Jews and many of the Greeks. He was the Messiah. And when, upon the accusation of the principal men among us, Pilate had condemned him to a cross, those who had first come to love him did not cease. He appeared to them spending a third day restored to life, for the prophets of God had foretold these things and a thousand other

> marvels about him. And the tribe of the Christians, so called after him, has still to this day not disappeared.

In 1971, Shlomo Pines, an Israeli philosopher and translator, discovered a tenth-century Arabic version of the *Testimonium Flavianum* by Josephus due to Agapius of Hierapolis, an Arabic Christian. He believed it to be the original Aramaic version.[383]

> At this time there was a wise man called Jesus, and his conduct was good, and he was known to be virtuous. Many people among the Jews and the other nations became his disciples. Pilate condemned him to be crucified and to die. But those who had become his disciples did not abandon his discipleship. They reported that he had appeared to them three days after his Crucifixion and that he was alive. Accordingly, he was perhaps the Messiah, concerning whom the prophets have reported wonders. And the tribe of the Christians, so named after him, has not disappeared to this day.

It is to be noted that the three controversial "deity" phrases have been either deleted ("if indeed one ought to call him a man") or softened ("He was the Messiah"; "He appeared to them spending a third day restored to life").

Paul L. Maier is a previous professor of ancient history at Western Michigan University and has previously served on the Lutheran Church–Missouri Synod. Meier points out the three phrases in the standard translations that are controversial: (1) "if indeed one should call him a man," (2) "He was the Messiah," and (3) "For he appeared to them on the third day, living again, just as the divine prophets had spoken of these and countless other wondrous things about him." Maier opines that since Josephus was a traditional non-Christian Jew, he would not have included the deity phrases in such confirmatory terms.[384]

This same criticism is expounded by John P. Meier[385] and echoed by most modern source critics.[386] Modern critics believe the original, non-Christianized, version from Josephus was as follows:

> At this time there appeared Jesus, a wise man. For he was a doer of startling deeds, a teacher of people who receive the truth with pleasure. And he gained a following both among many Jews and among many of Greek origin. And when Pilate, because of an accusation made by the leading men among us, condemned him to the cross, those who had loved him previously did not cease to do so. And up until this very day the tribe of Christians (named after him) has not died out.

The Emmaus Controversy

Some scholars have suggested that fourth-century Christians interpolated part of the Emmaus narrative of Luke 24 into the Testimonium. Goldberg contends that both the Testimonium and Luke's Emmaus narrative were taken from a common other Christian source.[387]

> And He said to them, "What things?" And they said to Him, "The things about Jesus the Nazarene, who was a prophet mighty in deed and word in the sight of God and all the people, and how the chief priests and our rulers delivered Him to the sentence of death and crucified Him. But we were hoping that it was He who was going to redeem Israel. Indeed, besides all this, it is the third day since these things happened.

> And He said to them, "O foolish men and slow of heart to believe in all that the prophets have spoken! Was it not necessary for the Christ to suffer these things and to enter into His glory?" Then beginning with Moses and with all the prophets, He explained to them the things concerning Himself in all the Scriptures. (Luke 24:19–21, 25–27 NASB)

Goldberg points out that two of the three controversial passages in the Testimonium ("if indeed one ought to call him a man" and "He was the Messiah") do not have parallels in the Emmaus passage.[388] While worded differently, confirmation of the resurrection after three days is confirmed by Jesus speaking to Cleopas and his companion.

So where does all this scrutiny of Josephus's Testimonium in *Antiquities* 18:3.3.63 leave us?

Given the fact that Josephus was not born until four years after the Crucifixion, he would have necessarily received his information from the early Christians who preserved verbal history in creeds. Luke also was not one of the original disciples. He likely was discipled by the apostle Paul in at least AD 50. Luke expressively comments that his information was obtained from research—not personal observation (Luke 1:1–4). Josephus's *Antiquities* was written in AD 94, so likely his research was near or slightly before that date. Luke is thought to have written his Gospel between AD 70 and 90, depending upon whose historical opinion you read. It is not at all unlikely that both Josephus and Luke would have gotten their information from the same root sources, and therefore, their reports would have similarities.

While no provable answer is possible, it is quite likely that writing from a common reference source, both Josephus's and Luke's accounts were originally written in the present translation form.

It is relevant that even the "softened" Pines's translation accepted by critics still documents that Jesus (1) existed, (2) was crucified by Pilate,

(3) was reported to have been seen three days later by His followers, and (4) perhaps was the Messiah. So the controversy is not over the presence of the beliefs but only their certainty.

Toledot Jesu (Yeshu)

The Toledot Jesu is a Jewish text mocking Jesus's birth, miracles, and death. The ancient rabbis were threatened by the rise of Christianity and rarely acknowledged Christianity.[389]

Analysis of the Toledot Yeshu is provided by H. I. Newman.[390] It apparently was committed to writing between the fourth and ninth centuries AD. The Toledot Yeshu is thought to be an evolution of contributions of various sources. Di Segni recognizes three sources: Pilate, Queen Helena, and Herod.[391] The Crucifixion references were apparently contributed by the "Pilate group."

Hillel quotes a specific pejorative description of the Crucifixion:

> He brought him before Rabbi Joshua b. Perachiah, and they lifted him up and crucified him on a cabbage stalk.23 But before they lifted him up to the cross (JOvU), he [sc. Jesus] recalled what is written in the Torah: 'You shall not leave his corpse overnight on the cross' (Deut. 21:23). At that moment he sent and called for the people he had deceived and said to them: 'If you come tomorrow and find neither me nor my corpse on the cross, I shall have ascended to the firmament of Heaven, and you will not see me.' They crucified him alive and stoned him with a rock.24He died on the cross, but they did not want to take him down from the cross. Rabbi Joshua said to them: 'On account of the wicked Jesus shall we change a statute of the Torah? For it is written: "You shall not leave his corpse overnight on the cross, etc." ' So they

> took him down from the cross and buried him in a water channel ... In the garden of Rabbi Judah the Gardener. And when those people whom he had deceived arrived and did not find him on the cross, they returned and seized the Jews and said to them: 'Our Lord Jesus said to us in truth that the Jews deal in lies. If you crucified him on the cross, where is his corpse? Truly he has gone to Heaven!' Immediately, Pilate called Judah the Gardener and said to him: 'What have you done with the corpse of Jesus?' Rabbi Judah responded and said to him: 'My lord, wicked Jesus knew what is written in the Torah—"You shall not leave his corpse, etc."—and deceived these people, saying to them: "If you come tomorrow and. do not find me on the cross, know that I have ascended to Heaven." Now if my lord so desires, I will bring him [i.e., Jesus] and reveal his corpse to them, and they will recognize that it is the wicked Jesus.' Rabbi Judah the Gardener went and removed him from his grave, tossed a rope around his legs, and dragged him through all the markets of Tiberias. And they declared over him: 'This is the wicked Jesus son of Pandera, who rebelled against Almighty God.' He ... and brought him before Pilate and called to all the disciples whom [Jesus] had deceived, and while some believed, others did not believe. Pilate the governor replied and said to Judah the Gardener: 'This is the wicked one whom you buried in the water course; now go bury him in a place for burying the dead.' Judah the Gardener went and buried him in a ... of water.

Newman theorizes that this cabbage and water framework is a comparison to the legend of Adonis. He also quotes references to Jesus in multiple other apocryphal books.

Newman further observes:

> As recognized by virtually all commentators on Toledot Yeshu, the bizarre crucifixion on a stalk of cabbage should be seen against the backdrop of John 19:41:
> 'In the place where he had been crucified there was a garden, and in the garden was a new tomb in which no one had yet been buried'
> What does the Toldot Yeshu contribute? No doubt the compendium was written from a mocking, negative Jewish viewpoint. Yet even in its distorted form, the Toledoth Yeshu validates that the Crucifixion of Jesus as a real historical event. On the other hand, it does not contribute to validation of the resurrection.

Lucian of Samosata (115–200 AD)

Lucian of Samosata was a second-century Greek satirist who was highly critical of Christians. In his satire, *The Death of Peregrinius*, he wrote,[392]

> The Christians, you know, worship a man to this day—the distinguished personage who introduced their novel rites, and was crucified on that account ... You see, these misguided creatures_start with the general conviction that they are immortal for all time, which explains the contempt of death and voluntary self-devotion which are so common among them; and then it was impressed on them by their original lawgiver that they are all brothers, from the moment that they are converted, and deny the gods of Greece, and worship the crucified sage, and live after his laws. All this they take quite on faith, with the result that they

> despise all worldly goods alike, regarding them merely as common property.

The Lucian reference documents that Jesus died by crucifixion and was worshiped by His followers after His death. It does not, however, explicitly document the resurrection.

Talmud (Probably Second-Century AD)

The Talmud is the central text of Rabbinic Judaism and the primary source of Jewish religious law. Most references are to the Babylonian version of the Talmud, which has two components, the Mishah and the Gemara.[393] It is the latter that contains potential references to Jesus of the New Testament.

Christians apparently began censoring the Talmud as early as AD 521. Apparently, beginning in the thirteenth century, alterations began, which throws into debate the authenticity of modern versions.[394]

The name used in the Talmud is Yeshu rather than the formal Jewish name Yeshua. While Jesus was common name in the ancient Middle East, there are specific references to Jesus of the Gospels. A sample reference follows:[395, 396]

> Babylonian Sanhedrin 43a–b (Editions or MSs: Herzog 1, Karlsruhe 2) is: "On (Sabbath eve and) the eve of Passover Jesus the Nazarene was hanged and a herald went forth before him forty days heralding, 'Jesus the Nazarene is going forth to be stoned because he practiced sorcery and instigated and seduced Israel to idolatry. Whoever knows anything in defense may come and state it.' But since they did not find anything in his defense they hanged him on (Sabbath eve and) the eve of Passover. Ulla said: Do you suppose that Jesus

> the Nazarene was one for whom a defense could be made? He was a mesit (someone who instigated Israel to idolatry), concerning whom the Merciful [God]says: Show him no compassion and do not shield him (Deut. 13:9). With Jesus the Nazarene it was different. For he was close to the government."

Among the various non-Christian references to Jesus of the New Testament, those in the Talmud are the most controversial.

Darkness at the Crucifixion

Matthew 27:45, Mark 15:33, and Luke 23:44 all record that darkness fell upon the land between the sixth and ninth hours as Jesus died.

Interestingly, there seem to be some non-Gospel accounts of that cosmic event.

Thallus was a Mediterranean historian who reportedly wrote around AD 50. His original manuscripts have been lost, but he is quoted by Julius Africanus, a Christian historian in AD 221.[397]

Apparently, in Thallus's third book, he affirms the episode of darkness and proposes a solar eclipse as the cause. Africanus is quoted as attempting to refute the Thallus mechanism:[398] "On the whole world there pressed a most fearful darkness; and the rocks were rent by an earthquake, and many places in Judea and other districts were thrown down. This darkness Thallus, in the third book of his *History*, calls, as appears to me without reason, an eclipse of the sun."

On the other hand, the fact that Julius Africanus argues this point indicates that knowledge of a real darkness event was circulating in the Mediterranean shortly after the time of the Crucifixion.

Further evidence of the darkness event is presented:[399] Tertullian claimed that this darkness was a "cosmic" or "world event," which he boasted was known by the Romans.[400] Africanus recorded Phlegon of

Tralles (a Greek author from Caria), regarding the "world darkness" in AD 137. Phlegon wrote that in the 202nd Olympiad (AD 33), there was "the greatest eclipse of the sun" and "it became night in the sixth hour of the day [i.e., noon] so that stars even appeared in the heavens. There was a great earthquake in Bithynia, and many things were overturned in Nicaea."[401]

Again, these references do not document the resurrection, but they do indicate that the Crucifixion, rather than routine, was apparently accompanied by a cosmic event of world darkness, just as attested in the three Gospels.

Conclusion

So where does all this historical documentation lead us?

First and foremost, the essential point is that there are no firsthand non-Christian historical records of the Crucifixion and resurrection. All were secondary or more distantly related accounts. On the other hand, there is very little existing history of anything in the first century AD. But there do exist a few non-Christian writings of late first century AD and the next few centuries that confirm the existence of Jesus and His Crucifixion.

And as has been pointed out, the number of Jesus's followers at the time of His ministry and Crucifixion were likely a few hundred at most. The explosive growth of Christianity began after the Crucifixion with the spreading Great Commission of the apostles, followed by the sanction of Christianity as the state religion of the Roman Empire in the fourth century AD.

Given the small size of the early followers of Jesus, particularly at the time of swelling of the population of Jerusalem during Passover, and the frequency of crucifixions, it would not be surprising that the trial by Pilate and the Crucifixion would go relatively unnoticed by the masses. And remember that post-resurrection, Jesus left Jerusalem to meet His followers in Galilee, where He was present for only about fifty days before the ascension.

Modern textural critics have discounted the historical validity of the Gospels. They cite contradictions in the modern translations as evidence that the Gospels are historically inaccurate. But is that conclusion truly valid?

The Gospels represent four firsthand accounts of Jesus's ministry, Crucifixion, and resurrection. And while the details of each account vary, the basic elements of the story are consistent. Do different recollections of an event mean the event didn't happen?

If we were to read different histories of the Second World War, say from the United States, from Germany, or France, or Russia, would they likely be identical in detail? I think not. So does that mean the Second World War didn't happen? Obviously not.

In conclusion, even the sparse history of the first century AD documents the ministry and Crucifixion of Jesus. Even critics accept that Jesus lived. The only firsthand accounts of the resurrection are the Gospels, and while they may vary in emphasized details, they tell a consistent story. Why not believe them?

If they were historical books assembled anywhere other than the Bible, I doubt they would be dismissed.

48

What Happened to the Apostles?

One of the controversial aspects of church history is the eventual fate of the apostles.

Before considering them individually, it is worthwhile to define terminology.

- A *disciple* is a student who is a follower of his/her mentor.
- An *apostle* is a disciple who is sent forth as a messenger to advance the mentor's teaching.
- A *martyr*, in this context, is someone killed for their Christian beliefs.

The original twelve were *disciples* of Jesus. Approximately halfway through His ministry, Jesus apparently felt that the disciples were sufficiently schooled to be sent out to carry the message as *apostles* (Matt. 10:1; Luke 6:12–13; Mark 6:7–13; Luke 9:1–6). Others were later sent as apostles (Luke 10:1). The most notable were Stephen (Acts 6:8), Mark (Acts 12:25; 2 Tim. 4:11), and Paul (Acts 9:15).

There is some confusion over identifying who the original twelve were. The listings in Matthew 10:2–4; Mark 3:16–19, Luke 6:13–16, and

Acts 1:13 are somewhat different. McDowell[402] concludes that Thaddeus (Matt. 10:4; Mark 3:16–19) and Judas, son of James (Luke 6:13–16; Acts 1:13), are the same person. McDowell similarly concludes that Bartholomew, found in all four lists in Matthew, Mark, Luke, and Acts, is the same person as Nathaniel mentioned in John 1:45–52. Finally, the list in Acts of those present after the resurrection omits Judas Iscariot for obvious reasons but fails to list Matthias, who has not yet been selected (Acts 1:26).

It appears that the apostles remained in and around Jerusalem for a while after the resurrection. After the stoning of Stephen (Acts 6–8) and the killing of James, the brother of John, by Herod Agrippa (Acts 12:12), the apostles fled Jerusalem.

Peter (Simon)

Peter, as the most mentioned apostle in the New Testament, has the most traditional history of his fate. There is some argument over Peter's ministry after leaving Jerusalem, but tradition states that he eventually ended up in Rome with Paul (see chapter 49). It appears that Paul had already established churches in Rome by AD 62 when Peter arrived.[403] Tradition states that he was crucified, along with Paul, in AD 64 by Nero (see chapter 30). His crucifixion is thought to have been foretold by Jesus:

> "Very truly I tell you, when you were younger you dressed yourself and went where you wanted; but when you are old you will stretch out your hands, and someone else will dress you and lead you where you do not want to go." Jesus said this to indicate the kind of death by which Peter would glorify God. Then he said to him, "Follow me!" (John 21:18–19)

In the ancient world, "stretch out your hands" often referred to crucifixion.[404] It is also considered that Peter's comment in 2 Peter 1:12–15 represents his farewell speech:

> So I will always remind you of these things, even though you know them and are firmly established in the truth you now have. I think it is right to refresh your memory as long as I live in the tent of this body, because I know that I will soon put it aside, as our Lord Jesus Christ has made clear to me. And I will make every effort to see that after my departure you will always be able to remember these things.

Peter's reference to "tent" is considered a common metaphor for the human body (Isa. 38:12; 2 Cor. 5:1, 4; John 1:14).[405]

When visiting Rome, one receives the explanation that Peter was crucified upside down, because he felt unworthy to be crucified the same as Jesus. While Peter's death by crucifixion seems to be validated by Clement of Rome writing near the end of the first century AD,[406] the upside-down version is not substantiated except by tradition. Peter was reported initially buried along the Appian Way, after which his bones were removed to a small cemetery by Emperor Constantine. The remains of Peter's bones are said to be in a sarcophagus beneath St. Peter's Basilica at the Vatican.

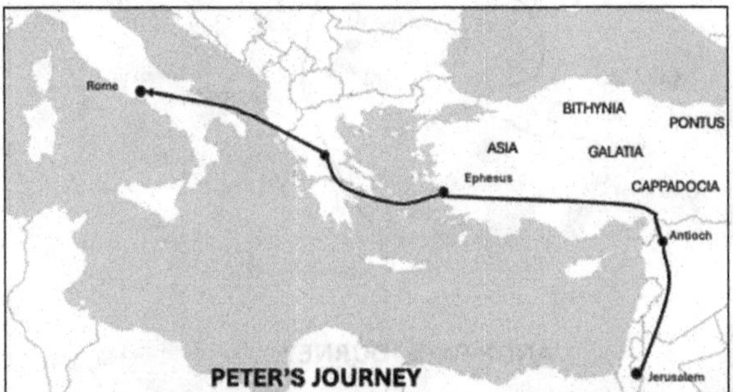

Andrew

Andrew, the brother of Peter, is mentioned only sparsely in the New Testament (Matt. 4:18; Matt. 10:12; Mark 1:16, 29–30; 3:18; 13:3; Luke 6:14; John 1:40, 44; 6:8; 12:22; 12:41; Acts 1:13). A quiet man, Andrew may have been the most widely traveled of the apostles. As such, his journeys are difficult to chronical. Most likely, Andrew traveled through Assyria (now Georgia), between the Black Sea and the Caspian Sea to Scythia. Ancient Scythia is now southern Ukraine. From there, he headed west through Romania, down through Byzantium (Istanbul), crossing into Achaia, Greece. No doubt he left influence in each of these locations, because he remains the patron saint of Georgia, Ukraine, and Russia.[407]

Andrew apparently ended up in Patras (Patrae) in Greek Achaia, where he ran afoul of the Porconsul, Aegeates. Andrew is reported to have converted Aegeates's wife, Maxamilla, who then rejected Aegeates. Aegeates then had Andrew crucified in AD 69.[408] Legend has it that that Andrew was roped to an X-shaped cross and died over several days. While creative, this detail cannot be substantiated. It is said that the skull of Andrew was temporarily removed to Byzantium, then returned to Patras.[409]

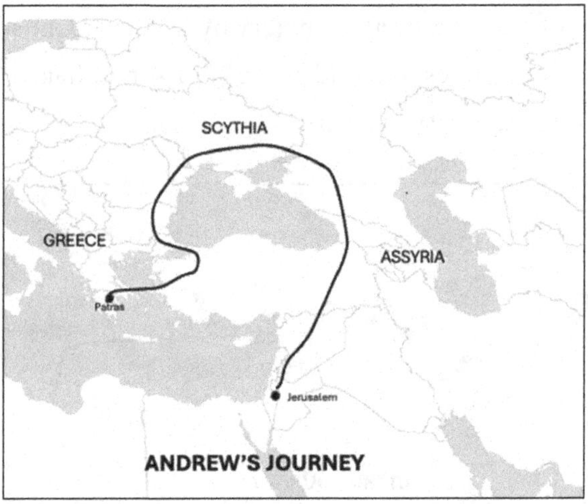

James, the Son of Zebedee

James, the brother of John, was in Jesus's inner circle, as indicated that he was with Jesus at the healing of Jairus's daughter (Mark 5:37), was chosen to accompany Jesus up the mountain at the transfiguration (Matt. 17:1–13; Mark 9:2–23; Luke 9:28–36), and accompanied Jesus at Gethsemane (Matt. 26:37). James is present at the upper-room meeting of Pentecost (Acts 1:13) but is not mentioned again until the report of his death (Acts 12:2). During that interval, a great deal happened—Peter's ministry, Stephen's stoning, and the beginning of Paul's ministry. Apparently, James left Jerusalem soon after Pentecost and went on a missionary journey to Spain. In AD 19, approximately four thousand young Jews were transported to Spain in slavery. It is possible that these youths were previously followers of John the Baptist, and James felt a calling to go minister to them.[410] Fourteen years later, James reappears in Jerusalem, where he is martyred by the sword. Mc Dowell suggests,[411]

> According to Jewish law, execution by sword was the punishment for murder or apostacy (*m. Sanhedrin 9:1*; Deut. 13:6–18). Herod lived as a faithful Jew, so he naturally would have been concerned to stop the growth of any heretical sect. According to Deuteronomy 13:6–18, if an individual entices the Jews to "go and serve other gods," then that person is to be stoned to death But if that person entices the whole city to follow other gods, then that person is to be killed by the sword.

Apparently, Herod felt that James was causing a city-wide uprising against the Jewish establishment. James was killed by the sword at the order of Herod Agrippa I in approximately AD 44.[412]

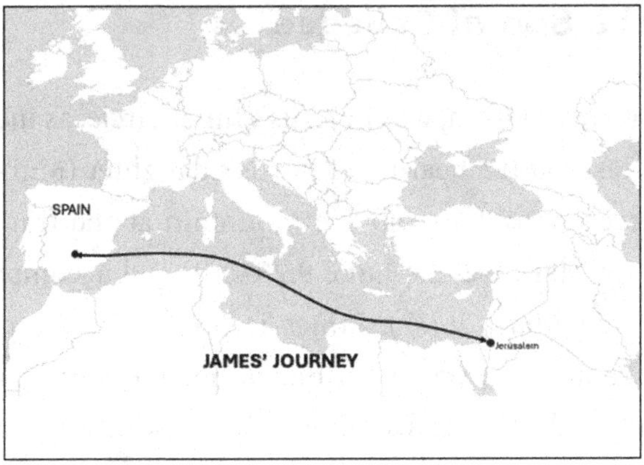

John, the Son of Zebedee

John, the younger brother of James (the Greater), was in Jesus's inner circle. He was with Jesus at the transfiguration (Matt. 17:1–13; Mark 9:2–23; Luke 9:28–36); nearest to Jesus at the Last Supper (13:23); was sent with Peter to prepare the Last Supper (Luke 22:8); accompanied Jesus to Gethsemane during the Olivet Discourse (Matt. 13:3) and at Jesus's capture (Matt. 26:37); was present at Jesus's trial before Caiaphas (John18:15); was present at the Crucifixion (John 19:26); was asked by Jesus to take care of Mary (John 19:27); ran to the empty tomb (John 20:4).

The subsequent history of John is detailed in chapter 29. Most likely, John ministered in Ephesus, then was banished to the island of Patmos, where he wrote the Revelation, 1 John, and 2 John, then died a natural death at an old age.

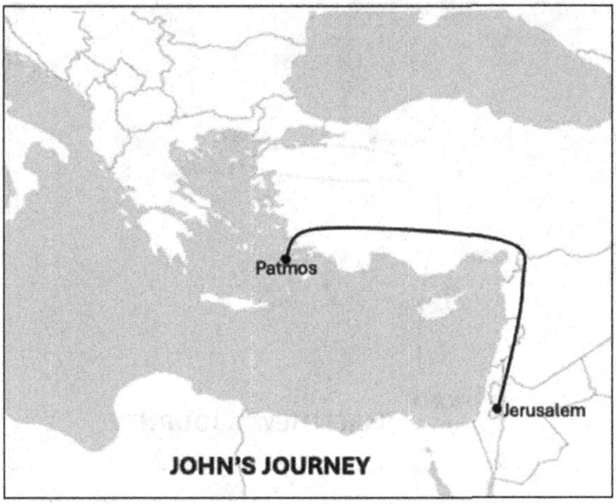

Matthew (Levi)

Matthew was the brother of James the Less. Both were sons of Alphaeus. Levi was a tax collector and, as such, was educated. He was not one of the original disciples of John the Baptist and entered the group of twelve later. After Pentecost, nothing more is heard about Matthew in the New Testament. All information on his fate comes from later church patriarchs and is somewhat conflicting.

The consensus opinion is that after Pentecost, Matthew remained in Jerusalem for fifteen years, preaching to the Jews about Christ. Church historians report that the apostles were assigned territories of ministry.[413] It appears that Matthew went to Persia (perhaps to the Jewish remnant in Babylon, since ancient Persia encompassed the whole area of modern Iraq and Iran), then focused his ministry in Ethiopia in north Africa. There are various reports of his death, either by martyrdom at the hands of the Alexandrian Sanhedrin[414] or a natural death.[415]

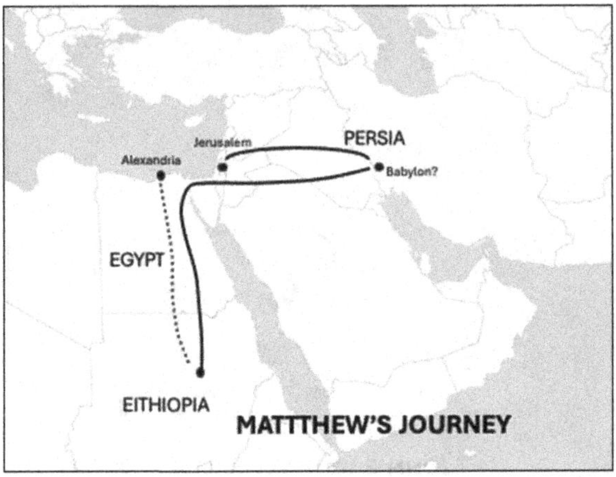

Philip

The apostle Philip was from the town of Bethsaida. He was an educated Hellenistic Jew who was called by Jesus, and he then recruited his friend Nathaniel (John 1:43– 45).

Philip is mentioned at the feeding of the five thousand (John 6:1–15); when Greeks sought Jesus (John 12:20–36); and at the Last Supper (John 14:8–21). The activities of Philip the apostle are recorded only in the Gospel of John.

When investigating the activities of Philip, one encounters the confusion between Philip the apostle and Philip the evangelist. The two encountered each other at the choosing of the seven to minister to the Hellenistic women (Acts 6:5). But the evangelist seems to have had more documented impact (Acts 8:4–8; 8:26, 21:8–9).

The missionary path of Philip is controversial. Some tradition states that he initially went to France.[416] There is consensus that he ended up in Hieropolis (southern Turkey), where he established his permanent ministry. The cause of his demise is based upon an AD 190 letter from Polycrates of Ephesus, who reported that after performing a healing miracle on the wife of the Roman proconsul Nicanora, she converted to Christianity. The proconsul was so enraged that he crucified Philip in about AD 62.[417]

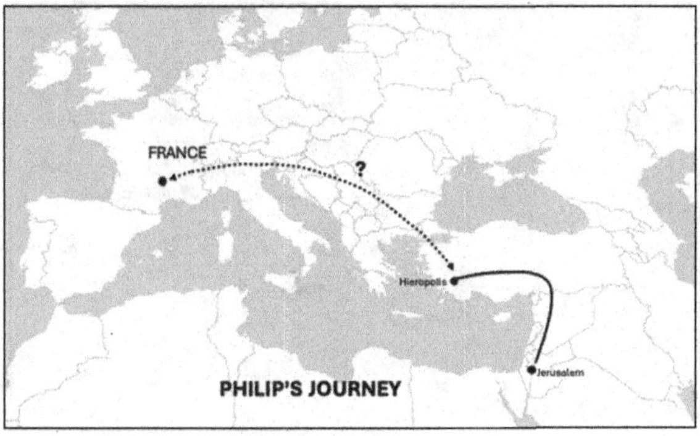

PHILIP'S JOURNEY

Bartholomew

Other than being listed as one of the twelve, the activities of Bartholomew are not mentioned in the New Testament. All history comes from conflicting apocryphal writings. What is known about Bartholomew is that he is likely the same person as Nathaneal—with Bartholomew as his last name.[418, 419, 420] The missionary travels of Bartholomew suggest that he spent time in India (AD 55), where he delivered the Gospel of Matthew. The specifics of this location are vague, however, since in ancient times the word *India* was used for the vast territory south and east of the Bosporus.[421] Bartholomew next appears in Hieropolis, where he accompanies the ministry of Philip. Tradition states that when Philip was martyred, Bartholomew escaped to Armenia, sometime around AD 70.[422] There seems to be consensus that the bulk of Bartholomew's ministry occurred in ancient Armenia, which at that time occupied most of the territory between the Caspian and Black Seas. Bartholomew is credited with furthering the work of Thaddeus in establishing the Christian church in Armenia.

The demise of Bartholomew also depends upon traditional sources, but the dominant theory is that he was martyred by flaying (skinned alive) in AD 70–71 at Alban (now Derbent in Azerbaijan),[423] on the edge of the Caspian Sea, at the order of king Sanadroug.[424]

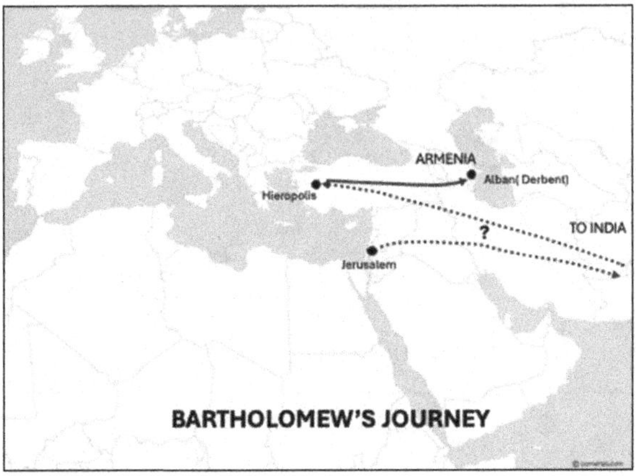

Thomas (Didymas)

While the New Testament has minimal historical documentation of Thomas, more is known about him than all the other apostles except Peter, John, and possibly Andrew. This is because of two apocryphal texts: *The Acts of Thomas* and *The Infancy Gospel of Thomas*. His name "Didymus" means "twin," but his other twin is not identified.

While Thomas is best known as "Doubting Thomas" for his refusal to believe Jesus was resurrected until seeing for himself (John 20:25–28), Thomas was apparently a man of courage. He was willing to risk death accompanying Jesus to raise Lazarus (John 11:16).

Thomas is known as the missionary to the East. Leaving Jerusalem about AD 44, after the death of James, Thomas headed east to the ancient nation of Parthia (now Iraq, Iran, Afghanistan, and Pakistan). Reportedly, his first stop was Babylon, likely to minister to the Jewish remnant. From there, Thomas went to northern India, arriving no later than AD 49.[425] He briefly returned to Jerusalem for the Apostolic Council Meeting in AD 50 (Acts 15:4), after which he returned to India in AD 52.[426]

Thomas's activity the next twenty years is unclear, although it has been suggested that he sailed the 5,028 nautical miles from India to

China, where he established the church in China between AD 65 and 68.[427]

Tradition states that he was martyred by lance stabbing outside Madras, India, in AD 72.[428]

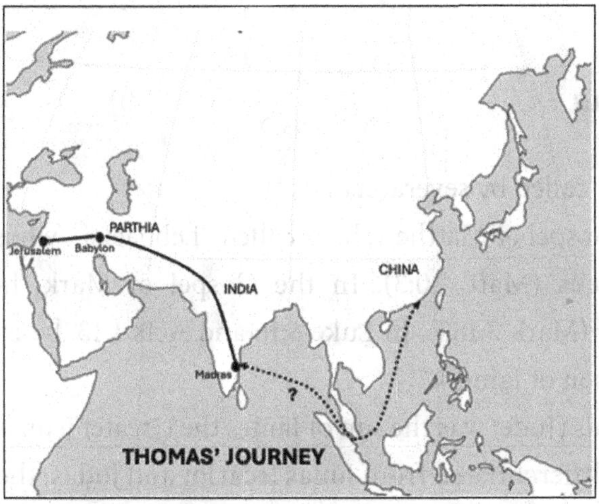

James, Son of Alphaeus

Very little is known about James, son of Alphaeus. Since Matthew's father was named Alphaeus, it was suggested that James and Matthew were brothers. However, Alphaeus was a common Hebrew name, so that is in doubt. It is probably that James came to be known as the "Lesser" and was the son of Mary Clopas, sister of Mary, the mother of Jesus.

More confusion arises due to the presence of three "James." James, the son of Zebedee and brother of the apostle John, is uncontroversial in identity. But church history has confused James the Lesser and James, the brother of Jesus. "Most of the ancient denominations, such as the Roman Catholic or Armenian Orthodox, identify James the Less and James the brother of Jesus as one and the same."[429, 430] Most scholars disagree.

The ministerial history of James the Lesser is brief and indistinct. He has variously been reported to have visited Spain and/or Persia.[431]

James's terminal fate is also unclear. Consensus holds that he was martyred for his faith, either by crucifixion or by stoning, but the where and how are unclear.[432]

Thaddeus

Thaddeus is called by several names.[433]

In the Gospel of Matthew, he is called "Lebbaeus," whose surname was Thaddeus (Matt. 10:3). In the Gospel of Mark, he is called "Thaddeus" (Mark 3:180). In Luke 6:16 and Acts 1:13, he is referred to as "Judas" (son of James).

Thaddeus (Jude) was the son of James the Greater (son of Zebedee). He is to be differentiated from Judas Iscariot and Judas, the brother of Jesus. Thaddeus was probably from Edessa, a city in ancient Amenia (now northern Iran).[434] Tradition establishes that he returned to his native Armenia, where he initially established the Christian church (AD 35–43) prior to being joined in ministry by Bartholomew (AD 46–60).[435]

He was reportedly martyred in Ardaze for converting the daughter of the local king in either AD 50[436] or 60.[437]

Simon the Zealot

Simon the Zealot is mentioned in the New Testament only in the listing of the apostles in the Gospels. He is not to be confused with Simon, son of Clopas, who became the successor to James as the bishop of Jerusalem. Reports of Simon's future ministry and fate are so varied as to be uninterpretable. It has been suggested that he visited Persia, Egypt, Spain, and, finally, Britain.

Matthias

Matthias was chosen to be the replacement twelfth apostle after the suicide of Judas Iscariot (Acts 1:26). Little is known about his ministry, but most tradition says that he focused his ministry first in Turkish Cappadocia, then finally in Georgia. He reportedly was martyred by stoning and being beheaded.[438]

John Mark

John Mark's home was in Jerusalem (Acts 12:12). He was the cousin of Barnabas (Col. 4:10). Mark was likely present at Jesus's capture in Gethsemane (Mark 14:51–52). The details of his Gospel account of Jesus's trials suggest that he might have been a close observer. He may also have been the "young man sitting at the right, wearing a white robe" in the empty tomb (Mark 16:5).

Mark accompanied Paul and Barnabas on the initial part of Paul's first missionary journey. In midjourney, Mark abruptly left the journey and returned to Jerusalem (Acts 13:13). It is not clear why Mark suddenly left the mission. Two years later, Paul refused to forgive Mark and include him in the second missionary journey (Acts 16:37–38). Barnabas took his cousin Mark on their own missionary journey (Acts 15:39).

It is not clear how Mark developed a close relationship with Peter, such that he became Peter's protégé and amanuensis. Peter was the oldest of the disciples, and Mark apparently was a youth (Mark 14:51). Peter refers to Mark as his "son" (1 Pet. 5:13). It is at Mark's mother's house that Peter came after the angel released him from prison (Acts 12:12–17).

Perhaps because of the development of Mark's relationship with Peter, Paul reinstated his relationship with Mark, which is demonstrated in Paul's prison epistles (Col. 4:10; 2 Tim. 4:11).

Apparently, after the death of James, Mark left Jerusalem and went to Alexandria. The year was about AD 49. There had been a large Jewish community in Alexandria since its founding by Alexander the Great. It was Jewish scholars in Alexandria who translated the ancient Hebrew Bible into the Greek *Septuagint* in 132 BC. It was a natural sailing route from Malta to Tunis, then along the north African coast to Alexandria. And the Jewish community in Alexandria provided a fertile missionary opportunity. There Mark established the Christian church, which would develop as part of the "Eastern Church," to be second only to Rome.

Mark is reported to have traveled back to Italy twice—first to Rome, from which he departed after the martyrdom of Peter and Paul in AD 64, then once more to Aquila, near Venice.[439]

Tradition states that Mark was martyred in AD 68 by being dragged through the city of Alexandria.[440]

Luke

Information on the history of Luke is provided in a summary by Dr. A. T. Robertson.[441]

Luke was a physician by education, who apparently met Paul in Antioch, just prior to Paul's first missionary journey. From that point onward, Luke became Paul's companion and "the beloved physician" (Col. 4:14). He is thought to have accompanied Paul during Paul's second imprisonment in Rome.

Luke's ultimate fate is not known. One tradition states he died peacefully in Boeotia, Greece.[442]

Paul

A detailed discussion the apostle Paul is provided in chapter 49. Therefore, only a brief summary of the end of his life will be presented here.

After his unsuccessful trial defense with Festus and Agrippa (Acts 25 and 26), Paul, as a Roman citizen, demanded to be sent to Rome for trial before Caesar (Acts 26:32).

Paul sailed to Rome, encountered a storm, and finally shipwrecked on the isle of Malta. Three months later, Paul sailed to Rome in AD 61 (Acts 28:11). In Rome, Paul was able to live by himself. Under house guard, Paul was able to continue preaching the Gospel (Acts 28:30–31). Paul was finally released after two years of confinement in AD 63. Tradition suggests he visited Spain, but upon return to Rome in AD 64, he encountered Nero's persecution of Christians. Paul was confined to Mamertine prison, an underground dungeon, then finally beheaded in AD 64.

Tradition states that since Paul was a Roman citizen, he was awarded a rapid death by the sword, rather than slow death by crucifixion, to which Peter was condemned.

49

Who Was the Apostle Paul?

Depending upon which epistles are accepted as truly written by the apostle Paul, he wrote thirteen or fourteen of the twenty-seven books of the Protestant New Testament. This comprises approximately 28 percent of the volume. Seven of Paul's letters have uncontested authorship: Galatians, 1 Thessalonians, 1 Corinthians, 2 Corinthians, Romans, Philippians, and Philemon. Those writings referred to as Deutero-Pauline include 2 Thessalonians, Colossians, Ephesians, 1 Timothy, 2 Timothy, Titus, and probably Hebrews.

Entire volumes have been written on the ministry and writings of Paul, so I will not try to repeat the details of doctrine, textural criticism, or specific encounters. Rather, this will be an overview of the apostle's life.

Background

The individual we came to know as Paul was born with the name Saul in the city of Tarsus, in the province of Cilicia, which is now the southeastern coast of Turkey. Paul's father was a Pharisee (Acts 23:6). As a youth, he was sent to Jerusalem to study in the rabbinic school of

Gamaliel (Acts 5). Gamaliel was a Pharisee, a member of the Sanhedrin, and the grandson of the founder of the Hillel school.[443]

Pharisees were group of pietists who believed in the supplemental oral laws supposedly given by God to Moses, as well as the written law—the Torah. They were contrasted to the Sadducees, who were priests who strictly believed in the written law.

Paul was also a Roman citizen, having been born the son of Roman citizens. Both his religious stance as a Pharisee and his Roman citizenship played significant later roles in Paul's life.

Conversion

In the New Testament, Paul first appears in Acts 7:58, where the witnesses stoning Stephen laid their robes at Saul's feet. Paul supported the stoning of Stephen (Acts 8:1). Saul then continues to "ravage" Christians and put them in prison (Acts 8:3). Saul then went to the high priest to authorize him to go to Damascus to seek out and bring Christians back to Jerusalem to prison (Acts 9:1–2). While on the road to Damascus, Saul is confronted by a Christophany of Jesus's voice asking Saul why he was persecuting Christians. Blinded, Saul was instantly converted to the living Lord, who sent him to Damascus. There Saul was directed to Ananias, who restored Saul's sight (Acts 9:18). Jesus confirmed that He had chosen Saul to be His messenger to the Gentiles (Acts 9:15).

When Saul starts preaching in Damascus, the Jews attack him, so he withdraws to Jerusalem and seeks council with the disciples. The disciples were initially suspicious of Saul, but Barnabas helped him recount the Damascus Christophany, so they accepted him. While the disciples continued to preach to their Jewish brethren, Saul proceeded to minister to the Gentiles.

How Did His Name Change?

Saul was raised a Jew in Tarsus. As such, his Hebrew name was "Saul," and he carried it proudly. When Saul became the "apostle of Gentiles" (Rom. 11:13), Saul stopped using his Hebrew name. He began using his Roman name, "Paul," during his first missionary journey (Acts 13:13).

How Did Paul Know What to Say about Christianity?

The question arises, since Paul never met Jesus during Jesus's ministry, how did he suddenly become an expert in the gospel message? Other than the direct words of Jesus, Paul's writings are the most detailed explanations of Christian theology and salvation. How did he know?

The answer is not entirely clear, but some clues can be found.

Paul did have several opportunities to learn from the original disciples. Shortly after Paul's conversion, he spent time with the disciples in Damascus (Acts 9:19). He later went to Jerusalem to spend time with and learn from the apostles (Acts 9:26–28). Three years later, Paul went to Jerusalem to be with the apostles again for fifteen days (Gal. 1:18). Acts 11:25–26 indicates Paul spent one year in Antioch with the "Christians."

Fourteen years later, Paul went to Jerusalem again (Gal. 2:1), but this may be the same visit as the Jerusalem Council of Acts 15.

Likely, Paul's explanation in Galatians is most important:

> I want you to know, brothers and sisters, that the gospel I preached is not of human origin. I did not receive it from any man, nor was I taught it; rather, I received it by revelation from Jesus Christ.

> But when God, who set me apart from my mother's womb and called me by his grace, was pleased to reveal his Son in me so that I might preach him among the Gentiles, my immediate response was not to consult any human being. I did not go up to Jerusalem to see those who were apostles before I was, but I went into Arabia. Later I returned to Damascus. (Gal. 1:11–12, 15–17)

Two points are very important in this text. First, Paul says, "I received it by revelation from Jesus Christ." Second, Paul says he went to Arabia. It is doubtful that even a good rabbinic student such as Paul could absorb the nuances of Christian doctrine merely through the brief encounters Paul had with the original apostles. The inescapable conclusion must be that while in Arabia, Paul spent direct time encountering the risen Jesus and being instructed by Him.

Ministry

Paul's ministry was based and supported by the church in Antioch. His journeys were around the northern Mediterranean, mainly modern-day Turkey and Greece.

In AD 46–47 was the first missionary journey (Acts 13–15:40). Paul, Barnabas, and Mark went through Cyprus to the (now Turkish) cities of Perga, Antioch of Pisidia, and Lystra. During that trip, Paul wrote the book of Galatians in AD 46–47. Mark unexpectedly left the journey midpoint.

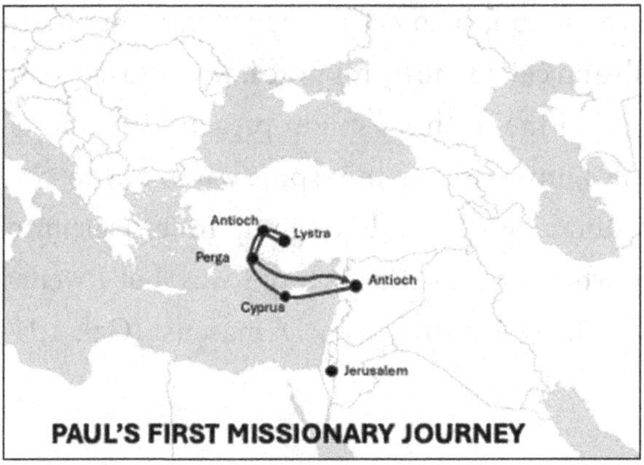

PAUL'S FIRST MISSIONARY JOURNEY

Paul then returned to Jerusalem in AD 49 to attend the Council of Jerusalem, where he was criticized for not requiring circumcision of the Gentiles. Peter and James, the brother of Jesus, defended Paul's decision.

In AD 49–52, the second missionary journey (Acts 15:40–18:23) started with conflict. Paul refused Barnabas's request to reinstate Mark (Acts 15:38), so Paul chose Silas to accompany him. Barnabas took Mark on a parallel mission (Acts 15:39). On this journey, Paul was blocked from going to Asia (Acts 16:9), so he ventured farther west to Philippi, Thessalonia, Athens, and finally Corinth, where he stayed for a year and a half. On this journey, Paul wrote the books of 1 and 2 Thessalonians from Corinth in AD 51–52.

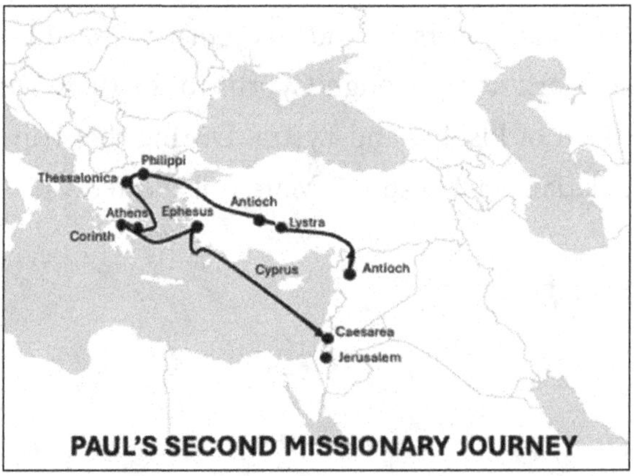

PAUL'S SECOND MISSIONARY JOURNEY

In AD 52–57 was the third missionary journey (Acts 18:23–21:14). He went to Ephesus, where he stayed three and a half years. Then on to Macedonia and Greece and Miletus. Paul wrote 1 Corinthians while in Ephesus in AD 52–57. He wrote 2 Corinthians from Macedonia.

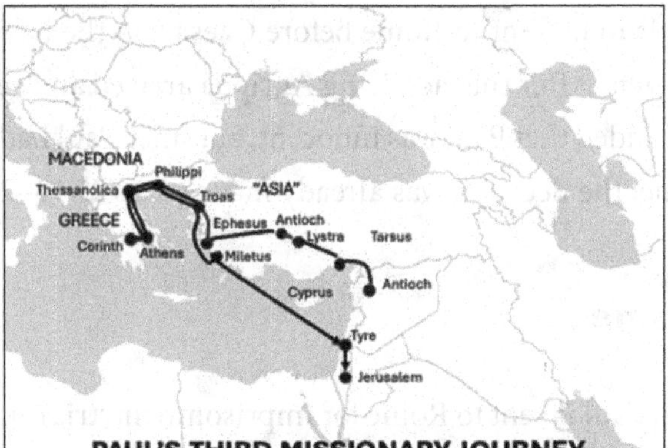

PAUL'S THIRD MISSIONARY JOURNEY

Betrayal

Returning by way of Tyre, Paul was warned not to return to Jerusalem (Acts 21:4). Then in Caesarea, the prophet Agabus again warns Paul against returning to Jerusalem, where he will be bound and handed over to the hands the Gentiles, meaning Romans (Acts 21:10–11).

Upon return to Jerusalem, James unexpectedly accused Paul of rejection of Moses (Acts 21:19–21) by teaching Gentiles that circumcision was unnecessary. Interestingly, this was the very issue that had instigated the initial Council of Jerusalem, where Peter defended Paul's approach and James concurred. James apparently had been intimidated into agreeing with Peter earlier, but now that Peter was gone from Jerusalem, James recanted.

Trials

Paul tries to defend himself—first to the crowd in Aramaic (Acts 2) and then to the Sanhedrin (Acts 23). Paul is then transferred to Caesarea to testify before Felix, who deferred the case for two years, with Paul remaining in prison (Acts 24). Festus succeeds Felix, and at that trial, Paul demands to be sent to Rome before Caesar on the basis that he is a Roman citizen. After the fact, King Agrippa arrived and reviewed the case. He concluded that Paul was innocent, but since Paul had demanded to go to Rome, the decision was already made (Acts 25:13–26:32).

On to Rome

At this point, Paul is sent to Rome for imprisonment, trial, and eventual martyrdom in AD 64. During his first imprisonment (AD 60–62), Paul wrote Philippians, Ephesians, Colossians, and Philemon. During his second imprisonment (AD 63–64), Paul wrote 1 Timothy, 2 Timothy, and Titus.

Paul's trial and execution in Rome are discussed in chapter 48.

50

Why Is the New Heaven on Planet Earth?

A renewed and cleansed earth as the location of heaven is extensively mentioned in the Bible, in both the Old and New Testaments (Isa. 65:17; 66:22; 2 Pet. 3:10–12; Rev. 21:1–22:9).

Why would God create the entire expanse of the universe and concentrate His presence on a tiny planet Earth?

Focus on the earth as the center of God's activities begins in the first chapter of Genesis. "In the beginning, God created the heavens and the earth" (Gen. 1:1). Throughout Old Testament times, humankind observed cosmologic changes (light, dark, rain, wind, sun, moon) and recognized that higher powers must be at work. For the most part, different gods were assigned to different actions—hence the practice of polytheism. The Old Testament refers to these as "pagan" gods, in deference to Yahweh, the single omnipotent God (Deut. 6:4).

In the Genesis account of the Garden of Eden, God seems to dwell in the garden directly, seeing and speaking to Adam, Eve, and the serpent (Gen. 3). Whether they could visualize God directly (as an anthropomorphism) or merely heard His voice is unclear. But God dwelt in the garden. So from the beginning of time, we have established God's specific interaction with planet Earth.

Throughout patriarchal history, there was no real understanding or focus on the matter of the universe (sun, moon, stars). Rather, as previously stated, humanity mere focused on the forces of nature.

Aristotle, who lived from 384 to 322 BC, believed Earth was round. He thought Earth was the center of the universe and that the sun, moon, planets, and all the fixed stars revolved around it. Aristotle's ideas were widely accepted by the Greeks of his time.

The Roman culture of the first century AD was heavily influenced by prior Greek philosophy. Is it any wonder, then, that the apostle John, writing the book of Revelation at the end of the first century AD, would visualize the future heaven on a renewed planet Earth?

In the second century AD, Claudius Ptolemy of Alexandria suggested that this discrepancy could be resolved if it were assumed that Earth was fixed in position, with the sun and other bodies revolving around it. As a result, Ptolemy's *geocentric* (Earth-centered) system dominated scientific thought for some 1,400 years. The geocentric model dominated until the sixteenth century when Polish astronomer Nicolaus Copernicus published his *De Revolutionibus Orbium Coelestium Libri VI* (*Six Books Concerning the Revolutions of the Heavenly Orbs*) in 1543 that heliocentrism began to be reestablished.[444]

From Genesis 1 until the publication of Copernicus's first theories of the universe, humankind was focused on planet Earth as the center of the universe—the geocentric model.

Conclusion

So how do we, in the twenty-first century AD, reckon with the eschatology describing the future heaven confined to a small planet, with God residing there at the exclusion of the rest of the universe? If earthly humans and the planet Earth are all that really matter, why did

God go to the trouble to create the vast universe rather than just planet Earth?

There are only so many options:

1. John's limited understanding of cosmology could have led him to visualize the future heaven on future earth in error.
2. Maybe our earth story isn't unique.

While there is no clear answer, one could theorize the following: Modern science has demonstrated the universe contains as many as forty billion planets like Earth with the potential for supporting human life.[445] Perhaps our Bible and our story are merely that of earthly creation, and our heaven will be on this renewed earth. That does not preclude God having created other earths and other heavens. Since God is omnipresent, he could dwell in multiple heavens.

51

Who Was John Mark?

John Mark, more often referred to as "Mark", is perhaps the most enigmatic individual in the New Testament. He is mentioned only five times in the New Testament. [446] Yet his Gospel of Mark is arguably the most important of the first three gospels.

As the central book of the "Synoptic Problem" issue, it is likely that the gospel of Mark was the first gospel to be formally written. While there remains some ambiguity regarding date and location, tradition holds that Mark's gospel was written during Peter's ministry in Rome sometime in the 50's or early 60's AD. Since Mark recorded the experiences of Peter, the composition had to be completed prior to Peter's martyrdom in 64 AD.

The prominence of Mark's writing is demonstrated by the extent of its use in the other gospels. Even though Mark's gospel is shorter than Matthew and Luke, it likely was used as a critical reference by both Matthew and by Luke when they composed their gospels. By proportion, 97.2% of Mark's words appear in Matthew, and 88.4% in Luke. [447]

Who was this very influential author who is barely mentioned in the New Testament?

Background

Very little is known about Mark's background. John Mark's home was in Jerusalem (Acts 12:12), and his mother was named Mary. Since Mary was a common name in first century Jerusalem, it is not known if she was one of the "Mary's" mentioned as followers of Jesus. She may well have been Mary Clopas, the mother of James the Lesser, and may have been the sister of Mary, the mother of Jesus. She was obviously in the "inner circle" due to fact that Peter was close friends with her (Acts 12:12). Mark was also the cousin of Barnabas (Col 4:10).

Relationship with Peter

Peter was the oldest of the disciples, and Mark apparently was a youth (Mk 14:51). It is not clear how Mark developed a close relationship with Peter, such that he became Peter's protégé and amanuensis (scribe). Peter refers to Mark as his "son" (1 Pet 5:13). It was to Mark's mother's house that Peter came after the angel released him from prison (Acts 12:12-17). The Acts reference indicates that Mary's house was a central gathering place for praying believers in Jerusalem. The fact that Peter went there for refuge seems to indicate that he was familiar with Mary, and therefore, acquainted with Mary's son John Mark. It is likely that through this relationship that Peter became the mentor of Mark.

Mark's Presence with Jesus' Ministry

During Jesus' ministry, Mark was apparently an adolescent boy. While his role is not obvious, there are little clues that Mark played a more prominent presence than has generally been appreciated. These clues were cleverly suggested by Albert Henry Ross, writing under the name "Frank Morison".[448]

The" Young Man" at Gethsemane

The first clue is present in Mark 14:51:

> [51] A *young man*, wearing nothing but a *linen garment*, was following Jesus. When they seized him, [52] he fled naked, leaving his garment behind.

These two short verses seem peculiarly inserted into the intense description of Jesus arrest. They are highly suggestive of being autobiographical – Mark likely was the "young man".

Removal of the Stone

Mark's description of the arrival of the women to the tomb on resurrection morning, again has the insertion of a superfluous detail:

> 4 But when they looked up, they saw that the stone, *which was very large*, had been rolled away. (Mark 16:4)

Why would Mark need to comment on the size of the stone? Perhaps Mark had helped Joseph of Arimathea roll the stone to close the tomb initially (Mk 16:46).

Or, even more intriguingly, could Mark have been the first to go to the tomb on resurrection morning, and have rolled the stone away, to see if Jesus body was still there?

The pericope of the angel moving the stone (Mt 28:2-4) is recorded only in Matthew, yet Matthew wasn't present to witness the angel action. He, along with the other disciples other than John, had fled from Gethsemane either into Jerusalem, or more likely, to the refuge in Bethany with Mary and Martha. Presumably, Matthew learned the detail of the earthquake and angel removing the stone from Mary Magdalene who Matthew reports as being present to witness the removal.

But interestingly, Mark records that on their way to the tomb, Mary Magdalene and the other women wondered how they would be able to roll the stone away to look for Jesus. Then, upon arrival, they found the stone to have already been rolled away (Mk 16:4). No mention is made of witnessing an earthquake or an angel.

Luke's account seems to be a partial parallel to Matthew (Luke 24:2). No description is made of an earthquake, although two angels are said to be present. It is well to remember that Luke was not present during the life or crucifixion of Jesus, so his account is second hand.

Finally, John's gospel also merely mentions that the stone had been removed (Jn 20:1). No mention is made of earthquakes or angels. His account carries weight because John, along with Peter, were still in Jerusalem even though they did not witness removal of the stone.

While there is no conclusive answer, does Mark's description suggests that he was the one who removed the stone?

The messenger in the tomb

While Matthew (Mt 28:5-7) and Luke (Luke 24:4) describe angels at the tomb, neither Mark nor John do so. John makes no mention of any messenger communication. However, Mark again offers a peculiar description:

> 5 As they entered the tomb, they saw a **young man dressed in a white robe** sitting on the right side, and they were alarmed. (Mark 16:5)

Mark clearly would know if he meant to be describing an angel, yet he used the term "young man" – the same term he used at Gethsemane. Could it have been Mark, sitting in the empty tomb, who told Mary Magdalene that Jesus had risen? The fact that Mark records the comment, "go tell his disciples, and Peter" (Mk 16:7) is also suggestive. Why would an angel specifically single out Peter. Mark, on the other hand, would want his mentor to be notified.

Detail of Jesus Trial

Finally, the detail of Jesus' arrest, trial, crucifixion, and resurrection suggests that Mark was a direct observer along with Peter and John. Neither Matthew nor Luke was present, so their accounts must have come from Mark's gospel. John was present at Jesus' trial before the high priest as "this disciple was known to the high priest" (Jn 18:15), at the crucifixion (Jn19:26-27), and at the empty tomb (Jn 20:3-5). Therefore, John's account is first-hand observation.

Post Resurrection Ministry

Approximately twenty years after Jesus' resurrection, Mark is next mentioned accompanying Barnabas in preparation for Paul's first missionary journey.

At Perga, Mark abruptly left the journey and returned to Jerusalem (Acts 13:13). It is not clear why Mark suddenly left the mission. Two years later Paul refused to forgive Mark and refused to include him in the second missionary journey (Acts 16:37-38). In response, Barnabas took his cousin Mark on their own missionary journey (Acts 15:39).

Perhaps because of the development of Mark's relationship with Peter, Paul reinstated his relationship with Mark. Paul's forgiveness is demonstrated in his prison epistles (Col 4:10; Philemon 1:24; 2 Tim 4:11).

Mark's final fate is discussed in *Chapter: What Happened to the Apostles*

Conclusion

Mark's role as the protégé and amanuensis (scribe) for Peter is clear. The Gospel of Mark is really Peter's gospel story, with a few insertions by Mark. As one of the three first-hand observers of Jesus' Passion Week (Peter, John, Mark?), Mark's gospel detail is foundational.

Second, the theory that Mark's gospel was significantly used as a reference by Matthew and Luke, in preparation of their own gospels (the "Synoptic Problem"), is generally accepted.

Finally, Mark's personal role in witnessing Jesus' arrest at Gethsemane and the empty tomb is conjectural. But as Frank Morison has inferred, Mark may have played a larger role than history has appreciated.

52

Why Was Augustine So Influential?

Biography

Aurelius Augustinus (Augustine of Hippo) was born in 354 AD and spent his youthful education in North Africa. Early in his life he adopted a hedonistic lifestyle following Manichaeism, the "dual cosmology" of the struggle between light and darkness espoused by the Parthian prophet Mani. [449], [450]

Moving from Africa to Rome, then to Milan, Augustine fell under the influence of Ambrose, which led to his conversion to Christianity in 386 AD. By 391 AD he was ordained a priest in Hippo Regius, Algeria. Augustine became full Bishop in 395. [451] He died in 430 AD.

Opportunity for Influence

From the death of Jesus until The Council of Chalcedon in 451 AD, the God-man nature and the doctrines of salvation (soteriology) were in debate. It was also a watershed historical period for the acceptance of Christianity in the western world. In 313 AD, the Roman Emperor

Constantine issued the Edict of Milan, which decriminalized Christianity. [452] Then, at the Edict of Thessalonica in 380, the Roman Emperor Theodosius I declared Christianity to be the only legitimate religion for the Roman Empire. [453] While Christianity had been widely fragmented during the patristic period of the early church fathers, it then became the religious authority of the powerful Roman Empire. This was the period in which Augustine lived (354 -430 AD). He was at the right place at the right time to have a major impact on future Christian doctrine.

Theology

While Augustine contributed broadly to the doctrines of Christianity, it is his evolution of the concept of predestination that is the topic of this review.

Augustine's initial theology was stimulated by resistance to *Pelagianism*, a heresy that proposed Adam's sin to be isolated to Adam (not original sin instilled in all subsequent mankind) and that man had the capability of choosing to do good to earn merit with God. One of Augustine's dilemmas, then, was the conflict between "works" of merit versus grace in the achievement of salvation.

As illustrated in his work, *Of Free Will*, Augustine concluded that God's foreknowledge of who would ultimately choose faith in Christ, was the determinate mechanism of "predestination".

However, Augustine became perplexed by two Biblical episodes.

First, was the story of Jacob and Esau. Augustine could not reconcile how God could have chosen Jacob, before either was born, with foreknowledge of free will choice. [454] Second, Augustin was troubled by 1 Cor 4: 7 "For what have you that you have not received? And if you have received it, why do you boast as though you have not received it?"

As result, Augustine reversed his previous theology to conclude that God's grace precedes faith and is the determining factor. Grace precedes and supersedes free will. His change of theology was explained in his 412 AD publication, *On Predestination of the Saints.*

Augustine concluded from scripture that the mechanism of grace is hardening the hearts of some, while unhardening the hearts of the elect so that they are enabled to choose faith. [455] Why God chooses some and not others remained a mystery to Augustine.

Was Augustine's Conclusion Correct?

Augustine's conclusions were based upon his exegesis of the writings of the apostle Paul.

Jacob and Esau

The story of Jacob and Esau occurs in Genesis chapters 25 and 27. the reference that disturbed Augustine was not uttered by Isaac, but rather by divine "oracle" to Malachi 1:2-3:

> "....Was not Esau Jacob's brother?" declares the LORD.
> "Yet I have loved Jacob, [3] but Esau I have hated,

The quote was then repeated by the apostle Paul in Romans 9:11-16:

> 11 Yet, before the twins were born or had done anything good or bad—in order that God's purpose in election might stand: 12 not by works but by him who calls—she was told, "The older will serve the younger." 13 Just as it is written: "Jacob I loved, but Esau I hated."
> 14 What then shall we say? Is God unjust? Not at all! 15 For he says to Moses,
> "I will have mercy on whom I have mercy,
> and I will have compassion on whom I have compassion."

> 16 It does not, therefore, depend on human desire or effort, but on God's mercy.

But the original quote from God in Malachi does not specify that God loved Jacob and hated Esau "before the twins were born or had done anything good or bad". The additional wording of Romans 9:11 was originated by Paul to justify his theology of predestination of the "elect".

Therefore, Augustine's conclusion was based upon the independent theology of Paul – not the Old Testament Scriptures. In fact, God's preference of Jacob over Esau in the Malachi reference could just as well have been because of God's foreknowledge of Esau's future deceit.

> *"For what have you that you have not received? And if you have received it, why do you boast as though you have not received it?" (1 Cor 4: 7)*

Augustine interpreted this Pauline statement to refer to "effective grace" in determining the "elect". While Paul often preached the preeminence of grace over "works" in achieving salvation (Eph 2:8-9), that does not seem to be the topic Paul is addressing in this reference.

In 1 Corinthians chapter four, Paul was addressing the problem of pride in the church at Corinth. Paul exhorted the Corinthian Christians to preserve humility. As interpreted by Walvoord and Bock:

> Paul concluded his address to the problem of division in the church by putting his finger unambiguously on their problem: pride.... But humility is the only acceptable posture of a person in relation to the God who gives a wide variety of gifts (v 7a) on the basis of grace (v 7b) and therefore alone is deserving of praise (v 7c; cf :4-9). [456]

Conclusion

While no one can know the mind of a past saint, it seems possible that Augustine's interpretation of the two dilemmas was faulty. Neither conclusively abrogated the doctrine of foreknowledge in election.

Nonetheless, with Augustine the concept of predestination of who would be among the elect – as opposed to foreknowledge of free will choice available to all – became firmly established in church doctrine. It would be a millennium later that the reformers, particularly Luther and Calvin, would amplify the predestination concept.

53

Does Man Have Free Will?

Few concepts in theology have stirred as much conflict and misunderstanding as the "free will" of humans and its role in salvation (soteriology).

What is Free Will?

To begin to understand the controversy, we must first define the terms. What exactly is meant by "free will"?

Merriam Webster's dictionary defines "will" as: "used to express desire, choice, willingness, consent, or in negative constructions refusal" "Free will" is then defined as:

1. voluntary choice or decision
2. freedom of humans to make choices that are not determined by prior causes or by divine intervention

Origin of Will

God created all creatures with the ability to make a choice – even in the pre-earth angelic realm. Lucifer had the capacity to choose rebellion, and many other angels apparently made similar decisions of "will" and followed him.

Then the first earthly humans - Adam and Eve - were given the capacity to choose. Even before they tasted the fruit from the Tree of Knowledge of Good and Evil, they made the decision (will) to do so.

Having chosen the Hebrews as His chosen people, God declared on Sinai:

> 3 "You shall have no other gods before me.
> 4 "You shall not make for yourself an image in the form of anything in heaven above or on the earth beneath or in the waters below. 5 You shall not bow down to them or worship them; for I, the Lord your God, am a jealous God, punishing the children for the sin of the parents to the third and fourth generation of those who hate me, 6 but showing love to a thousand generations of those who love me and keep my commandments. (Exodus 20:3-6)

Obviously, God recognized that the Hebrews had been given the ability to make a choice to follow Him or other gods.

When the Law was given, both in the original Ten Commandments as well as hundreds of additional "oral laws". Deuteronomy 26: 16-18, God commands his people to obey His laws:

> 16 The LORD your God commands you this day to follow these decrees and laws; carefully observe them with all your heart and with all your soul. 17 You have declared this day that the LORD is your God and that you will walk in obedience to him, that you will keep his decrees, commands, and laws—that you will listen to him. 18 And the LORD has declared this day that you are his people,

his treasured possession as he promised, and that you are to keep all his commands.

Then, in Deuteronomy 28, God further explains the consequences. They will be blessed for obedience (Deut 28:1) and be cursed for disobedience (Deut 28:15-30).

Once again, the people are given the ability to choose their course of actions, as well as the responsibility for disobedience. Throughout the entirety the Old Testament, the Hebrews battle with making obedient and disobedient decisions.

There can be no dispute that God gave humans the ability to choose – "will".

Whether man has the capacity to choose between good and evil

During Augustine's era, several competing doctrines of man's capacity and the effect of Eden arose. Adherents to *Manichaeism* believed that Adam was born sinful, even before he ate the forbidden fruit. As such, Adam's descendants irrevocably evil and had no willful escape.

Of greater popularity was *Pelagianism*. Pelagius (354-418 AD) advocated that Adam's transgression affected only him and did not transmit to his progeny. Accordingly, man has the moral ability ("free will") to choose good. Grace may facilitate achieving righteousness but is not essential. A variation of the doctrine is *Semi-Pelagianism*, which accepts that man's inherent nature is toward sin, but that he retains the capacity to do good and cooperate with God's grace. Responsiveness is a cooperation between God's facilitating grace and man's exercise of "free will." [457] Unfortunately, the actual writings of Pelagius have been lost, such that his theology is only validated through the descriptions of his detractors. Augustine organized the Council of Carthage in 418 AD at which Pelagius was excommunicated and all his writings were burned.

The reaction to the self-determination theology of Pelagianism led Augustine, Luther, and Calvin to appear to overstate the limitation of the role of man's capacity to decide – "will". The hyperbolic style of their writings could lead one to conclude that man has no control over his decisions.

In his polemic "magnum opus", *On the Bondage of the Will*, Luther tends to overstate the limitation of man's will. " ... with regard to God, and in all that bears on salvation or damnation, he has no 'free will', but is captive, prisoner, and bondslave, either to the will of God, or to the will of Satan." [458] . Further, Luther states, " ... we do everything of necessity, and nothing by 'free will'; for the power of 'free will' is nil, and it does no good, nor can do without grace." [459]

Calvin declared, "We deny that choice is free, because through man's innate wickedness it is of necessity driven to what is evil and cannot see anything but evil." [460]

What is not so clear from the comments of the reformers is the limitation of the "bond-slave" of will (Luther) [461] or the "bondage" of the will (Calvin) [462] . Their comments suggest that man not only cannot resist doing evil, he also is unable to choose to do good. However, history has shown that even "reprobates" sometimes do good things.

Sproul explains that Augustine tried to differentiate the specific areas of limitation of man's will:

> Augustine did not deny that fallen man still has a will and that the will is capable of making choices. He argued that fallen man still has a free will (*liberium arbitrium*) but has lost his moral liberty (*libertas*). The state of original sin leaves us in the wretched condition of being unable to refrain from sinning. We still are able to choose what we desire, but our desires remain chained by our evil impulses. He argued that the freedom that remains in the will always leads to sin. [463]

Barrett summarizes a more modern explanation of the Reformed position on limitation of man's will:

> Through his common grace, God restrains evil so that man does not always commit the worst possible sin. Second, total depravity does not mean that man has no innate knowledge of God's will or that man no longer possesses a conscience that can discern between good and evil. Third, total depravity does not mean that man is incapable of appreciating the good deeds or character of others. Though societies are corrupt they still retain remnants of altruism and civil good (or *civil virtue* as the Reformers titled it). God's common grace ensures that men can still perform civil responsibilities that benefit others (such as a doctor helping a patient in need of surgery.). [464]

What Causes Bondage – Original Sin or God?

It was widely accepted among the patristic church Fathers that Adam's original sin was transmitted to future mankind, it was this "original sin" that put man's will in "bondage", making him incapable of understanding and accepting salvific faith. However, it is not clear that only "original sin" causes the tendency to evil. Both Luther and Calvin point out that God actively "hardened" Pharoah's heart, which apparently prevented him from making a positive decision. Of course, this raises the question, "Who is responsible for the will "bondage"? God through "necessity" or the individual?

Calvin assigns responsibility exclusively to fallen man:

> According to these definitions we allow that man has choice and that it is self- determined, so that if he does

> anything evil, it should be imputed to him and to his voluntary choosing. [465]....We assign the blame for this corruption to man; we do not ascribe it to God. [466]

Both Luther and Calvin subscribe to the concept of transmission of "original sin" from Adam's transgression. And both hold the individual responsible for doing evil.

Free Will and Faith

The issue of will and faith centered around whether man, of his own accord ("will"), is independently able to decide to have faith in Christ.

Despite the apparent overstatements on restriction of action of man's will, the issue was not about the will being able to make "civic" decisions. Rather, the "will" controversy concerned two specific actions: (1) whether man could will sufficiently pious works (merit) as to earn salvation, (2) whether man was independently capable ("free will") of making a "moral' (theological salvific) decision to accept faith; or whether original sin has so hampered his ability to discern that he is unable to choose to have faith.

Regarding whether man, through his "free will", retained the ability to choose faith without the necessary freeing of his will from the "bondage" of original sin through grace, the Pelagians said, "Yes". Pelagius advocated that man has the moral ability ("free will") to choose to have faith in God. Grace may facilitate the choice but is not essential (Synergism). A variation of the doctrine is *Semi-Pelagianism*, which accepts that man's inherent nature is toward sin, but that he retains the capacity to do good and cooperate with God's grace. Responsiveness is a cooperation between God's facilitating grace and man's exercise of "free will." [467] Erasmus and Arminius became the continuation of Pelagianism.

Augustine said, "No". Man is unable to independently choose to have faith due to "bondage of his will to sin". The capacity to choose faith is totally dependent ("necessity") on God's prior grace to liberate man's will for him to have the capacity to choose faith (Monergism). Augustine wrote, "…if any one dare say, "I have faith of myself, I did not, therefore receive it," he directly contradicts this most manifest truth – not because it is in the choice of man's will to believe or not believe, but because in the elect the will is prepared by the Lord."[468]

Reformed theology (Augustine, Luther, Calvin) focused on three doctrines: (1) man's will was no longer "free" to make the decision of faith due to "bondage" from transmission of Adam's original sin, (2) in order for man to will assent to salvific faith, man's will had to be freed from bondage by necessary grace from God, and (3) once freed from bondage, man's will was not coerced to assent to faith; rather, the regenerated will would be enlightened, empowered, and would then voluntarily seek (will) faith.

The Continuation of "Bondaged Will"

One could surmise from Calvin's comments that once God released the hardened heart from bondage of the will to inevitably choose sin, that the regenerate Christian would no longer choose to sin:

> 6 For we know that our old self was crucified with him so that the body ruled by sin might be done away with,[a] that we should no longer be slaves to sin— 7 because anyone who has died has been set free from sin. (Romans 6:6-7)

But multiple New Testament verses confirm otherwise:

> 15 I do not understand what I do. For what I want to do I do not do, but what I hate I do. (Romans 7:15)

> 15 Here is a trustworthy saying that deserves full acceptance: Christ Jesus came into the world to save sinners—of whom I am the worst. (1 Timothy 1:15)
>
> 17 In the same way, faith by itself, if it is not accompanied by action, is dead. (James 2:17)
>
> 22 You see that his faith and his actions were working together, and his faith was made complete by what he did.
> 24 You see that a person is considered righteous by what they do and not by faith alone.
> 26 As the body without the spirit is dead, so faith without deeds is dead. (James 2:22-26)

Conclusion

The debate over the role of "free will" has created confusion for centuries. Despite the vigorous polemic against "free will" by Augustinian "Reformed" theologians (Augustine, Luther, Calvin, Sproul), they eventually acknowledge that man's will must play an active role in accepting faith.

Augustine acknowledged a person's participation in faith:[469]

> For who cannot see that thinking is prior to believing? For no one believes anything unless he has first thought it is to be believed…it is necessary that everything which is believed should be believed after thought has preceded; although even belief itself is nothing else than to think with assent. For it is not every one thinks that believes, since many think in order that they may

> not believe; but everybody who believes, thinks – both thinks in believing and believes in thinking.

In reality, the polemic of Augustine, Luther, and Calvin against "free will" is not whether man's will (mind, thinking) is necessary to assent to faith, but rather whether man's will is "free" from the impact of inherited Adamic sin to have the capacity to decide to accept faith without the pre-conditioning release from "bondage" by efficacious (irresistible) grace.

Reformed Theology teaches that once "irresistible grace" frees the human will from "bondage" of Adamic original sin (Rom 6:6-7) to do only evil, man's will is then "regenerated". After being freed from "bondage" by the "necessity"' of God's grace, the "will" ultimately has to act to "assent" to faith.

Arminians believe man has the "free will" to respond to the assent to faith provided by prevenient (preparatory, resistible) grace. Augustinian "Reformed" theologians believe that only the elect are bestowed with "irresistible grace" which first regenerates their soul from bondage to original sin (Rom 6:6-7), after which their "will" ("free"?) is motivated to assent to faith.

It appears that the question is not whether man retains a "will", but rather, how "free" that will really is. Whether the response of the "will" is "free" or "coerced" is open to debate.

Believers are admonished to demonstrate their renewed "will" by good deeds (James 2:22-26). But apparently, the "bondage" of original sin, causing tendency to choose sinful deeds, is not completely removed. So, while salvation is secured through assent to faith in Christ, because retained original sin, even regenerated believers still struggle with sinful actions (Rom 7:15; 1 Tim 1:15).

54

What Is the Role of Grace?

The word "grace' occurs one hundred and seventy times in the Bible. Thirty-eight occurrences are in the Old Testament; one hundred thirty-two are in the New Testament. [470]

Webster's dictionary defines "grace": [471]

> a: unmerited divine assistance given to humans for their regeneration or sanctification.
> b: a virtue coming from God.
> c: a state of sanctification enjoyed through divine assistance.

How Many Kinds of Grace?

The *Pocket Dictionary of Theological Terms* list three types of grace:

> *Common grace* speaks of God's extension of favor to all people through providential care, regardless of whether or not they acknowledge and love God. *Efficacious grace* refers the special application of grace to a person

> who comes by faith to Christ for salvation. It is the special act of God that brings about the true salvation of a person. *Prevenient grace*, though often thought to be synonymous with common grace, refers more specifically to the Wesleyan idea that God has enabled all people to respond favorably to the gospel if they so choose. [472]

Augustine obliquely suggests that there are two kinds of "calling". One he describes as "not the calling with which they were called who would not come to the marriage, since with that calling were called also the Jews, to whom Christ crucified is an offense, and the Gentiles, to whom Christ crucified is foolishness;" Then, an apparent stronger calling "….there is a certain sure calling of those who are called according to God's purpose, whom he has foreknown and predestined….with that calling wherewith a man is made a believer." [473]

Barrett interprets Augustine's reference:

> Augustine demonstrates from texts like 1 Corinthians 1:24; Romans 8:28-29; 9:12-13; and 11:25-29 that there are two distinct callings, one universal and the other particular. The former is the gospel call that many people reject while the latter is efficacious, so that those who the Father draws always come to Jesus. " [474]

Luther also appears to describe two different actions of grace:

> "What I maintain is this; that where God works apart from the grace of His Spirit, He works all things in all men, even the ungodly; for He alone moves, makes to act, and impels by the motion of His omnipotence, all those things which He alone created; they can neither avoid nor alter this movement, but necessarily follow

> and obey it, each thing according to the measure of its God-given power. Thus, all things, even the ungodly co-operate with God. And then God acts by the Spirit of His grace in those whom he has justified, that is, in His own kingdom, He moves and carries them along in like manner; and they, being a new creation, follow and co-operate with Him, or rather, as Paul says, are made to act by Him (Rom 8:14)" [475]

Calvin's descriptions of different types of grace are also vague. He describes God's "true doctrine of Providence" by which God controls the natural forces of creation. [476] He then goes on to describe two types of calling of men":

> "there are two species of calling: for there is a universal call, by which God, through the external preaching of the word, invites all men alike, even those for whom he designs the call to be a savor of death, and the ground of a severer condemnation. Besides this there is a special call for which, for the most part, God bestows and believers only, when by the illumination of the Spirit he causes the word to be preached to take deep root in their hearts. [477]

Erasmus describes four varieties of grace…

> The first kind of grace we possess by nature. some call it the natural influence…which is common to all mankind.
>
> A secondary variety is extraordinary grace. God through mercy moves the undeserving sinner to contrition. The goodness of God does not refuse any mortals the second grace. The mercy of God offers everyone favorable

> opportunities for repentance. One need only attach the rest of one's own will to God's help, which merely invites to, but does not compel to betterment. Furthermore, one finds the opinion, that it is within our power to turn our will to or away from grace….
>
> … third and efficient grace, which we have called cooperative, and which promotes that which is begun…
>
> … and a fourth grace which leads to the final goal.
>
> The last three are supposedly one and the same grace, even though according to its operation in us, we call it by different names. Thus, the first excites, the second promotes, and the third leads to the goal. [478]

While common grace refers to God's general maintenance of order in creation, prevenient (universal) grace and efficacious (particular) grace refer to God's calling mankind to salvific faith in Christ.

Common Grace

Essentially all Christian denominations accept the concept of common grace.

Common grace is manifest in God's control of nature (Ps 145:9; Matt 5:45). Calvin, in referring to God controlling nature, concludes that "creation and providence are joined".

> After learning that there is a Creator, it must forthwith infer that he is also a Governor and Preserver, and that, not producing a kind of general motion in the machine of the globe as well as in each of its parts, but by a special providence sustaining, cherishing, superintending, and all the things which he has made, to the very minutest, even to a sparrow. [479]

Common grace is also described to influence general human interaction – restraining evil (Gen 20:6; 1 Sam 25:14, 26, 34); as well as encouraging "civic righteousness of the unregenerate." [480]

Prevenient Grace

Prevenient grace is the most controversial and is the center of the Calvinism vs Arminianism conflict. Prevenient, resistible grace is a central tenet of Arminianism.

There are several proposed variations of prevenient grace. [481] In the classical Arminian doctrine at the time of gospel presentation the Holy Spirit frees a person from the bondage of sin, opens his heart, and enables the sinner's will to place faith in Christ. A second variation is a general prevenient grace which calls all men, followed by a "particular prevenient grace" which frees man's will to accept faith at the presentation of the gospel. Finally, there is a Wesleyan-Arminian variation in which Christ's crucifixion dispensed universal prevenient grace to all men which fully negates bondage of the will from sin (universal atonement). Man is then free to accept faith in Christ or reject it.

Those espousing prevenient grace interpret Jn 12:32 as indicating a general gracious call directed to all men.

It appears even Calvin recognized a universal (prevenient?) grace that is a calling to all mankind: "universal call, by which God, through the external preaching of the word, invites all men alike, even those for whom he designs the call to be a savor of death". [482] Many scriptural verses describe this general (universal) call inviting all to accept in Christ (Rom 10:8-13; Mt 10:32; Mt 11:28; 2 Pet 3:9). These references seem to infer that acceptance of faith is available to all men, not just the "elect".

Efficacious Grace

The concept of "efficacious grace" is inextricably connected to the doctrine of predestination of the elect. Predestination, however, will be discussed separately.

Until the fourth century time of Augustine the mechanism of salvation was considered to be prevenient grace cooperating with the free will of man to accept or reject faith in Christ. But Augustine, particularly in his exegesis of Paul's writings, reversed his theology. Augustine concluded "....there is a certain sure calling of those who are called according to God's purpose, whom he has foreknown and predestined....with that calling wherewith a man is made a believer."

Augustine's theology was adopted by Luther, "And then God acts by the Spirit of His grace in those whom he has justified, that is, in His own kingdom, He moves and carries them along in like manner; and they, being a new creation, follow and co-operate with Him, or rather, as Paul says, are made to act by Him (Rom 8:14)". [483] Calvin followed suit, ".... he steers the mind to choose what is right, he moves the will also effectively to obedience, he arouses and advances the endeavour until the actual completion of the work is attained. " [484] Biblical references Isaiah 54:13; Ezekiel 36:44-45; John 6:44-45; and Eph 2:8-9 were used to evidence action of efficacious grace.

This calling became known as "efficacious", meaning irresistible, and further became the keystone of Calvinistic doctrine I the "I" in the TULIP acronym. It is further confirmed in the *Westminister Confession of Faith* Chapter 10.4 and Chapter 14.1. Scriptural support for irresistibility was professed from Rom 9:19 (NIV), "who is able to resist his will".

The claim that such grace was irresistible led to protests from Erasmus and Pighius that such action rendered the Christian to be robotic, with coerced will. [485] Using the same verses in Romans, they pointed out the complete pericope, "Then why does God still blame us? For who is able to resist his will?" (Rom 9:19 (NIV). To counter this criticism the Reformers argued that while efficacious grace is irresistible, response is not coerced. Rather efficacious grace regenerates the sinner to desire acceptance of faith. Luther rebuts, "...when God works in us, the will is changed under the sweet influence of the Spirit of God. It desires and acts not from compulsion, but responsively of its own desire and inclination." [486]

Of central importance to the doctrine efficacious grace was the order in which it occurs in achieving salvation (*order salutis*). This issue changed Augustine's thinking. [487] Augustine, and subsequently the Reformers, insist that efficacious grace necessarily precedes any act of the will to assent to faith. Such doctrine essentially eliminates man's free will to respond to a common (prevenient) grace call as proposed by Arminian theology.

Finally, the Reformers argued while *common grace* was offered to all mankind, *efficacious grace* leading to salvation was offered only to the predestined "elect".

What's the Point of Evangelism?

Jesus issued the "Great Commission" in Matthew 28:19:

> 19 Therefore go and make disciples of all nations, baptizing them in the name of the Father and of the Son and of the Holy Spirit,

One of the great conundrums of Reformed Christian doctrine is why one would bother preaching an invitation to faith when the outcome has already been decided - the chosen "elect" must "irresistibly" respond with assent to faith and the non-chosen "reprobates" are unable to respond?

The Calvinist Barrett argues that exposure to the gospel message through the Word is the mechanism through which elect are converted. He observes that with a general calling, no one knows who has been chosen to respond. [488] Jesus appears to suggest a universal call. "For many are called, but few are chosen" (Mt 22:14)

This coincides with Paul's explanation:

> 13 for, "Everyone who calls on the name of the Lord will be saved."
> 14 How, then, can they call on the one they have not believed in? And how can they believe in the one of whom they have not heard? And how can they hear without someone preaching to them? 15 And how can anyone preach unless they are sent? As it is written: "How beautiful are the feet of those who bring good news!"
> 17 Consequently, faith comes from hearing the message, and the message is heard through the word about Christ. (Rom 10:13-15, 17)

Conclusion

Grace is the unmerited favor of God in dealing with His creation.

There apparently are three types of grace: (1) *common grace* through which God manages nature; (2) *prevenient* (resistible) grace which is God's universal invitation to assent to faith in Christ; and (3) *efficacious (irresistible) grace* by which God changes the heart of the elect, causing them to seek assent to faith in Christ.

The role of grace separates the two dominant protestant theologies – Arminianism and Calvinism. Both theologies accept the presence of *common grace.*

Arminians believe in *prevenient (resistible) grace* available to all (universal atonement) to accept or reject. Grace, delivered by hearing the gospel Word exposes all to the option to choose faith. By this order, man's will can assent to faith if he independently chooses to do so. As such assent to faith occurs through cooperation with grace.

Calvinists appear to recognize the presence of *prevenient (universal)* grace. But they deny its effectiveness in leading to a decision of faith unless God has previously removed the "bondage of inherited sin" and freed the will to desire to assent to faith through *efficacious (irresistible)* grace. Further, they believe that God bestows *efficacious (irresistible)* grace only to the "elect".

Both groups espouse that hearing the gospel presented through evangelism is the mechanism through which a decision to assent to faith occurs. Finally, both theologies agree that man has the capacity (will) to evaluate the decision to assent to faith. Even Augustine acknowledged a person's participation in faith: "For it is not every one who thinks that believes, since many think in order that they many not believe; but everybody who believes, thinks – both thinks in believing and believes in thinking." [489]

So, what's the difference?

Calvinists believe inherited total depravity of the will precludes man's ability to respond to the invitation of *prevenient grace* calling and assent to faith unless they have been pre-conditioned by *efficacious grace,* after which they irresistibly chose to believe. In contrast, Arminians believe even though man's inherited sinful nature tends to lead them to sinful behavior, man still retains enough independence of will to respond to the invitation of *prevenient grace* calling by either acceptance or rejection of faith.

How does a believer know if he or she was "chosen"?

In practicality, after hearing the gospel invitation, if a person assents to faith in Christ, then his or her salvation is secured. He or she will not know whether he or she chose faith through independent will (Arminianism) or whether the assent to faith was due to preparation by "irresistible" grace (Calvinism) as one of the chosen "elect". The explanation waits for eternity.

55

What is a Personal Relationship With Jesus?

The Christian relationship with Jesus is repeatedly described as a "personal relationship". The term "personal relationship" indicates an intimate, interaction as opposed to an "acquaintance", meaning a person one knows slightly, but who is not a close friend. The key difference is interaction with communication. A key component of a "relationship" is mutual communication.

Deere points out that "with the exception of Chapter 17, every chapter of Acts contains an example of, or a reference to, supernatural revelatory communication from God to his servants."[490] Yet with the extinction of the first-generation apostles, there would appear to be a significant decrease in direct communication from the Holy Spirit after the end of the first century. This leads us to the core discussion of this review: Do Christians really have a direct interactive communication with Jesus, and if so, how do they know?

Hearing God's "Voice"

The metaphor "hearing God's voice" is frequently used:

> "In silence and in meditation on the eternal truths, I hear the voice of God which excites our hearts to greater love." [491] (C.S. Lewis quote)

Yet most Christian leaders acknowledge that it is a metaphor:

> Charles Swindoll observed, "We serve a head we cannot see and listen to a voice we cannot literally hear " [492]

> Antony Flew, the noted atheist turned Christian, similarly has not been able to identify communication from the Spirit: "Some claim to have made contact with this (intelligent) Mind. I have not—yet. But who knows what could happen next? "[493]

> N.T. Wright, the Anglican bishop of Dunham, England, and noted Christian writer describes "living by the Spirit" in terms of how the indwelling of the Spirit involves changing the internal character of the believer to desire to live differently. But Wright does not indicate specific communication from the Spirit. [494]

Traditional View

The so-called "Traditional View" is that while spending meditative time reading the Bible, God implants His thoughts to us.

Deere agrees that the primary method of communication with God is through the Bible, not just reading or academic study, but quiet meditation. It is through meditation with "availability, willingness, and humility" that one can receive direction from God. He agrees that during such meditation one might receive implantation of thought. Deere raises an interesting point regarding the limitation of using the Bible alone as a source of Godly communication. The "problem with the view that God speaks only through the Bible is that it leaves God with nothing to say about large areas of our lives." Deere also suggests that dreams are like meditation and could be an interval of communication.

But Deere goes a step further. He believes that during Biblical meditation one could hear God's voice. Deere describes "voice" in several forms. The most common voice apparently was discrete thought. The second voice was an inaudible complete sentence, which Deere reports to have heard "perhaps fifteen or twenty times over the last ten years." Deere has never heard an audible voice.

Mark Batterson, Min.D., who is the lead pastor of the National Community Church in Washington, D.C., has also written on hearing the voice of the Holy Spirit. He lists seven "love languages" as vehicles through which God communicates: (1) scripture, (2) desires, (3) doors, (4) dreams, (5) people, (6) prompting, and (7) pain. While he repeatedly refers to God speaking, and frequently converts God's message to sentence form, he never refers to an inaudible or an audible voice. His whispered voice appears to be implanted thought or arrangement of circumstances (open vs. closed doors). Like Deere, Batterson emphasizes the importance of spending quiet time, particularly in prayer, to be receptive to receiving God's message.[495]

But how do you know these meditative thoughts are God's thoughts and not our own?

Spiritual leaders find this question difficult to answer:

C.S. Lewis found it difficult to definitively identify communication from the Spirit:

> It is quite right that you should feel that "something terrific" has happened to you (it has) and be "all glowy."

> Accept these sensations with thankfulness as birthday cards from God, but remember that they are only greetings, not the real gift. I mean, it is not the sensations that are the real thing. The real thing is the gift of the Holy Spirit which can't usually be—perhaps not ever—experienced as a sensation or emotion. The sensations are merely the response of your nervous system. Don't depend on them. Otherwise, when they go and you are once more emotionally flat (as you certainly will be quite soon), you might think that the real thing had gone too. But it won't. It will be there when you can't feel it. May even be most operative when you can feel it least.[496]

Saucy also questions how a believer can be sure an implanted thought is truly a revelation from God:

> The present work of God in us surely uses all the external means of guidance mentioned, especially the truth of Scripture. But the final product is the thought in our mind that emanates from the heart, with all of its feeling and impulse. If we believe the Spirit of God is at work in this process, then we must acknowledge that the thought within us is in some way produced by him and is not simply the product of our own minds.
>
> In practical terms, as we use all the means of guidance at our disposal, especially meditation on Scripture, we should carefully probe our hearts and minds for God's voice. But we should also remember that this voice of God is in our hearts and mind, which are still a mixture of the new works of God and our old sinful egos. Thus, the thought in our hearts may

> be the word of self rather than of God. In this age of an imperfect heart, one cannot confidently assert, "God told me…."[497]

Wisdom View

Friesen[498] advocates the "wisdom view" in detail. He argues there are three wills of God:

1. God's *sovereign* will: God's secret plan that determines everything in the universe
2. God's *moral* will: God's revealed commands in the Bible that teach how men ought to believe and live
3. God's *individual* will: God's ideal, detailed life plan uniquely designed for each person

Friesen describes the pursuit of knowledge of God's *individual* will as the "traditional view" and argues that such pursuit is fruitless and frustrating. He argues there is no scriptural basis for believing the Holy Spirit communicates through implantation of thoughts on daily decisions. Rather, he interprets "leading by the Spirit" to mean the Holy Spirit helps Christians obey the *moral* will of God defined in the Bible. Direct communication from the Holy Spirit would be special revelation, which Friesen believes largely ended with the close of the canon.

He further argues the principles of decision making are according to "the way of wisdom": [499]

1. Where God commands [in the Bible] that we must obey.
2. Where there is no command, God gives us freedom (and responsibility) to choose.
3. Where there is no command, God gives us *wisdom* to choose.

4. When we have chosen what is moral and wise, we must trust the sovereign God to work all the details together for good.

In summary, Friesen believes that knowledge of the scriptures leads to wisdom in making individual decisions in accordance with obedience. He rejects the "traditional view" that more specific "leading" is possible.

Conclusion

Even among Christian leaders, there is not a clear-cut consensus on how one is to be sure he or she is "hearing" from Jesus.

First, even though the risen Jesus appeared directly to Paul (Acts 9:3-5), Jesus explained that with His ascension back to heaven, the Holy Spirit would be the communicator to humans in His stead (Jn 14:26; Acts 2:1-4). So, is a "personal relationship with Jesus" really a relationship with the Holy Spirit?

Second, if we as Christians are to have a "personal relationship with Jesus", that personal application to our lives implies being "led" in directed service in our daily lives. Otherwise, why should we pray for decisional direction? In my interview of several seminary professors and pastors, none could specifically identify how they knew they were being "led" by Jesus.

If one accepts the "Wisdom" viewpoint, then the term "relationship" would seem to be a misnomer. Just follow the rules.

If one accepts the "traditional" viewpoint, the most likely communication from Jesus is either implanted thought or arrangement of circumstances (the "open door"). Yet how do we know those thoughts are from God, or how do we know the "open door" wasn't coincidental?

With either approach, having a "personal relationship with Jesus" is less distinct than is commonly suggested in Christian circles. Of course, the fact that relating to God is a mystery, does not mean that the relationship does not exist. But expressing the relationship in more discrete terms than actually occurs can lead Christians to stumble into doubt, "Am I the only one who cannot discern a direct relationship communication?"

Perhaps the pragmatic observation of Charles Swindoll best sums up reality:

"We serve a head we cannot see and listen to a voice we cannot literally hear."

56

Are There Messianic Prophecies in Matthew?

It is generally agreed that Matthew directed his gospels to the Jewish community. His gospel is thought to have had two purposes: (1) to show that Jesus was truly the Messiah prophesied in the Old Testament, and (2) to encourage Jewish believers that even though the current generation had killed the Messiah they were long expecting, God was not abandoning a future for the Jewish people as a whole. [500]

To prove Jesus was the Messiah, Matthew quoted fifteen Old Testament prophecies which he claimed were fulfilled by Jesus. The Jews were expecting a coming Messiah as prophesied by Moses (Deut 18:18-19).

What qualifies as a prophecy?

Lockyer quotes the following criteria from D.A Pierson's *God's Living Oracles*: [501]

1. It must be such and unveiling of the future that no mere human foresight or wisdom could have guessed it

2. The prediction must deal in sufficient detail to exclude shrewd guesswork
3. There must be such a lapse of time between the prophecy and the fulfillment as precludes the agency of the prophet himself in effecting or affecting the result.

There are at least eighty- eight prophets in the Bible. There are sixty-three in the Old Testament and twenty-five in the New Testament. [502] The grouping of prophets with books included in the Old Testament is based not upon importance, but rather, is based upon the length of their writings. The Major Prophets (5) are: Isaiah, Jeremiah, Lamentations, Ezekiel, and Daniel. The Minor Prophets 12) are: Hosea, Joel, Amos, Obadiah, Jonah, Micah, Nahum, Habakkuk, Zephaniah, Haggai, Zechariah, and Malachi.

Due to the impact of prophets in the Old Testament, as well as the problem of false prophets, God instituted risk in prophesying. When a "prophet" spoke untruths in the name of the Lord was subjected to death. (Deut 18:20).

In examining Old Testament passages for Messianic predictions, it must also be remembered that the doctrine of Christianity interprets the Old Testament through a Christ-centered lens. Lockyer concludes that there are over 300 Messianic prophecies and that the chance of Jesus fulfilling them by chance is 1:537,000,000. [503]

There is a risk of reading more into the comments of prophets than they intended. The Old Testament prophets were active in the period from the divided kingdom (931 BC) to the completion of rebuilding the Temple (516 BC). It was a time of great turmoil for the Hebrews. Thus, many of the prophecies were aimed a current events. The challenge is to discern the present from the future.

The side-by-side comparisons are:

Matthew 1:22-23 English Standard Version 22 All this took place to fulfill what the Lord had spoken by the prophet: 23 "Behold, the virgin shall conceive and bear a son, and they shall call his name Immanuel"	Isaiah 7:14 English Standard Version 14 Therefore the Lord himself will give you a sign. Behold, the virgin shall conceive and bear a son, and shall call his name Immanuel.
Matthew 2:5-6 English Standard Version 5 They told him, "In Bethlehem of Judea, for so it is written by the prophet: 6 "'And you, O Bethlehem, in the land of Judah, are by no means least among the rulers of Judah; for from you shall come a ruler who will shepherd my people Israel.'"	Micah 5:2 English Standard Version 2 But you, O Bethlehem Ephrathah, who are too little to be among the clans of Judah, from you shall come forth for me one who is to be ruler in Israel, whose coming forth is from of old, from ancient days.

Matthew 2:15 English Standard Version 15 and remained there until the death of Herod. This was to fulfill what the Lord had spoken by the prophet, "Out of Egypt I called my son."	Hosea 11:1 English Standard Version The Lord's Love for Israel 11 When Israel was a child, I loved him, and out of Egypt I called my son.
Matthew 2:16-17 English Standard Version Herod Kills the Children 16 Then Herod, when he saw that he had been tricked by the wise men, became furious, and he sent and killed all the male children in Bethlehem and in all that region who were two years old or under, according to the time that he had ascertained from the wise men. 17 Then was fulfilled what was spoken by the prophet Jeremiah:	Jeremiah 31:15 English Standard Version 15 Thus says the Lord: "A voice is heard in Ramah, lamentation and bitter weeping. Rachel is weeping for her children; she refuses to be comforted for her children, because they are no more."
Matthew 3:1-3 English Standard Version John the Baptist Prepares the Way 3 In those days John the Baptist came preaching in the wilderness of Judea, 2 "Repent, for the kingdom of heaven is at hand." 3 For this is he who was spoken of by the prophet Isaiah when he said, "The voice of one crying in the wilderness: 'Prepare the way of the Lord; make his paths straight.'"	Isaiah 40:3 English Standard Version 3 A voice cries: "In the wilderness prepare the way of the Lord; make straight in the desert a highway for our God.

Matthew 4:5-6 English Standard Version 5 Then the devil took him to the holy city and set him on the pinnacle of the temple 6 and said to him, "If you are the Son of God, throw yourself down, for it is written, "'He will command his angels concerning you,' and "'On their hands they will bear you up, lest you strike your foot against a stone.'"	Psalm 91:11-12 English Standard Version 11 For he will command his angels concerning you to guard you in all your ways. 12 On their hands they will bear you up, lest you strike your foot against a stone.
Matthew 4:13-16 English Standard Version 13 And leaving Nazareth he went and lived in Capernaum by the sea, in the territory of Zebulun and Naphtali, 14 so that what was spoken by the prophet Isaiah might be fulfilled: 15 "The land of Zebulun and the land of Naphtali, the way of the sea, beyond the Jordan, Galilee of the Gentiles— 16 the people dwelling in darkness have seen a great light, and for those dwelling in the region and shadow of death, on them a light has dawned."	Isaiah 9:1-2 English Standard Version For to Us a Child Is Born 9 But there will be no gloom for her who was in anguish. In the former time he brought into contempt the land of Zebulun and the land of Naphtali, but in the latter time he has made glorious the way of the sea, the land beyond the Jordan, Galilee of the nations. 2 The people who walked in darkness have seen a great light; those who dwelt in a land of deep darkness, on them has light shone.
Matthew 8:17 English Standard Version 17 This was to fulfill what was spoken by the prophet Isaiah: "He took our illnesses and bore our diseases."	Isaiah 53:4 English Standard Version 4 Surely he has borne our griefs and carried our sorrows; yet we esteemed him stricken, smitten by God, and afflicted.
Matthew 12:17-21 English Standard Version 17 This was to fulfill what was spoken by the prophet Isaiah: 18 "Behold, my servant whom I have chosen, my beloved with whom my soul is well pleased. I will put my Spirit upon him, and he will proclaim justice to the Gentiles. 19 He will not quarrel or cry aloud, nor will anyone hear his voice in the streets; 20 a bruised reed he will not break, and a smoldering wick he will not quench, until he brings justice to victory; 21 and in his name the Gentiles will hope."	Isaiah 42:1-4 English Standard Version The Lord's Chosen Servant 42 Behold my servant, whom I uphold, my chosen, in whom my soul delights; I have put my Spirit upon him; he will bring forth justice to the nations. 2 He will not cry aloud or lift up his voice, or make it heard in the street; 3 a bruised reed he will not break, and a faintly burning wick he will not quench; he will faithfully bring forth justice. 4 He will not grow faint or be discouraged till he has established justice in the earth; and the coastlands wait for his law.

Matthew 13:35 English Standard Version 35 This was to fulfill what was spoken by the prophet: "I will open my mouth in parables; I will utter what has been hidden since the foundation of the world."	Psalm 78:2 English Standard Version 2 I will open my mouth in a parable; I will utter dark sayings from of old,
Matthew 21:4-5 English Standard Version 4 This took place to fulfill what was spoken by the prophet, saying, 5 "Say to the daughter of Zion, 'Behold, your king is coming to you, humble, and mounted on a donkey, on a colt, the foal of a beast of burden.'"	Zechariah 9:9 English Standard Version 9 Rejoice greatly, O daughter of Zion! Shout aloud, O daughter of Jerusalem! Behold, your king is coming to you; righteous and having salvation is he, humble and mounted on a donkey, on a colt, the foal of a donkey.
Matthew 21:42 English Standard Version 42 Jesus said to them, "Have you never read in the Scriptures: "'The stone that the builders rejected has become the cornerstone; this was the Lord's doing, and it is marvelous in our eyes'?	Psalm 118:22-23 English Standard Version 22 The stone that the builders rejected has become the cornerstone. 23 This is the Lord's doing; it is marvelous in our eyes.
Matthew 26:31 English Standard Version 31 Then Jesus said to them, "You will all fall away because of me this night. For it is written, 'I will strike the shepherd, and the sheep of the flock will be scattered.'	Zechariah 13:7 English Standard Version The Shepherd Struck 7 "Awake, O sword, against my shepherd, against the man who stands next to me," declares the Lord of hosts. "Strike the shepherd, and the sheep will be scattered; I will turn my hand against the little ones.

Matthew 26:64 English Standard Version 64 Jesus said to him, "You have said so. But I tell you, from now on you will see the Son of Man seated at the right hand of Power and coming on the clouds of heaven."	Daniel 7:13 English Standard Version The Son of Man Is Given Dominion 13 "I saw in the night visions, and behold, with the clouds of heaven there came one like a son of man, and he came to the Ancient of Days and was presented before him.
Matthew 27:9-10 English Standard Version 9 Then was fulfilled what had been spoken by the prophet Jeremiah, saying, "And they took the thirty pieces of silver, the price of him on whom a price had been set by some of the sons of Israel, 10 and they gave them for the potter's field, as the Lord directed me."	Zechariah 11:12-13 English Standard Version 12 Then I said to them, "If it seems good to you, give me my wages; but if not, keep them." And they weighed out as my wages thirty pieces of silver. 13 Then the Lord said to me, "Throw it to the potter"—the lordly price at which I was priced by them. So I took the thirty pieces of silver and threw them into the house of the Lord, to the potter.

There are several other times in Matthew, as in the other Gospels, that Jesus quotes Old Testament references to validate His own role: [504]

Mt 9:13	Hos 6:6
Mt 10:35-36	Micah 7:6
Mt 11:10	Mal 3:1
Mt 11:29	Jer 6:16
Mt 12:7	Hos 6:6
Mt 12:39	Jonah 1:17; 2 Chron 9:1-12
Mt 13:14-15	Isa 6:9-10
Mt 15:8	Isa 29:13; Ezek 33:31
Mt 21:13	Isa 56:7
Mt 24:15	Dan 12:11

Additionally, there are three references to fulfillment of prophecies in Matthew which do not have a specific Old Testament passages specified. Two are direct quotes from Jesus.

> 23 And he went and lived in a city called Nazareth, so that what was spoken by the prophets might be fulfilled, that he would be called a Nazarene. (Matthew 2:23 ESV)

This comment (Mt 2:23) that Jesus would be called a Nazarene because he was from Nazareth is repeated in Mk 14:67. In fact, there is no specific OT prophecy foretelling Jesus living in Nazareth. There is a potential play on words in this reference since Nazarene is similar to the word "Nazarite" (Num 6:1-21). Matthew may have intended this term to identify Jesus with the "single-minded devotion to God" which characterized Nazarites. [505]

> 17 "Do not think that I have come to abolish the Law or the Prophets; I have not come to abolish them but to fulfill them. (Matt. 5:17 ESV)

This quotation (Mt 5:17) is the words of Jesus from the Sermon on the Mount. It is not fulfillment of OT prophecy, but rather it is a statement to the Pharisees that only He was able to fulfill the laws without fail, and that belief in Him, rather than futile attempt to fulfill all the laws, was the path to salvation. [506]

> 52 Then Jesus said to him, "Put your sword back into its place. For all who take the sword will perish by the sword. 53 Do you think that I cannot appeal to my Father, and he will at once send me more than twelve legions of angels? 54 But how then should the Scriptures be fulfilled, that it must be so?" 55 At that hour Jesus said to the crowds, "Have you come out as against a robber, with swords and clubs to capture me? Day after day I sat in the temple teaching, and you did not seize me. 56 But all this has taken place that the Scriptures of the prophets might be fulfilled." Then all the disciples left him and fled. (Matt. 26:52-56 ESV)

Again, this passage (Mt 26:52-56) is a direct quote from Jesus. The specific OT prophecy to which He was referring is not identified. It could have been to Isaiah, chapter 53, or to other Messianic prophecies.

Interpretations

Isaiah 7:4
This passage is one of the most controversial of all Messianic prophecies. The background story is that Ahaz was an apostate King of Judah. His adversaries, Pekah (King of Israel) and Rezin (King of Aram) formed an alliance to overthrow Judah. Isaiah told Ahaz that God would protect Judah, and that Ahaz was to ask for a sign from God to validate God's commitment. Ahaz refused to ask for a sign. Isaiah told Ahaz that God would show him a sign anyway: a boy named Immanuel (which means "God is with us".) The controversy arises over whether this Immanuel was a prophecy of the Messiah to come, or whether it was a boy in Ahaz's

current time. A second controversy is whether the mother was a virgin. The Hebrew word alma is defined as a young woman – not necessarily a virgin. The conflicting views make this verse questionable as a strong Messianic prophecy.

Micah 5:2

Micah lived and prophesied in the same period as Isaiah. As opposed to the above reference, the Micah 5:2 reference is to a coming Messiah to be born in the relatively insignificant town of Bethlehem. The historical insignificance of Bethlehem ("not even mentioned in the list of towns in Josh 15 or Neh 11 [507]) makes this specific prophecy even more powerful.

Hosea 11:1

Hosea was a prophet during the end of the Northern Kingdom, Israel. Lamenting the apostacy of Israel, Hosea reminds them of God's love to deliver them from Egypt in the Exodus. There is no evidence that this passage was intended to be a Messianic prophecy. Matthew creatively applied the passage to Jesus' return from safety in Egypt.

Jeremiah 31:15

Jeremiah was a prophet in the Southern Kingdom of Judah who witnessed the destruction of the Northern Kingdom of Israel by the Assyrians in 722 BC. Ramah was a small town five miles from Jerusalem. Rachael was the mother of two of the Northern Kingdom kings. Thus, Jeremiah probably described Rachel watching the weeping of Northern Kingdom mothers as their children were captured into exile. On the other hand, the town of Ramah was the staging area for Nebuchadnezzar's later deportation of the children from Judah, so Rachel may have been mourning that event. Either way, there was no Messianic intention in the text. Matthew, again, creatively applied the story to the mourning of mothers from Herod's massacre of the two-year old children (Mt 2:17-18). [508]

Isaiah 40:3

This passage was written by Isaiah prior to the conquering of Judah and the Jewish captivity in Babylon. He was assuring the Jews that even though destruction and captivity lay ahead, God would be faithful and later deliver them back to their Promised Land. The passage is a metaphor recalling the Exodus when God led them through the desert to the Promised Land. Isaiah is foretelling that God will lead them back from Babylonian captivity to their home in Judah. Matthew drew the comparison of "A voice cries. 'In the wilderness prepare the way of the Lord.'" to the wilderness ministry of John the Baptist. There is no evidence that Isaiah intended the passage to be such a prophecy.

Psalm 91:11-12

The anonymous author of Psalm 91 was making the point that God and His angels will protect those who have made God their refuge. The Messianic application is that Satan is reported to have taunted Jesus with the passage at the time of Jesus temptation to jump from the pinnacle of the Temple (Mt 4:6). As such, this passage is not specifically a Messianic prophecy.

Isaiah 9:1-2

The entirety of Chapter 9:1-7 is a prophecy that the people of Galilee, who had been walking in darkness will have a "light" shown on them in the person of a child who will be called. "Wonderful Counselor, Mighty God, Everlasting Father, Prince of Peace" (v 6). Therefore, it can be assumed that the entire passage – not just verses 1 and 2 as quoted by Matthew (4:13-16) is clearly a Messianic prophecy.

Isaiah 53:4

Just as Isaiah chapter 9:1-7 foretold of a Messianic child, Chapter 16:5 announced the Messiah to be from the house of David (16:5). But contrary to the Hebrew's expectation that the Messiah would be a conquering king, Isaiah launches into a detailed description of a suffering servant. The 53rd chapter of Isaiah is by far the longest and most widely accepted of the Messianic prophecies.

Isaiah 42:1-4

This passage describes God's "servant" who is empowered by God's Spirit and who will bring justice to the world. The Hebrew term for "servant" connotes "chosen one' or "trusted envoy". [509] This is clearly a Messianic reference.

Psalm 78:2

The Psalmist, Asaph, is extolling the people to remember the teachings God had given them from old. There is no indication that this prophetically referred to the later teachings of Jesus.

Zechariah 9:9

Zechariah was a post-exilic priest, a Levite born in Babylon. He was both a prophet and a priest. [510] The book of Zechariah is one of the most important prophetic books in the Bible. It is referenced forty-two times in the New Testament. [511] The reference to the king arriving riding on a donkey is a clear Messianic prophecy. The fact that the king was astride a donkey rather than a war stallion connoted intention of peace. [512]

Psalm 118:22-23

The Psalmist likely was referring to his king as the capstone, a practice common in ancient Israel. [513] Once again, Jesus' quotation of the verse brings it into Messianic usage.

Zechariah 13:7

It is possible that the original reference was to the scattering of the Jews at the destruction of the Temple (AD 70) or during the last half of the Tribulation. [514] But this Old Testament reference was uttered by Jesus himself (Mt 26:31; Mk 14:26) in predicting that his followers would scatter. It also appears to show that God himself arranged for His "shepherd" (Jesus) to be stricken. Jesus' usage defines it as a Messianic prophecy from Zechariah.

Daniel 7:13

This passage is Daniel's dream where he sees the "son of Man", presumably a Christophany. Not only is this a Messianic prophecy from Daniel, but Jesus, himself, uses the "son of Man" term to prophesy His own future arrival to earth as King.

Zechariah 11:12-13

Due to the presence of the specific amount (30 pieces of silver) and the term "potter" Matthew applied this to Judas Iscariot's payment and the subsequent "Potter's Field". However, it is not clear in the original passage that these two facts were Messianic prophecies. It is possible that the shepherds were the religious leaders of time. [515]

Conclusion

Of the fifteen Old Testament passages referenced as Messianic by Matthew, only six seem to be clearly intended to be so by their Old Testament authors (Micah 5:2; Isa 9:1-2; Isa 42:1; Isa 53:4; Zech 9:9; and Daniel 7:13). Jesus conscripted Psalm 118:22-23 and Zech 13:7 to be Messianic. The remaining seven passages in Matthew (Isa 7:4; Hosea 11:1; Jer 13:15; Isa 40:3; Ps 91:11-12; Ps 778:2; and Zech 11:12-13) do not have a solid Messianic basis.

Of conspicuous note is the absence of any resurrection prophecy in Matthew's selections. While predictions of the birth, ministry, and crucifixion were important, the entirety of the Christian faith centers upon the resurrection. This absence is likely due to the fact that the ancient Hebrews of the Old Testament did not have a clear concept of the afterlife. Resurrection, if existing at all, was to be a group event at the end time when God re-established the nation of Israel. In fact, Jesus' individual and immediate resurrection was a surprise and mystery even to the disciples. For this reason, there were no definite Old Testament prophecies of the Messiah's resurrection from which Matthew could choose to include.

57

Did Daniel Prophesy the Future?

Other than the Revelation of John, the book of Daniel is the most prophetic book in the Bible. On the other hand, Daniel is also one of the most controversial books in the Old Testament. Who was Daniel, and what is his "seventy weeks" prophecy?

Biography

Daniel was reportedly born during the reign of King Josiah in approximately 641-609 BC. At that time Judah was "experiencing a spiritual revival". [516] According to the historian Josephus, Daniel came from a royal line, so we can suppose he also had an excellent education and social standing." [517]

As had been prophesied by Isaiah, Daniel was one of the sons of Judah who were taken to Babylon as slaves in the first of the Babylonian invasions of Judah in 605 BC.

> 17 The time will surely come when everything in your palace, and all that your predecessors have stored up

> until this day, will be carried off to Babylon. Nothing will be left, says the Lord. 18 And some of your descendants, your own flesh and blood who will be born to you, will be taken away, and they will become eunuchs in the palace of the king of Babylon." (2 Kings 20:17-18)
>
> 6 The time will surely come when everything in your palace, and all that your predecessors have stored up until this day, will be carried off to Babylon. Nothing will be left, says the Lord. 7 And some of your descendants, your own flesh and blood who will be born to you, will be taken away, and they will become eunuchs in the palace of the king of Babylon." (Isaiah 39:6)

The ESV translation of Daniel 1:3 suggests that Daniel was under the authority of Ashpenaz, the "chief eunuch". Since Isaiah's prophecy had foretold it, Daniel very likely was castrated to become a eunuch. The practice was common among male servants of a king's court, to prevent them from interacting with the female harem. [518]

Captured along with Daniel were his three companions Hananiah, Mishael, and Azariah. Due to their attractiveness and intellects, the four Jewish youths were chosen for service in the court. Daniel, who's Hebrew name meant "God (El) is my judge" [519] was renamed Belteshazzar. His companions were given the Babylonian names Shadrach, Meshach and Abednego. (Daniel 1:7).

While Daniel's steadfast faith led him to be tested in the lions' den (Daniel 6: 16), it was his ability to interpret dreams and to prophesy future events that is most important to eschatology.

Neither the Bible nor history record where Daniel died. Ezra 8:2 mentions a "Daniel" among those returning to Jerusalem from Babylon, but the preponderance of tradition is that he died in Babylon (Persia), and never returned to Judah. [520]

Dream Prophecies

In chapter 2, Daniel interpreted Nebuchadnezzar's dream to mean the sequential rule of four empires. Babylon (2:32,38); Medo-Persia (2:32,39); Greece (2:32, 39); and Rome (2:33, 40-43). [521] These geopolitical changes are described in more detail in four more dreams in chapters 7-11.

While the geopolitical predictions correlated with history, it is the Messianic timing prophecy of Daniel 9:24-27 that is most striking:

> 24 "Seventy 'sevens' are decreed for your people and your holy city to finish transgression, to put an end to sin, to atone for wickedness, to bring in everlasting righteousness, to seal up vision and prophecy and to anoint the Most Holy Place.
>
> 25 "Know and understand this: From the time the word goes out to restore and rebuild Jerusalem until the Anointed One, the ruler, comes, there will be seven 'sevens,' and sixty-two 'sevens.' It will be rebuilt with streets and a trench, but in times of trouble. 26 After the sixty-two 'sevens,' the Anointed One will be put to death and will have nothing. The people of the ruler who will come will destroy the city and the sanctuary. The end will come like a flood: War will continue until the end, and desolations have been decreed. 27 He will confirm a covenant with many for one 'seven.' In the middle of the 'seven' he will put an end to sacrifice and offering. And at the temple[h] he will set up an abomination that causes desolation, until the end that is decreed is poured out on him." (Daniel 9:24-27)

This reference describes three periods totaling "seventy sevens": seven sevens (49); sixty-one sevens (61); and one seven (1). Evangelical scholars have interpreted this sequence to predict arrival of the Messiah, a gap of the "church age", the seven years of the "tribulation", followed by the return of Christ.

The math calculation is as follows. The time-period began with Artaxerxes' decree to rebuild the city of Jerusalem in 445 BC (Nehemiah 2:1). [522] The precedent for using days to signify years was established in Numbers 14:34 and Ezekiel 4:6. The seven weeks to complete rebuilding Jerusalem, followed by sixty-two weeks until arrival of the Messiah, equals sixty-nine weeks. With each figurative "week" day interpreted as a year, there is a total of 483 years until the arrival of the Messiah. David Jeremiah clarifies that the ancient Hebrew calendar consisted of a 360-day year – not 365 as we use in the Gregorian calendar. [523] By this calculation, 69 x 360 = 24,840 days.

Jeremiah quotes Sir Robert Anderson, "Starting from March 14, 445 B.C., we can calculate the date of Christ's Triumphal Entry to be April 6, 32 A.D." [524] A slightly different date calculation of AD 33 is concluded when using the date of Artaxerxes's decree as 444 BC. [525] This minor difference is insignificant given the uncertainty of both Artaxerxes's decree as well as the date of Jesus entry. The variation represents two-tenths of a percent (.0002).

Verse 26 is interpreted as the crucifixion ("Messiah will be cut off"), followed by destruction of the temple ("destroy the city and the sanctuary"). After an apparent gap in time (The "church age"), a seven-year period of "tribulation is predicted. Finally, the Messiah is to return to "make an end to sin, …bring everlasting righteousness" as described in Daniel 9:24.

In chart form: [526]

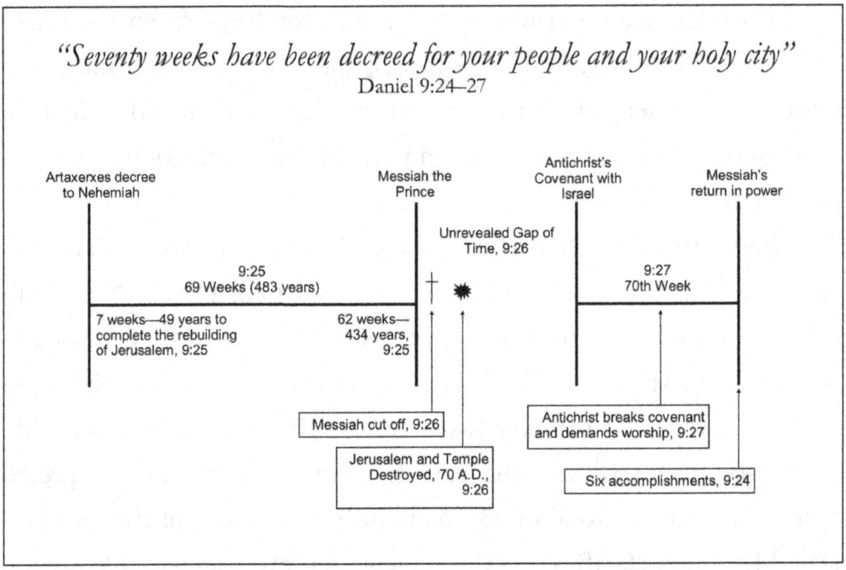

Dating Controversy

Starting with the bias that supernatural prophetic revelations do not exist, liberal scholars have argued that the book of Daniel was written in the late second century BC, around 164 BC during the Maccabean revolt by several different authors. [527] Daniel is described as a fictional character who prophesizes after the fact.

Textural critics propose that the book of Daniel was written by multiple authors, in the second century BC, as a resistance to the cruel Hellenistic oppression by the Seleucid king, Antiochus IV Epiphanes. Their theory is that Daniel is a fictional character constructed after the Danel, a pious figure described in the 13th century BC Aqhat legend from Ugarit (a Canaanite city in which the tablet describing the legend was found). [528]

Daniel being mentioned three times in the book of Ezekiel (Ezk 14:14,20;28:3) further confirms the early dating. Like Daniel, Ezekiel was taken into captivity in Babylon. They likely knew each other. The notion that Ezekiel was referring to a pagan mythological hero, Danel, is beyond imagination. [529]

Other Criticisms

Other criticisms include: (1) lack of mention of Daniel in the writings of Jesus ben Sirach in 180 BC, (2) Belshazzar called king of Babylon in Daniel 6, when the king actually was Nabonidus, (3) Darius the Mede in chapters 5 and 6 is otherwise not known, (4) three Greek words of musical instruments are mentioned, but the Greek influence was mainly in the third century BC, (5) half of Daniel was written in Aramaic (2:4-7:28), a language used by the Jews of the intertestamental period, and (6) the first six chapters of the book of Daniel are written in the third person, whereas the subsequent five chapters are written in the first person.

Evangelical theologians, however, date the book of Daniel to the period of captivity in Babylon, around 503 BC. [530] They counter the above criticisms. [531]

Belshazzar as King

"Belshazzar had been known only from the biblical Book of Daniel (chapters 5, 7–8) and from *Xenophon's Cyropaedia* until 1854, when references to him were found in Babylonian cuneiform inscriptions." [532] Although Daniel refers to him as the son of Nebuchadressar (Dan 5:18), Belshazzar was the son of Nabonidus, who succeeded Nebuchadressar. When Nabonidus went into exile, Balthazzar was left in charge of the throne. [533] It is possible that Balthazzar was serving as king in Daniel chapter 5. However, the confusion of Daniel calling Balthazzar the son of Nebuchadressar is unexplained.

Language

The Aramaic language issue could possibly be explained by the fact that, " the Aramaic of Daniel is 'official,' or 'imperial'— the standardized Aramaic used in official correspondence when Aramaic was the lingua franca of the Near East (see 2 Ki 18: 26 ; Ezk 4: 7 ; Dan 2: 4), not the colloquial, regional Aramaic of second-century B.C. Palestine, at which time the common language of the region was Greek." [534]

Further evidence is the reference in 2 Kings 18:26 when Eliakim requested the field commander of the Assyrians to speak in Aramaic since he didn't understand Hebrew language. This event occurred when Hezekiah (741-687 BC) was King, and as such, validates the use of Aramaic in that era.

A similar time reference occurs in Ezra 4:7. Ezra, writing in about 458 BC reports that in the days of Artaxerxes, king of Persia, received a letter written in Aramaic. This provides another time reference of the ancient use of the Aramaic language.

Daniel himself comments that astrologers answered Nebuchadnezzar in Aramaic (Dan 2:4).

However, the portion of the book of Daniel that is written in Aramaic (2:4-7:28) also happens to be the first seven chapters that are written in the third person. The remaining apocalyptic chapters (8-12) are the first-person portions which were written in Hebrew.

The issue of the split language and split grammar suggests separate authors but could have occurred from translators. It remains an unexplained conundrum.

Greek Instruments

The issue of the three Greek named instruments seems trivial. While the Greek empire had not yet become dominant, one cannot assume that they did not contribute a few instruments to Hebrew culture.

Darius

"Darius" is mentioned by Daniel eight times: 5:31; 6:1; 6:6; 6:9; 6:25; 6:28; 9:1; 11:1. Darius is mentioned by Ezra 10 times; Haggai 3 times; Zechariah 3 times; and Nehemiah once. [535]

What is not clear is whether these are all the same person – Darius the Mede mentioned by Daniel. An exhaustive analysis of potential identities of Darius the Mede is provided by the Spirit and Truth website: [536]

> Correlating Darius the Mede with rulers known to extra-biblical history has proven to be a complex task, made all-the-more challenging because the name "Darius" is applied within historic inscriptions to at least five Persian rulers. The frequency with which the name appears suggests "Darius" was a title, like "Pharaoh" (used of Egyptian rulers) or "Caesar" (used of Roman rulers). An added complication is the practice of some rulers who took on additional throne names in honor of relatives or previous leaders whom they admired.

While exact identification of Darius the Mede is not yet clear, it is premature to assume such an individual, as described by Daniel, did not exist.

Conclusion

The issues of Balthazzar's identity, the first-versus-third-person narratives, the ancient Hebrew versus Aramaic language, and the identity of Darius the Mede remain unclear. These have led to considerable textural criticism.

However, the accuracy of the prophecies, particularly the dating of Messianic arrival, are difficult to explain away. The Messianic arrival was two hundred years after even a proposed second century BC date of authorship. How could a second century BC author accurately predict an event which occurred two hundred years later "after the fact"? It still required remarkable forward time projection.

Finally, the most powerful validation of Daniel's story is that Jesus himself acknowledge the existence of Daniel and his prophecies (Mt 24:15; Mt 26:64; Mk 13:14; Mk 14:62; Luke 22:69; Heb 11:33-34).

58

Did Scribes Write the Bible?

Webster's dictionary defines amanuensis as "one employed to write from dictation or to copy manuscript". [537] The term amanuensis does not appear in the Bible. In the Hebrew culture, the function was performed by "scribes".

Scribes

God chose and appointed the Levites, the descendants of Aaron, in Numbers 8:16-18. Their main responsibility was care of the Tabernacle, but they also were the scribes of the ancient era. [538]

The ancient Hebrew word for scribe was sō·p̄êr (רֵפֹס:). [539] The term sō·p̄êr first appears in Judges 5:14 in the King James and Interlinear translations as "writer". [540] The term is again used in 2 Samuel 8:17, where Seraiah is described as "secretary'. Scribes are then mentioned throughout 2 Kings (12;10; 18:18; 18:37; 19:2; 22:3; 22:8-10; 25:19); 1 Chronicles (18:16; 24:6; 27:32); 2 Chronicles (24:11; 26:11; 34:15; 34:18; 34:20), Ezra (4:8-9; 4:17; 4:23; 7:6; 7:11-12; 7:21); Nehemiah (8:1; 8:4; 8:9; 8:13; 12:26; 12:36; 13:13); Isaiah (33:18; 36:3; 37:2) and Jeremiah (36:4;

36:10; 36:12; 36:20; 36:26; 36:32; 37:15; 37:20; 52:25); Matthew (8:19; 13:52) Mark (12:32); and 1 Cor (1:20).

Scribes as a group are mentioned in 1 Kings 4:3; 1 Chronicles 2:55; 2 Chronicles 34:13; Esther 3:12 and 8:9; and Jeremiah 8:8. Finally, scribes are mentioned sixty-two additional times in the New Testament, frequently as adversaries of Jesus. [541]

Need for a Written Record

Prior to the Exodus and establishment of the nation of Israel, there likely was no perceived need for a written history to be provided for posterity. Oral transmission was adequate for daily life.

But on Sinai, God gave Moses not only the Ten Commandments, but also a long list of laws ("ordinances") the Israelites were to follow (Ex21:1). Moses spent forty days on the mountain receiving these detailed instructions (Ex 34:28). The ordinances are detailed in Exodus chapters 20:23 through chapter 31, in the whole book of Leviticus; in Numbers chapters 28-30, and in Deuteronomy 5:1-21; 10:1-27:26, and 20:23-31- a total of 613 of them. Two hundred forty-eight are positive; three hundred sixty-five are negative. A full 30% of the Pentateuch is devoted to enunciation of the Laws.[542] While the Ten Commandments might have been brief enough to commit to memory, the number and detail of the" ordinances" were too long to reliably remember. As such there was a need to for compilation of a written record.'

I Kings 6:1 states that the Exodus occurred 480 years before Solomon started building the Temple (960 BC). That would make the Exodus date 1440 BC. If Moses wrote the Pentateuch, it had to have been written between 1440 and 1360 BC during the two sojourns in the wilderness of Sinai. Modern textural critics have adopted the "Documentary Hypothesis" of Graf -Wellhausen [543] to suggest that the Pentateuch was written by different authors and compiled in the fifth century BC, long after Moses lived. [544] The evangelical viewpoint would argue; (1) remembering 613 specific laws for nine-hundred years would be a mental stretch, even for the Israelites, and (2) Moses would have incentive to have constructed a written record to be followed by the new nation of Israel in the Promised Land. Finally, it likely is not coincidence that the institution of scribes occurred at this same time. And even more "coincidental" is that fact that Moses picked the tribe of Levi, his own family, to become the scribes. Who better to undertake a new writing project than your own close family?

Moses had a period of eighty years (Num 14:33-34) to interview the Egyptian Israelites, to learn their oral history, and to compose the Pentateuch. The original tablets containing the Ten Commandments were placed within the Ark of the Covenant (Deut 10:2). Exodus 24:2-4 documents that Moses wrote down the "ordinances," then gave the scrolls to the priests who carried the Ark of the Covenant (Deut 31:9). Within the laws was direction that a future king in the Promised Land was to "write for himself a copy of the law on a scroll. (Deut 17:18).

The Ark of the Covenant was captured by the Philistines (1 Sam 4:11). It is likely that the scrolls of the book of the laws were captured by the Philistines along with the Ark of the Covenant. The Ark was then returned to Kiriath-jearin (1 Sam 7:2) for twenty years, then taken to Jerusalem (2 Sam 6:12) by David (1010-970 BC). Solomon (970-931) BC then placed the Ark in the Temple.

The fate of the book of the laws is unclear during part of the divided kingdom period. *The Expositor's Bible Commentary* is quoted, "'The Book,' however seems to have become misplaced during the apostate administrations of the previous kings, Manasseh and Amon, under whom the ark had been moved about " [545]

It is clear from 2 Kings 22:8 that a written book of the "law" was in existence during the time of King Josiah of Judah (640-609 BC). The narrative that it was "found" by the priest Hilkiah (2 Kings 22:8; 2 Chron 34: 15) during restoration of the Temple suggests that the original was missing within the Temple for some time interval. The presence of a written book of the law of Moses is again mentioned in Nehemiah 8:1, dating around 400 BC.

There are two reasons the ancients utilized scribes for manuscript construction: literacy and convenience.

Literacy

Prior to 3400 BC, all history was maintained and transmitted orally. The first evidences of writing were imprinting wet clay with reed stylus in Mesopotamia. [546] Initial "writing" was cuneiform picture symbols, which evolved into the Phoenician script by 1200 BC. Therefore, some primitive method of written history, likely Akkadian, [547] was present by the time of Moses.

It is also of note that Moses, himself, was from the tribe of Levi (Ex 2:1) and he was raised within the court of Pharoah. Moses was likely educated, or at least familiar with writing. It would be natural that he would have taught his family, the tribe of Levi, whom he would later assign the duty to be scribes.

Education was a priority in the Sumerian culture (c. 4500 – c.1900 BC) in Mesopotamia, but due to the difficulty of the primitive language, it took years to perfect. [548] Literacy was achieved through apprenticeship with the scribes. The apprenticeship system became more formalized during the time of Ezra. Interestingly, there is no word in the ancient Hebrew language for "school". [549] Literacy in the generally population during the ancient period has been assumed to have been rare. Even as late as the first century, the general population literacy rate in Palestine was less than 10%.

Convenience

It is not clear upon what medium the Pentateuch was written, but given the length, it is impractical to think it was written in clay. Papyrus scrolls were present in Egypt, and it is likely that the Pentateuch was written on papyrus, leather, or parchment scrolls. [550], [551] Even so, the process would have been tedious and laborious.

The writing process on papyri was tedious and time-consuming. It is therefore not surprising that the duty would be delegated to an amanuensis (scribe) who had the materials, skill, and time to produce written documents.

The process of employing a "secretary" to transcribe and manage documents persists even today.

Role of the Amanuensis

The role of the amanuensis is defined by Payes : [552]

- Secretarial Freedom.
  In addition to verbatim transcription of dictation, the amanuensis had a degree of freedom to construct the grammar or phrasing, and perhaps, to edit somewhat. This secretarial freedom no doubt explains the different literary styles among the various writings of the same author.

- Authorial Control
  The final draft was read and edited to satisfaction by the controlling author.

Grammatical Perspective

Except for Nehemiah, Psalms, Ecclesiastes, Song of Solomon, and parts of Lamentations, the Old Testament is written in the third person.

Similarly, all four of the New Testament gospels are written in the third person. With the onset of Acts, use of the first person becomes much more common.

Luke inserts the first person "I" in his introduction of Acts, then inserts "we" throughout his narrative of Paul's journeys to indicate his presence with Paul.

The first person is heavily used by the apostle Paul in his letters, even though he used amanuenses to do the transcription. The amanuensis is specifically identified for Romans: Tertius (Rom 16:22). The identity of the amanuensis is not specifically identified in Paul's other letters; however, it is clear that Paul reviewed and approved the writings. This is evidenced by Paul's attestations in his own handwriting in Gal 6:11; 2 Thes 3:17; 1 Cor 16:21; 2 Cor 10:1, Col 4:18; and Philemon 19.

Finally, the letters of James; 1 and 2 Peter; 1, 2, and 3 John; Jude; and the Revelation utilize the first person.

As discussed, the use of the first person does not exclude the role of an amanuensis transcribing dictation.

Conclusion

Given the issues of literacy and convenience, it is not surprising that most of the Bible is written in the third person.

The widespread use of an amanuensis for constructing the writings of the Bible easily explains differences in grammatic style, perspective, and possibly even the language (Hebrew, Aramaic, Greek) used. To conclude that grammatic and language differences negate the authenticity of the authors would be erroneous.

The multiple references to the "book of the law" throughout the Pentateuch and subsequent Old Testament books strongly supports the belief that it was written by Moses after the Exodus. The historical reference to it being "found" in the Temple restoration during the reign of King Josiah of Judah (640-609 BC) negates the textural criticism theory that the Pentateuch was written in during the Second Temple period.

59

How Did the Popes Dominate Christianity?

Roman History

From the perspective of Christianity, the history began with the establishment of the Roman Empire from the previous Roman Republic in 27 BC. [553]

For the three hundred years after the crucifixion, Christians of all persuasions were persecuted by the Roman emperors. But organized persecution was terminated in 311 AD by the Galerius' edict of toleration. Then, the emperor Constantine, perhaps under the influence of his mother Helena, converted to Christianity. At the Edict of Milan in 313, Constantine declared Christianity to be acceptable in the Roman empire. [554] Christianity was later designated as the "state religion" of the Roman Empire by the Edict of Thessalonica in 380 AD. [555]

The Roman Empire split into Western and Eastern factions in 395 AD. [556] The Western Roman Empire was overrun by the Germanic Visgoths in 476 AD. [557] The Eastern (Byzantine) Empire survived another one thousand years until it was conquered by the Ottoman Turks in 1453 AD. [558]

The structure of the Roman Catholic church followed the pattern of the Empire. Beginning shortly after the fall of the Western Empire, the Eastern (Byzantine) church gradually became estranged. This trend eventuated into the schism of 1054. [559]

The history of the Papacy relevant to western Christianity centers around the residual western Roman Catholic church.

Establishment of the Papacy

The basis for the papacy in Roman Catholicism is the "Keys of the Kingdom" reference by Jesus to the apostle Peter in Matthew 16:17-19 (NASB):

> 17 And Jesus said to him, "Blessed are you, Simon Barjona, because flesh and blood did not reveal *this* to you, but My Father who is in heaven. 18 I also say to you that you are Peter, and upon this rock I will build My church; and the gates of Hades will not overpower it. 19 I will give you the *keys of the kingdom of heaven; and whatever you bind on earth shall have been bound in heaven, and whatever you loose on earth shall have been loosed in heaven."*

It was this reference from which Roman Catholicism began the succession of Popes after the martyrdom of the apostle Peter in 64 AD. Roman Catholics assumed that they were the exclusive and direct intermediary between God and mankind since they held the "power of the keys".

For the first three hundred years after the crucifixion, the Roman Catholic Popes were of little consequence. [560] But with the influence of the Emperor Constantine and the subsequent Edicts of Milan (313 AD) and Thessalonica (30 AD), the importance and authority of the Pope in Rome became dominant in western Roman Catholicism. The most influential Pope of this period was Leo the Great (440-461 AD), who established the Pope's "power of the keys."

After the fall of the western Roman Empire in 476 AD, there was political instability in Rome due to various "barbaric" invasions. Finally, with rise of the Frankish Empire, [561] Pope Leo III crowned Charlemagne as Emperor of what would be come to be known as the Holy Roman Empire in 800 AD. This loosely assembled coalition of kingdoms would persist as an effort to reconstitute the old Roman Empire until 1808. [562] In practicality, it was an effort of the Papacy to maintain not only spiritual, but also political influence.

Papacy Problems

> The first known use of plenary indulgences was in 1095 when Pope Urban II remitted all penance of persons who participated in the crusades and who confessed their sins. Later, the indulgences were also offered to those who couldn't go on the Crusades but offered cash contributions to the effort instead. In the early 1200s, the Church began claiming that it had a "treasury" of indulgences (consisting of the merits of Christ and the saints) that it could dispense in ways that promoted the Church and its mission. In a decretal issued in 1343, Pope Clement VI declared, "The merits of Christ are a treasure of indulgences." [563]

Pope Sixtus IV (1414- 1484) applied the opportunity of indulgences not only to the living to but to "alleviate the sufferings of their relatives in purgatory." [564] Then Leo X, in need of funds to complete St Peter's Basilica in 1517, established a system of commissions for those collecting indulgences. [565] It was this practice, especially by Tetzel, that infuriated Martin Luther and led to his posting the Ninety-five Theses. [566]

Besides objecting to collecting "indulgences", Luther challenged two other elements of the Papacy: (1) their authority to institute policies of their authority and exclusivity not directly based on Scripture (Sola Scripta), as well as (2) their emphasis on salvation by works rather than by grace alone (Sola Gratia, Sola Fide). These concepts would become central to the principles of the Protestant Reformation.

60

How Did the Gospel Writers Remember The Exact Quotes Of Jesus?

According to the NIV Study Bible, the gospel of Matthew was written between 50-70 AD; Mark was written mid 50's to 60's; Luke was written 60's to 80's; and John was written between 50-85 AD. Paul's letter to the Galatians was his earliest New Testament epistle, and was written between 48 to 50's AD. [567]

Hinds observes the King James Version of the New Testament to contain:

> The number of words in the New Testament is 181,253. Only 36,450 of these 181,253 words are the words of Christ—barely over 20 per cent. Considered as verses, the New Testament has 7,959 verses, of which but 1,599 are sayings of Christ.
>
> These relatively few sayings of Jesus have not a place apart but run in an uneven distribution through the four Gospels (a few in other Books); and in each of the four

> Gospels—Matthew, Mark, Luke, John—the "sayings" are unevenly distributed through the narrative. Often a "saying" recorded, it may be, by Matthew, is paraphrased, or even duplicated, by one or more of the other three biographers, none of whom seems to have intended either a chronological harmony with the others, or even a sustained sequence of his own. [568]

The "red letter" verses quoting Jesus in the King James Version of the Bible total 1928 - Matthew 649; Mark 283; Luke 584; and John 412. [569]

Content Overlap

From the time of the patriarchs, the overlapping of text among the first three gospels has been noticed. Beginning in the 1780s, Matthew, Mark, and Luke have been referred to as the Synoptic Gospels (from *synoptikos*, "seen together"). [570] How the overlap occurred has been dubbed the "Synoptic Problem."

Stein [571] quotes Tyson [572]

1. .... 97.2 percent of the words in Mark have a parallel in Matthew and 88.4 percent have a parallel in Luke...Of the 18,293 words that appear in Matthew, 7392 (40.4%) have no parallel in Mark, and of the 19,376 words that appear in Luke, 10,259 (52.9%) have no parallel in Mark.
2. Matthew and Luke share 235 verses in common that they did not get from Mark. [573]

Markan Priority

From early second century AD, the prevailing opinion was that the gospel of Matthew was the first to be written. Matthew was the most popular writing within the early Christian church since it was written in Hebrew to a Jewish audience. It also was more complete, in that it covered the virgin birth, Jesus' ministry, role of the law, and the crucifixion. Later endorsed by Augustine and the Roman Catholic church, the Augustinian hypothesis theorized that Matthew's gospel was written first, then was subsequently used by Mark and Luke.

The discipline of analyzing the Bible, and particularly the New Testament, was gestated by a group of German Protestants, Burr in Tubingen, Germany, led by Ferdinand Christian during the late 18th and early 19th century. [574] This came to be known as "textural criticism".

Griesbach (1745-1812) adopted the opinion of Matthew being the first gospel but changed the subsequent order to Luke and then Mark. Lachmann, in 1835, observed that "Matthew and Luke agree only when they also agree with Mark and that, where material is introduced that is not in Mark, it is inserted in different places." This led Lachman to conclude the priority of Mark. [575]

"Late" Writing of the Gospels

One of the perplexing questions in New Testament study, is "why did the gospel authors wait over twenty years to put the Jesus story into writing?"

Stein surmises that Jesus' followers were expecting the Parousia (second coming) to be immediate. As such, those who had experienced Jesus' teaching were still alive. The Jewish culture had a long tradition of maintenance of history by orally by memory. It was, therefore, only when they realized that the Parousia was delayed, and the original observers began to die off, that the need for a written recorded realized.[576] It is thought that the gospel of Mark was stimulated by the death of Peter, and that Matthew penned his gospel in anticipation of his own death. [577]

Source of Mark's Information

Accepting that Matthew and Luke had Mark's gospel as reference, where did Mark obtain his initial information? It was at least twenty years between Jesus' ministry and the writing of Mark's gospel. While it is well known that the first century Jews were proficient at memorizing history, to assume that they could merely remember Jesus's exact words and the historical details of all His encounters is a stretch.

Stein quotes Redlich in concluding that "before the gospels were written there did exist a period in which the gospels were passed on orally. That is generally accepted as having influenced the production of all four gospels. However, Stein argues that only the presence of written sources could explain: (1) the exactness of wording among the gospels, (2) parenthetical statements the gospels have in common, and (3) extensive agreement in the order of the materials. [578]

Academic consensus is that there likely were fragmented notes recorded by Jesus' followers. Mark then assembled these notes into his gospel. This is thought to be partially evidenced by the sudden transitions from one pericope to the next in Mark. [579]

The Two Source Hypothesis

The fact that Matthew and Luke share 235 verses that are not found in Mark, led scholars to suggest a second written source used by Matthew and Luke. It appears that the first scholar to hypothesize a second source was Herbert Marsh in 1801. He labelled the theoretical document the Hebrew letter *beth* (ב). In 1832 German scholar, Friedrich Schleiermacher, interpreted the writings of the patriarch, Papias of Hierapolis, to infer the presence of a separate document of Jesus' sayings that was used by Matthew. The mystery document was referred to as *Logia*, in deference to Papias. Then in 1838 another German scholar of the Tubingen school, Christian Herman Weisse, combined Schleiermacher's suggestion of a separate source with the concept of Markan priority to create the "Two Source Hypothesis." [580]

Heinrich Julius Holtzman was an influential liberal Bible scholar, associated with Tubingen school, who sanctioned Weisse's theory in 1863 and re-named the mystery document Lambda (Λ). However, late in the 19th century scholars became uncomfortable with associating the unknown document with Papias. Johannes Weiss then came up with the symbol Q, as an abbreviation of the German word *Quelle* – meaning "source".

Finally, B.H. Streeter, an English Anglican theologian of the early twentieth century, expanded the Two Source Hypothesis'. In noticing material in Matthew and Luke which was unique to each gospel, Streeter proposed that two additional source documents must exist, M and L. [581]

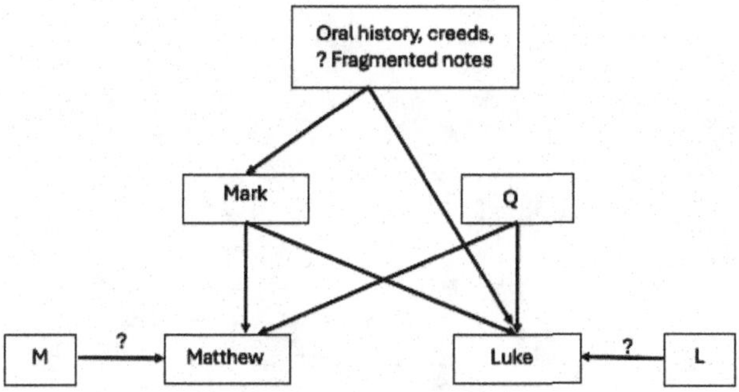

Conclusion

It is probable that the delay from Jesus' death and the writing of the gospels was due to (1) tradition of oral history, and (2) expectation of immediate Parousia.

The concept of "Markan Priority' – that is, Mark was written first and was later referenced by Matthew and Luke, - is generally accepted. It is likely that Mark drew his material from fragmented recordings. While Matthew and Luke both utilized Mark's gospel, they likely did not know or interact with each other. Finally, the commonality of information in Matthew and Luke (235 verses) that is not found in Mark, suggests a second common source. This source, which has come to be known as Q (Quelle), is theorized but has never been found. Finally, Streeter has proposed that both Matthew and Luke utilized other sources other than Mark and Q. He referred to these theorized other sources as M and L, respectively.

Endnotes

Chapter 1

1 https://www.maa.org/external_archive/devlin/devlin_12_99.html.
2 https://www.livescience.com/46558-8laws-of-motion.html.
3 https://www.space.com/36273-3theory-special-relativity.html.
4 https://www.space.com/17661-1theory-general-relativity.html.
5 https://www.scientificamerican.com/author/gabriele-veneziano/.
6 http://homepages.wmich.edu/~korista/hawking-time.html.
7 https://www.youtube.com/results?search_query=richard+dawkins+vs+john+lennox+has+science+buried+god+debate+.

Chapter 2

8 Bill Bryson, *A Short History of Everything* (New York: Broadway Books, 2003), 2911–293.
9 Fred Hoyle, *The Intelligent Universe* (New York: Holt, Rinehart, and Winston, 1983), 177.
10 https://www.seti.org/press-release/how-many-habitable-planets-are-out-there, October 29, 2020, Mountain View, CA. The findings will be published in *The Astronomical Journal*.
11 https://www.seti.org/drake-equation-index.
12 Bryson 27.
13 Hawking, *Brief Answers*, 85.

Chapter 3

14 https://www.google.com/search?hl=en&authuser=0&biw=870&bih=661&tbm=isch&sa=1&ei=YbVyXJ_C OdKEsAXBpuYDA&q=land+promised+to+abraham+map&oq=land+promised+to+&gs_l=img.1.1.0l7j0i8i30j0i24l2.79683. 82763..85617...0.0..0.102.1008.11j1......1....1..gws-wiz-img.nUnT7IV78t4#imgrc=Gyv5vSEtey-5lM:

15 https://www.google.com/search?hl=en&authuser=0&tbm=isch&source=hp&biw=870&bih=661&ei=SrVyXIraBuLLjgST8KnwCg&q=land+of+canaan+bible+map&oq=land+of+canaan&gs_l=img.1.8.0l10.2350.13133.23461...5. 0..0.121.1410.16j1......1....1..gws-wiz-img.....0..35i39j0i30j0i8i30j0i5i30j0i10i24.osH6v8_mTis#imgrc=PaW6iYoO-Tv1GM:

16 https://www.google.com/search?hl=en&authuser=0&tbm=isch&source=hp&biw=933&bih=692&ei=kx90XKKNJ8G4gSs8bwQ&q=land+of+the+midianites&oq=Land+of+the+midian&gs_l=img.1.0.0i24.2589.8099.11455...0.0..0.195.1902.14j4......1....1..gws-wiz-img.....0..35i39j0j0i8i30.Ch41mmZrgsY#imgrc=hHpER_h49ILNxM:

17 http://www.historyworld.net/wrldhis/PlainTextHistories.asp?historyid=aa60

18 https://www.google.com/search?hl=en&authuser=0&biw=866&bih=687&tbm=isch&sa=1&ei=kiBzXKq3J8yAtgXexK3oBQ&q=philistine+migration&oq=philistine+migration&gs_l=img.3...18251. 25526..28254...4.0..0.115.2331.18j6......0....1..gws-wiz-img.......35i39j0i10i67j0j0i67j0i5i30j0i10i24j0i24j0i10j0i8i30.xcX1Cd4TPzQ#imgrc=S1GB-t6NZh9zOM:

19 https://www.britannica.com/place/Palestine/media/439645/3078

20 http://www.ismaili.net/histoire/history03/history302.html)

21 ibid

Chapter 4

22 https://www.britannica.com/print/article/184625

23 https://www.christianity.com/wiki/people/who-was-elijah-in-the-bible

24 NIV Study Bible. Zondervan. Grand Rapids, MI. 2008. Note p 21822–3.

25 https://en.wikipedia.org/wiki/Elijah

26 https://www.brandeis.edu/jewish-experience/holidays-religious-traditions/2022/march/elijah-passover-matt.html

27 Kay, Glenn. When Was Yeshua Born? https://messianicfellowship.50webs.com/yeshuabirth1.html

Chapter 5

28 https://www.biblestudy.org/bible-study-by-topic/people-killed-by-god.html:)
29 Brian Patrick Byrne, Leon Markovitz, Jody Sieradzki and Tal Reznik. https://www.vocativ.com/news/309748/all-the-people-god-kills-in-the-bible/index.html
30 Byrne, et al.
31 https://isthatinthebible.wordpress.com/2015/09/20/canaanites-amorites-and-hittites-in-history-and-the-bible/
32 Bowman, Robert Joshua's Conquest: Was It Justified? - Apologetics https://www.namb.net/apologetics/resource/joshua-s-conquest-was-it..justified?.
33 http://godswarplan.com/occupation-of-canaan-promised-land-12-2tribes-at-war-disobedience-death-of-joshua-judges-1-12
34 Bowman, Robert Joshua's Conquest: Was It Justified?

Chapter 6

35 Gamble, Harry Y. *The New Testament Canon: Its Making and Meaning.* Wipf and Stock Publishers. Eugene, OR. 1985.
36 Gamble 15
37 Gamble 17
38 Gamble 200–21
39 Gamble 21
40 Gamble 23
41 Gamble 35
42 Gamble 28
43 Gamble 29
44 Gamble 47
45 Gamble 41
46 Gamble 47
47 Gamble 52
48 Gamble 46
49 Gamble 555–56

50 Gamble 677–72
51 Gamble 72
52 Gamble 67

Chapter 7

53 Metzger, Bruce M. and Ehrman, Bruce D. *The Text of the New Testament (4th Ed).* Oxford University Press. Oxford, NY. 2005. P 50
54 https://library.duke.edu/papyrus/texts/manuscripts.html
55 Enns, Peter. *Inspiration and Incarnation. Baker Academics. Grand Rapids, MI. 2015. P488–49.*
56 Mounce, William D. *https://missingbibleverses*.com/how-were-copies-made
57 Metzger and Ehrman, p.111–15.
58 Metzger and Ehrman, p.24.
59 Mounce. https://missingbibleverses.com/verse-references
60 Metzger and Ehrman, p 1511–152.
61 https://www.britannica.com/topic/King-James-Version
62 https://www.tcseagles.org/faculty/nchilds/editoruploads/files/Timeline_of_Bible_Translation_History.pdf
63 Metzger and Ehrman, p 165.
64 Ehrman, Bart D. *Misquoting Jesus.* Harper One. New York. P. 89.
65 Bart D. Ehrman and Wallace, Daniel. *The Reliability of the New Testament.* Fortress Press. Minneapolis, MN.P 41.
66 Ehrman and Wallace and Ehrman, p 33.
67 https://en.wikipedia.org/wiki/List_of_New_Testament_verses_not_included_in_modern_English_translations#The_sixteen_omitted_verses

Chapter 8

68 Metzger, Bruce M. and Ehrman, Bart D. The Text of the New Testament. Oxford Press. New York. 2005. P 1377–138.
69 https://victorianweb.org/religion/higher.html
70 https://www.theopedia.com/biblical-criticismß
71 Craig, William Lane. Reasonable Faith. (3rd Ed). Crossway. Wheaton, IL. 2008. p 343.
72 https://en.wikipedia.org/wiki/Biblical_criticism
73 https://en.wikipedia.org/wiki/Biblical_criticism

74 https://en.wikipedia.org/wiki/Biblical_criticism

75 https://www.newworldencyclopedia.org/entry/Jesus_Seminar

76 Ehrman, Bart D. Jesus: Apocolyptic Prophet of the New Millennium.Oxford University Press. New York. 1999

77 Meier, John P. A Marginal Jew. Doubleday. New York. 1991.

78 Hume, David. In David Hume Collected Writings. Section X. Of Miracles. Benediction Classics. Oxford University Press. New York. 2013. P 5555–556

79 Craig 345.

80 Haberman, Gary R. Risen Indeed. Lexham Academic. Bellingham, WA. 2021.

81 Craig, William Lane. Reasonable Faith. (3rd Ed). Crossway. Wheaton, IL. 2008

82 Morison, Frank. Who Moved the Stone. Faber and Faber. Zondervan. Grand Rapids, MI. 2002

Chapter 9

83 https://www.history.com/topics/renaissance/renaissance

84 https://www.britannica.com/topic/Deism

85 Craig, William Lane. Reasonable Faith. Crossway. Wheaton, IL. P 342

Chapter 10

86 https://www.gotquestions.org/Abimelech-Bible.html

87 https://www.gotquestions.org/Abimelech-Bible.html

88 *NIV Study Bible.* p 592

89 https://www.gotquestions.org/Abimelech-Bible.html

90 Wallace, Daniel B. *Mark 2:26 and the Problem with Abiathar.* Presentation to the Evangelical Theological Society, Southwest Regional Meeting, 2004. https://bible.org/article/mark-226-6and-problem-abiathar

91 Fabry, Merrill. https://time.com/4462775/bc-ad-dating-history/. August, 2016

Chapter 11

92 https://knowingscripture.com/articles/covenant-theology-vs-dispensationalism

93 https://knowingscripture.com/articles/covenant-theology-vs-dispensationalism

94 https://exploringthetruth.org/the-covenants-of-works-and-grace-what-is-covenant-theology/
95 https://www.thegospelcoalition.org/essay/covenant-theology/
96 Garris, Zachary. https://knowingscripture.com/articles/covenant-theology-vs-dispensationalism
97 Chafer, Lewis Sperry. *Systematic Theology,* 8 vols. Dallas Seminary Press, 1948 4:40

Chapter 12

98 https://biblescan.com/search.php?q=soul
99 https://biblescan.com/searchnt.php?q=Spirit
100 https://biblehub.com/hebrew/5315.htm
101 https://biblehub.com/hebrew/nafshi_5315.htm
102 https://godventure.co.uk/news/psalm-23-3exploring-the-hebrew
103 Newman, Lester. MA Thesis, Boston University, 1958 https://open.bu.edu/handle/2144/6233
104 Cooper, John W. Body, Soul & Life Everlasting. William Eerdmans Publishing. Grand Rapids, MI. 1998. P 43
105 https://biblehub.com/hebrew/7585.htm.
106 Robinson, H. Wheeler. The Christian Doctrine of Man. Edinburgh: Clark. 1911. P 92 referenced in Cooper, p 522–53
107 Cooper 118
108 Cooper 744–74
109 https://biblehub.com/hebrew/refaim_7496.htm
110 Cooper 622–63
111 Cooper 64
112 Steiner, Richard C. Disembodied Souls. SBL Press. Atlanta, GA. 2015. p 124
113 Cooper 74
114 https://ntwrightpage.com/2016/04/05/the-resurrection-of-resurrection/
115 https://study.com/academy/lesson/the-immortal-soul-ideas-of-socrates-plato-augustine.html
116 https://study.com/academy/lesson/the-immortal-soul-ideas-of-socrates-plato-augustine.html)
117 Steiner 126
118 https://biblehub.com/greek/5590.htm
119 Newman, Lester.

120 https://study.com/academy/lesson/the-immortal-soul-ideas-of-socrates-plato-augustine.html
121 https://www.discovermagazine.com/planet-earth/how-we-know-ancient-humans-believed-in-the-afterlife
122 Science Vol 358, No 6363, p6599–662, 2017
123 https://www.smithsonianmag.com/arts-culture/the-skeletons-of-shanidar-cave-7028477/

Chapter 13

124 Steiner, Richard C. *Disembodied Souls* . SBL Press. Atlanta, GA p 855–86
125 Scofield, C. I., ed. *The Scofield Reference Bible.* Oxford University Press, NY. 1909, p 1270.
126 G. H. Pember. *Earth's Earliest Ages.* Grand Rapids: Kregel Publications, 1942, p 77.
127 Luther, Martin. Luther's Works. American Edition. 21:3033–304. As quoted: https://wolfmueller.co/martin-luther-on-body-soul-spirit/
128 Steiner 866–87.
129 Grudem, Wayne. *What is the Soul? Is it Different form the Spirit?* Online Systematic Theology Course. http://www.waynegrudem.com/test/2007/041507.pdf)

Chapter 14

130 Tertullian. Treatise Against Praexas 2 (https://www.tertullian.org/articles/evans_praxeas_eng.htm)
131 Grantz, Stanley J; Guretzki, David J; and Nordling, Cherith Fee. *Pocket Dictionary of Theological Terms* .p 42
132 Grantz 40.
133 Ehrman, Bart D. *How Jesus Became God.* Harper One. New York. 2014.

Chapter 15

134 www.ancientscripts.com/writing
135 Wells, Spencer. *The Journey of Man.* Random House. New York. 2003.
136 Cann, Rl, Stoneking, M Wilson, AC. "mitochondrial DNA and human evolution." *Nature.* 325 (6099): 311–36, 1987.

137 Zimmer, Carl *(10 September 2019).* "Scientists Find the Skull of Humanity's Ancestor, on a Computer – By comparing fossils and CT scans, researchers say they have reconstructed the skull of the last common forebear of modern humans." The New York Times. *Retrieved 31 December 2019.*

138 Mounier, Aurélien; Lahr, Marta (2019*).* "Deciphering African late middle Pleistocene hominin diversity and the origin of our species." Nature Communications. **10** (1): 3406.

139 Maca-Meyer N, González AM, Larruga JM, Flores C, Cabrera VM (2001). "Major genomic mitochondrial lineages delineate early human expansions"

140 https://en.wikipedia.org/wiki/Early_human_migrations#cite_note-NYT-20190910-038

Chapter 16

141 Ehrman, Bart D. *Jesus: Apocalyptic Prophet of the New Millenium.*Oxford University Press. 1999. pp 366–39.

142 Ehrman 39.

143 Hunt, Robert D. "Herod and Augustus: A Look at Patron-Client Relationships." *Studia Antiqua* 2, no.1 (2002)

144 The *NIV Study Bible.* Zondervan Publishers. Grand Rapids, MI. 2008. Notes p 21066–2107

145 https://reasons.org/explore/publications/tnrtb/read/tnrtb/2002/12/01/the-christmas-star

146 https://community.logos.com/cfs-filesystemfile.ashx/__key/CommunityServer.Discussions.Components.Files/124/4035.atlas-babylon-1.jpg

147 https://en.wikipedia.org/wiki/Day%27s_journey

Chapter 17

148 Lanser, Rick. https://biblearchaeology.org/abr-projects/the-daniel-9-924-427-7project-2/4366-6when-did-herod-the-great-die-part-1

149 Lanser, Rick. https://biblearchaeology.org/abr-projects/the-daniel-9-924-427-7project-2/4367-7when-did-herod-the-great-die-part-2

150 https://wol.jw.org/en/wol/d/r1/lp-e/1001072004

151 https://wol.jw.org/en/wol/d/r1/lp-e/1102005162).

152 https://weatherspark.com/s/98811/3/Average-Winter-Weather-in-Bethlehem-Palestinian-Territories#Figures-Rainfall

153 https://weatherspark.com/m/98811/12/Average-Weather-in-December-in-Bethlehem-Palestinian-Territories#Figures-Temperature
154 https://www.patheos.com/blogs/davearmstrong/2020/12/jesus-december-birth-grazing-sheep-in-bethlehem.html
155 Kay, Glenn. https://messianicfellowship.50webs.com/yeshuabirth1.html
156 Lanser, Rick https://biblearchaeology.org/abr-projects/the-daniel-9-924-427-7project-2/4368-8 pinpointing-the-date-of-christ-s-birth
157 Lanser
158 Strong: https://biblehub.com/interlinear/luke/2-22.htm
159 NIV Study Bible. Zondervan. Grand Rapids, MI. 2008. P2106)
160 Wallace, Daniel B. The Problem of Luke 2:2 " This was the first census taken when Quirinius was governor of Syria." https://bible.org/article/problem-luke-22-2ithis-was-first-census-taken-when-quirinius-was-governor-syria
161 Lanser, Rick. https://biblearchaeology.org/abr-projects/the-daniel-9-924-427-7project-2/4368-8 pinpointing-the-date-of-christ-s-birth
162 Kay, Glenn. https://messianicfellowship.50webs.com/yeshuabirth1.htm
163 Kay, Glenn. http://messianicfellowship.50webs.com /yeshuabirth1.html
164 Kay, Glenn. https://messianicfellowship.50webs.com/yeshuabirth1.html
165 Lanser, Rick https://biblearchaeology.org/abr-projects/the-daniel-9-924-427-7project-2/4368-8pinpointing-the-date-of-christ-s-birth

Chapter 18

166 https://www.iranicaonline.org/articles/magi
167 https://www.britannica.com/summary/astrology
168 Humphreys, Colin J. The Star of Bethlehem – a comet in 5 BC – and the Date of the Birth of Christ. Q.Jl astr. Soc 32:3899–407. 1991) https://articles.adsabs.harvard.edu/cgi-bin/nph-iarticle_query?db_key=AST&bibcode=1991QJRAS..32..389H&letter=0&classic=YES&defaultprint=YES&whole_paper=YES&page=389&epage=389&send=Send+PDF&filetype=.pdf
169 Molnar, Michael R. The Magi's Star from the Perspective of Ancient Astrological Practices. Q. J. R. Astr. Soc. 36:1099–126, 1995. p109)
170 https://www.spiritoflifeag.com/how-many-miracles-are-there-in-the-bible/
171 https://starwalk/space/en/news/ the -great-conjunction-jupiter-and Saturn-appear-the-closest-since-1623
172 https://jofj.net/info-popup/triple-conjunction/
173 Humphreys 405

174 Molnar, Michael R. 121

175 Lanser, Rick. Pinpointing the Date of Christ's Birth. https://biblearchaeology.org/abr-projects/the-daniel-9-924-427-7project-2/4368-8pinpointing-the-date-of-christ-s-birth

176 Strobel, Nick https://www.astronomynotes.com/history/bethlehem-star.html

177 Joseph Henry Thayer, A Greek-English Lexicon of the New Testament (Grand Rapids, MI: Baker, 1977): 81–82.

178 https://reasons.org/explore/publications/articles/astronomy-sheds-new-light-on-the-christmas-star

179 Humphreys 392.

180 Humphreys 392

181 Humphreys 393

182 Humphreys 397

183 Humphreys 392

184 Humphreys 399

185 Humphreys 400

Chapter 19

186 Whiston, William (ed). *Josephus: The Complete Works : The Wars of the Jews.* 1.14.4

187 Whiston. Josephus, *Antiquities* 18.1.1

188 Whiston. Josephus. Antiquities. 18.1.6

189 https://www.britannica.com/topic/Zealot

Chapter 20

190 Ehrman, Bart D. *Jesus Before the Gospels.* Harper One. New York.2016 .p209

191 Ehrman, Bart D. *How Jesus Became God.* Harper One . New York. 2014. Chapter 3.

192 https://www.npr.org/transcripts/300246095

193 Ehrman, Bart D. *How Jesus Became God.* P2688–269.

194 *NIV Study Bible.* Zondervan. 1995 Edition. P 2357.

Chapter 21

195 Ehrman, Bart D. *Jesus Interrupted.* Harper One. New York. 2009. P 39.

196 https://www.bible-researcher.com/codex-d1.html

197 https://cudl.lib.cam.ac.uk/view
198 https://documents.adventistarchives.org/Theses/GeorgeRiceDiss.pdf
199 Metzger, Bruce M. and Ehrman, Bart D. *The Text of the New Testament: Its Transmission, Corruption and Restoration* (4th ed). Oxford Press. New York. 2005. p71.
200 More Arguments over Luke 3:22 - The Bart Ehrman Blog. https://ehrmanblog.org .Aug 11, 2013)
201 Ehrman, Bart D. *The Orthodox Corruption of Scripture.* Oxford University Press. New York, 2011. p59
202 Ehrman, Bart D. *How Jesus Became God.* Harper One. New York. 2014. P 5.
203 If Jesus Never Called Himself God, How Did He Become One? : NPR https://www.npr.org/transcripts/300246095
204 Ehrman, Bart D. *Jesus Before the Gospels.* Harper One. New York. 2016. P 213.

Chapter 22

205 Strong" Concordance. (https://biblehub.com/greek/3439.htm.)

Chapter 23

206 F.F. Bruce, H.L. Ellison, and G.C. D Howley. The International Bible Commentary. Zondervan. Grand Rapids, MI. 1986. P 588.)"
207 https://biblehub.com/hebrew/yelidticha_3205.htm
208 https://biblehub.com/hebrew/3205.htm
209 International Bible Commentary. P 588.
210 Strong, James . the New Strong's Expanded Exhaustive Concordance of the Bible. Thomas Nelson. Nashville, TN. 2010. P 49.
211 https://biblehub.com/greek/3439.htm:
212 https://biblehub.com/greek/1080.htm
213 Landow, George P. ttps://victorianweb.org/religion/type/typo10.html)
214 Barker, Kenneth L. NIV Study Bible. Zondervan. Grand Rapids, MI. 2008. P 2540.
215 Meir, John P. *A Marginal Jew.* Vol1. Doubleday. New York. 1991. PP1688–169.
216 https://jewsforjesus.org/publications/newsletter/newsletter-jan-1991/ritual-washings-and-baptism/
217 https://www.gotquestions.net/Printer/kingdom-of-God-within-you-PF.html
218 *Smith's Bible Dictionary.* Barbour Publishers. Uhrichsville, OH. P 260

Chapter 24

219 Walvood, John F and Zuck, Roy B. *The Bible Knowledge Commentary.* New Testament Victor Books. Wheaton, IL. 1983. P 25.

220 Bailey, Mark and Constable, *Tom Nelson's New Testament Survey.* Thomas Nelson. Nashville, TN. 1999. P 10.

Chapter 25

221 https://www.thebiblejourney.org/biblejourney1/3-3jesuss

222 https://www.gotquestions.org/already-not-yet.html

223 https://www.thecharaproject.com/parables

Chapter 26

224 https://en.wikipedia.org/wiki/Clopas

225 https://en.wikipedia.org/wiki/Clopas

226 http://www.livingwithfaith.org/blog/who-was-the-other-mary-at-the-tomb

227 https://www.gotquestions.org/Salome-in-the-Bible.html

228 https://www.biblicalcyclopedia.com/M/mary-the-(wife)-of-clopas.html

Chapter 27

229 Meier, John P. *A Marginal Jew.* Doubleday. New York. 1994. Vol 2. Pp1166–117.

230 https://www.revisedenglishversion.com/Matt/4/20

231 Philostratus, *The Life of Apollonius of Tyana* 4.45. The translation is that of Christopher P. Jones (Loeb Classical Library, vol.16. Harvard University Press, 2005).

Chapter 29

232 Strong, James. Strong's Expanded Exhaustive Concordance of the Bible. Thomas Nelson. Nashville, TN. 2010. P 457

233 https://www.biblicalcyclopedia.com/M/mary-the-(wife)-of-clopas.html

234 https://www.biblicalcyclopedia.com/J/john-the-apostle.html

235 https://www.biblestudytools.com/dictionary/boanerges/

236 https://christianity.stackexchange.com/questions/79835/what-were-the-ages-of-the-apostles-peter-and-john-when-jesus-was-crucified
237 https://www.gotquestions.org/when-did-Mary-die.html
238 https://amazingbibletimeline.com/blog/john-exiled-to-patmos/
239 https://www.britannica.com/biography/Herod-Agrippa-I
240 https://www.meandertravel.com/biblical_asia_minor/biblical_asia_minor.php?details=stjohnandsevenchurches&m=3&md=sc3
241 Jeremiah, David. https://davidjeremiah.blog/seven-churches-of-revelation-bible-study/).
242 https://biblearchaeology.org/research/new-testament-era/3080-0the-king-and-i-the-apostle-john-and-emperor-domitian-part-1
243 https://biblearchaeology.org/research/new-testament-era/3080-0the-king-and-i-the-apostle-john-and-emperor-domitian-part-1
244 NIV Study Bible. Kenneth Barker, ed. Zondervan. Grand Rapids, MI. 2008. P26299–2630.
245 https://www.meandertravel.com/biblical_asia_minor/biblical_asia_minor.php?details=stjohnandsevenchurches&m=3&md=sc3
246 https://www.britannica.com/print/article/305163

Chapter 30

247 Strong, James. Strong's Expanded Exhaustive Concordance of the Bible. Thomas Nelson. Nashville, TN. 2010. Pp 662,817,101, 451,454
248 https://www.biblicalarchaeology.org/daily/biblical-sites-places/biblical-archaeology-sites/the-house-of-peter-the-home-of-jesus-in-capernaum/
249 CATHOLIC ENCYCLOPEDIA: St. Peter, Prince of the Apostles https://www.newadvent.org/cathen/11744a.htm#I
250 Schecter, Solomon and Greenstone, Julius. H. https://www.jewishencyclopedia.com/articles/10435-5marriage-laws).
251 Michael L. Satlow, *Jewish marriage in antiquity*. Princeton: Princeton University Press, 2001).
252 https://christianity.stackexchange.com/questions/79835/what-were-the-ages-of-the-apostles-peter-and-john-when-jesus-was-crucified
253 (https://christianity.stackexchange.com/questions/79835/what-were-the-ages-of-the-apostles-peter-and-john-when-jesus-was-crucified
254 https://www.newadvent.org/cathen/11744a.htm#I
255 https://www.revisedenglishversion.com/Matt/4/20

256 https://www.thebiblejourney.org/biblejourney1/7-7journeys-of-jesuss-followers/peters-journeys/
257 Strong, James. The New Strong's Exhaustive Concordance of the Bible. Thomas Nelson. Nashville, TN. 2010
258 https://biblehub.com/greek/932.htm
259 Pentecost, J. Dwight. *Thy Kingdom Come.* Kregal Publications. Grand Rapids, MI p 2900–291.
260 House, H. Wayne. " The Church's Appropriation of Israel's Blessings, in *Israel, The Land and the People*, p 77
261 Blaising, Craig and Bock, Darrell. Progressive Dispensationalism.p 251
262 Sauer. From Eternity to Eternity. P 1766–176. Quoted in Toussaint, Stanley D. The Contingency of the Coming of the Kingdom from Integrity of the Heart, Skillfulness of the Hands: Biblical Leadership
263 Meier, John P. A Marginal Jew. Doubleday. New York.1994. Vol 2. P 2388–239
264 Pentecost 2822–283
265 Pentecost 291
266 Pentecost 283
267 https://en.wikipedia.org/wiki/Kingdom_theology

Chapter 32

268 https://www.merriam-webster.com/dictionary/parable
269 *http://www.differencebetween.net* › Language
270 https://www.thefreedictionary.com/Similes-Metaphors-Analogies-Allegories
271 https://www.thecharaproject.com/parables
272 Viljoen, F.P., 2019, 'Why Jesus spoke in parables', In die Skrifig 53(1), a2523. htps://doi.org/10.4102/ids. v53i1.2523
273 Viljoen, F.P.
274 Hooker, M.D., 2000, 'Mark's parables of the kingdom (Mark 4:1–4)', in R.N. Longenecker (ed.), *The challenge of Jesus's parables*, Eerdmans, Grand Rapids, MI. pp. 79–101

Chapter 33

275 Ehrman, Bart D. *Jesus Interrupted.* Harper Collins. New York. 2009. P 255–27.

Chapter 34

276 Holoubek, J.E. and Holoubek, A.B. Blood, sweat and fear. "A Classification of hematidhidrosis.J Med. 1996;27(33–4):1155–33.

277 Saugato Biswas, Trupti Surana, Abhishek De, and Falguni Nag. A Curious Case of Sweating Blood Indian J Dermatol. 2013 Nov-Dec; 58(6): 478–480

278 Raksha M. Patel, Stuti Mahajan. Hematohidrosis: A rare clinical entity Indian Dermatology Online Journal -December 2010 -Volume 1 - Issue 1. P300–32.

279 Maglie, Roberto and Caprioni, Marzia. A Case of Blood Sweating: hematohidrosis. CMAJ 23:189, 2017.

280 Kluger, Nicolas. Hematohidrosis (bloody sweat): a review of the recent literature (19966–2016). Acta Dermatovenerol Alp Pannonica Adriat. 2018 Jun;27(2):855–90.

281 https://www.webmd.com/a-to-z-guides/hematidrosis-hematohidrosis

Chapter 35

282 Grudem, Wayne. Systematic Theology, Second Edition. Zondervan Academic. Grand Rapids, MI. 2020. p706.

283 Bird, Michael. Evangelical Theology. Zondervan Academic. Grand Rapids, MI. p443

284 Demarest, Bruce. The Cross and Salvation. Crossway. Wheaton, IL. 1997. p153

285 Grudem 725.

286 Bird 455

287 Bird p451–452

288 Demarest, p157

289 Ryrie, Charles. Basic Theology. Moody Press. Chicago, IL. 1999. p 356-7.

Chapter 36

290 https://www.andrews.edu/library/car/cardigital/Periodicals/AUSS/2008/2008-82/2008-82-203.pdf

291 https://pediaa.com/what-is-the-difference-between-julian-and-gregorian-calendars/

292 https://en.wikipedia.org/wiki/Hebrew_calendar

293 https://en.wikipedia.org/wiki/March_equinox

294 https://www.wake-up.org/time-periods/passover-week-chronology.html
295 http://hcscchurch.org/wp-content/uploads/2014/08/How-did-People-Tell-Time-in-Jesus%E2%80%99-9Day.pdf
296 https://www.gotquestions.org/Saturday-Sunday.html)
297 https://en.wikipedia.org/wiki/Hebrew_calendar
298 https://www.quora.com/Why-does-Judaism-celebrate-Sabbath-on-Saturday
299 https://bustedhalo.com/ministry-resources/why-isnt-the-sabbath-on-saturday
300 https://en.wikipedia.org/wiki/Sabbath
301 https://www.gotquestions.org/what-year-did-Jesus-die.html
302 http://jesus-messiah.com/html/passover-dates-26-634ad.html
303 (http://www.hebrewcalendar.net/htdocs/main.en.html
304 https://peacecrusader.wordpress.com/tag/day-of-week/
305 http://www.csgnetwork.com/julianmanycalconv.html
306 http://biblelight.net/pasover.htm
307 https://www.wake-up.org/time-periods/passover-week-chronology.html ;
308 http://www.agapebiblestudy.com/documents/The Biblical Chronology
309 https://www.agapebiblestudy.com/documents/The Passover Feast and...
310 https://www.cgg.org/index.cfm/fuseaction/Library.sr/CT/BQA/k/169/Is-high-day-weekly-Sabbath.htm
311 http://historicchristianity.blogspot.com/2006/05/chronology-of-easte
312 https://www.quora.com/When-did-Jesus-die-What-day-of-the-week-...;
313 https://worldsymbolsblog.wordpress.com/2015/04/03/the-origins-of-passover-and-easter)
314 http://jesus-messiah.com/html/passover-dates-26-634ad.html
315 https://www.cgg.org/index.cfm/fuseaction/Library.sr/CT/BQA/k/169/Is-high-day-weekly-Sabbath.htm
316 Coulter, Fred R. The Day Jesus the Christ Died. York Publishing. Hollister, CA. 2008.p 81.

Chapter 37

317 Ehrman, Bart. D. *Jesus Interrupted*. Harper One Publishers. New York. 2008. p 255–27.
318 https://www.biblegateway.com/versions/New-International-Version..
319 http://www.biblewebapp.com/reader
320 http://www.scripture4all.org/OnlineInterlinear/Greek_Index.htm

321 https://en.wikipedia.org/wiki/Roman_timekeeping

322 http://blog.adw.org/2014/08/how-did-people-tell-time-in-jesus-time/

323 http://www.agapebiblestudy.com/charts/jewishtimedivision.htm

324 Geisler, Norman and Howe, *Thomas. When Critics Ask.* Baker Books. Grand Rapids, MI. 1992. P 376

325 Archer, Gleason L. Jr. *The Encyclopedia of Bible Difficulties.* Zondervan. Grand Rapids, MI. 1982.p 363

326 Mc Dowell, Josh and Mc Dowell, Sean. *The Handbook of Bible Difficulties.* Harvest House Publishers, Eugene, OR. 2013. P208.

Chapter 38

327 https://bible.org/question/are-there-verses-missing-luke-2450-053-3some-manuscripts

328 Snapp, James. https://www.thetextofthegospels.com/2014/12/the-bible-so-mispresented-its-sin-part.html

Chapter 39

329 https://bible.knowing-jesus.com/topics/Three-Days

330 https://www.agapebiblestudy.com/documents/The%20Symbolic%20Significance%20of%20the%20third%20day.htm

331 https://www.gotquestions.org/why-three-days.html

332 https://www.jewish-funerals.org/shemira/

333 Patristic Bible Commentary: Litteral's Catena on Jonah, Chapter2 https://sites.google.com/site/aquinasstudybible/home/jonah/litteral-s-catena-on-jonah/chapter-1/chapter-2

334 Lenker, John Nicholas, Editor. Translated by John Nicholas Lenker and others. Martin Luther Sermons.Vol 2 Easter Sunday.Second Sermon Mark 16:11–8 The Story of Christ's Resurrection.p202

Chapter 40

335 Alcorn, Randy. Heaven. Tyndale House Publishers. Carol Stream, Il. 2004.p42

336 https://biblehub.com/greek/3857.htm

337 Thayer's Greek Lexicon (https://biblehub.com/greek/3857.htm)

338 Alcorn 55
339 https://biblehub.com/hebrew/strongs_7585.htm
340 https://en.wikipedia.org/wiki/Sheol
341 https://biblehub.com/greek/3857.htm
342 https://www.bibleinfo.com/en/questions/thief-on-cross
343 https://www.revealedtruth.com/bible-study/where-did-jesus-go/

Chapter 41

344 https://www.definitions.net/definition/harrowing+of+hell)
345 https://www.pcabookstore.com/samples/11589.pdf
346 https://biblehub.com/topical/h/hell.htm)
347 https://biblehub.com/topical/h/hell.htm)
348 Emerson, Matthew. https://ps.edu/did-jesus-go-to-hell-matthew-emerson
349 Alcorn, Randy. *Heaven*. Tyndale House Publisher. 2004. p47.
350 Allen, R. Michael. *Reformed Theology*,2012, pp. 67,68
351 Calvin, John. *The Institutes of the Christian Religion* . (Translated by Thomas Norton, 1581). Published by Pantianos Classics. Book Four. Ch 16. P 187
352 Sam Storms https://www.crosswalk.com/slideshows/10-0things-you-should-know-about-hell.html

Chapter 42

353 Strong, James/ The New Strong Expanded Exhaustive Concordance of the Bible. Thomas Nelson. Nashville, TN. 2010. P 760
354 Strong p 183
355 https://www.britannica.com/topic/Satan
356 https://www.christianity.com/wiki/angels-and-demons/how-did-lucifer-fall-and-become-satan-11557519.html
357 Stewart, Don. https://www.blueletterbible.org/faq/don_stewart/don_stewart_79.cfm
358 https://biblehub.com/hebrew/1966.htm).
359 https://www.biblestudytools.com/topical-verses/demons-in-the-bible/

Chapter 43

360 Cooper, John W. *Body, Soul and Everlasting Life.* William Eerdmans Publisher. Grand Rapids, MI. 1998. p622–63

361 Cooper 64

362 Whiston, William. *Josephus: The Complete Works. The Antiquities of the Jews.* Thomas Nelson. Dallas. 1998. 18.1.4. P 572

363 Whiston, Josephus 18.1.3. p 572

364 https://www.myjewishlearning.com/article/jewish-resurrection-of-the-dead/

Chapter 44

365 https://www.britannica.com/topic/Easter-holiday

366 *https://www.cgi.org/new-page-56*

367 *https://www.cgi.org/new-page-56*

368 Church History (Socrates Scholasticus). Book V, Ch 22.

Chapter 45

369 https://believersportal.com/120-0recorded-miracles-in-the-bible

Chapter 46

370 NIV Study Bible. Barker, Kenneth L. (ed). Zondervan. Grand Rapids, MI. 2008. p 2096

371 https://jimmyakin.com/2017/01/how-the-resurrection-narratives-fit-together.html

Chapter 47

372 *The Wars Of The Jews* Book VI Ch 9 Sec 3

373 Wilkinson, "*Ancient Jerusalem, Its Water Supply and Population,*" PEFQS 106, pp. 33–51 (1974)

374 *Estimating the Population of Ancient Jerusalem*, Magen Broshi, BAR 4:02, Jun 1978

375 Rocca, "*Herod's Judaea: A Mediterranean State in the Classical World,*" p. 333 (2008). Mohr Siebeck.

376 Hillel Geva (2014) *Jerusalem's Population in Antiquity: A Minimalist View,* TelAviv, 41:2, 1311–160, DOI: 10.1179/0334435514Z.00000000041

377 Retief, F.P.L Cilliers *The history and pathology of crucifixion* S Afr Med J 2003 Dec;93(12):9388–41.

378 White, Matthew.https://necrometrics.com/romestat.htm

379 Origen, *Commentary on Matthew,* Book X, Chapter 17

380 Maier, Paul L. Josephus and Jesus -Apologetics. https:// www.namb.net/apologetics/resource/josephus-and-jesus/

381 Eusebius on Josephus: *Demonstratio evangelica* Translated by W.J.Ferrar. Society for Promoting Christian Knowledge. The MacMillan Company. New York, 1920, pp1422–143.

382 Feldman, Louis H. *Jewish Antiquities, Books XVIII-XX,* Published by London, Heinemann., 1965):

383 Schlomo Pines, *An Arabic Version of the Testimonium Flavianum and its Implications* [Jerusalem: Israel Academy of Sciences and Humanities, 1971

384 Meier, John P. Jesus in Josephus: A Modest Proposal. The Catholic Quarterly. Vol 52, NO 2 (January 1990), pp766–103

385 Meier, John P. *A Marginal Jew: Rethinking the Historical Jesus.* Vol 1: 566–62. Doubleday.New York. 1991.

386 Ehrman, Bart D. *Jesus: Apocalyptic Prophet of the New Millennium.* Oxford University Press. New York. 1999. P 611–62

387 Goldberg, Gary J. *The Coincidences of the Emmaus Narrative of Luke and the Testimonium of Josephus.* Journal of Pseudographia 13 (1995), pp 599–77

388 Goldberg, Gary J.

389 https://www.ancientjewreview.com/articles/2014/12/25/a-quick-introduction-to-toledot-yesh

390 Newman, Hillel. *The Death of Jesus in the Toledot Yeshu.*1999. https://academic.oup.com › jts › article-pdf)

391 Di Signa, Vangelo 218

392 Rochford, James http://christianapologeticsalliance.com/2016/02/12/did-jesus-exist-part-4-4lucian-and-thallus

393 Goldberg, Abraham (1987). "*The Palestinian Talmud.* In Safrai, Shmuel (ed.). The Literature of the Jewish People in the Period of the Second Temple and the Talmud, Volume 3 The Literature of the Sages. Brill. pp. 303–322

394 https://en.wikipedia.org/wiki/Jesus_in_the_Talmud#cite_note-100
395 Schäfer, Peter. " *Jesus in the Talmud* .Princeton University Press, 2007, p 13, 85–92, 98–100, 113, 174.;
396 Pick, Bernhard. *The Talmud: What It Is and What It Knows of Jesus and His Followers*, publisher? 1887 (reprint Kessinger Publishing, LLC, 2007. p 115)
397 Rochford, James. http://christianapologeticsalliance.com/2016/02/12/did-jesus-exist-part-4-4lucian-and-thallus/)
398 Julius Africanus, *History of the World.*
399 Rochford, James. http://christianapologeticsalliance.com/2016/02/12/did-jesus-exist-part-4-4lucian-and-thallus
400 Tertullian *Apologeticus* Chapter 21:19
401 Maier, Paul L. *Pontius Pilate*,. Garden City, NY: Doubleday, 1968. Footnote. Cited in Strobel, Lee. The Case for Christ: a Journalist's Personal Investigation of the Evidence for Jesus. Grand Rapids, MI: Zondervan, 1998. P. 85

Chapter 48

402 McDowell, Sean. *The Fate of the Apostles.* Routledge. Taylor and Francis Group. New York. 2018.p 266–27.
403 Orzeck, Richard. *The Twelve Apostles of Jesus: Their Forgotten History.* Perfect Love Publishing. Trumansburg, NY. 2021.p 37.
404 McDowell. 63.
405 McDowell 65.
406 1 Clement 5.11–4.
407 Orzeck 68.
408 McDowell 180.
409 Mc Birnie, Willam. S.*The Search for the Twelve Apostles.* Tyndale House Publishers. Carol Stream, IL. 1973.P 56
410 Mc Birnie 71.
411 Mc Dowell 191.
412 M BIrnie 61
413 Orzeck 162
414 McBirnie 137
415 Mc Dowell 2266–227.
416 Orzeck 124
417 Orzeck 126
418 Orzeck 85

419 McDowell 211
420 McBirnie 102.
421 McBirnie 106
422 Orzeck 90.
423 McBirnie 107
424 Orzeck 97
425 Mc Birnie 119
426 Orzeck 193.
427 Orzeck 197.
428 Orzeck 195
429 Mc Birnie 140.
430 Orzeck 114.
431 McDowell 2322–233.
432 McDowell 235
433 McBirnie 150.
434 Orzeck 104.
435 McBirnie 154.
436 McBirnie 154
437 Orzeck 107
438 Orzeck 178.
439 McBirnie 197.
440 McBirnie 196
441 McBirnie 2033–206
442 McBirnie 207

Chapter 49

443 https://www.biblestudy.org/apostlepaul/life-epistles-of-apostle-paul/religious-schools.html

Chapter 50

444 https://www.britannica.com/science/geocentric-model
445 https://en.wikipedia.org/wiki/Earth_analog

Chapter 51

446 Strong, James. *The New Strong Expanded Exhaustive Concordance of the Bible.* Thomas Nelson. Nashville, TN. 2010. p 570

447 Stein, Robert H. *The Synoptic Problem.* Baker Books. Grand Rapids, MI. 1987. P48

448 Morison, Frank. *Who Moved the Stone.* Zondervan. Grand Rapids, MI. 1958.

Chapter 52

449 https://en.wikipedia.org/wiki/Augustine_of_Hippo

450 https://en.wikipedia.org/wiki/Manichaeism

451 https://en.wikipedia.org/wiki/Augustine_of_Hippo

452 https://en.wikipedia.org/wiki/Constantine_the_Great_and_Christianity

453 https://en.wikipedia.org/wiki/Augustine_of_Hippo

454 Augustin. *On Predestination of the Saints.* Aeterna Press Coppell, Texas. 2023. Ch 7 (III). P 8.

455 Augustin. *On Predestination of the Saints* Ch 15-16, p 17-18.

456 Walvoord, John and Bock, Roy B. *The Bible Knowledge Commentary; New Testament Edition.* Victor Books. Wheaton, IL. 1983. P 512-513.

Chapter 53

457 Sproul. R. C. https://www.monergism.com/augustine-and-pelagius

458 Luther, Martin. *The Bondage of the Will.* Translated by J.I.Packer and O.R. Johnston. Baker Academic. Grand Rapids, MI. 1957. P107.

459 Luther, Martin. *The Bondage of the Will.* P 105.

460 Calvin, John . *The Bondage and Liberation of the Will.* Edited by Lane, A.N.S. Translated by G.I. Davies. Baker Books. Grand Rapids, MI. P 69

461 Luther, Martin. *The Bondage of the Will.* P107

462 Calvin, John . *The Bondage and Liberation of the Will.* P47.

463 Sproul https://www.monergism.com/augustine-and-pelagius

464 Barrett, Matthew. Salvation by Grace. P&R Publishing. Phillipsburg, NJ. 2013. P 40.

465 Calvin *The Bondage and Liberation of the Will* p 69.

466 Calvin *The Bondage and Liberation of the Will* p 40.

467 Sproul. R. C. https://www.monergism.com/augustine-and-pelagius

468 Augustine. *Preservation of the Saints*, p 13.

469 Augustine. *Preservation of the Saints*, p 4.

Chapter 54

470 Strong, James. *The New Strong's Expanded Exhaustive Concordance of the Bible*. Thomas Nelson. Nashville. 2010. P 339.

471 https://www.merriam-webster.com/dictionary/grace

472 Grenz, Stanley J., Guretzki, David, and Nordling, Cherityh Fee. *Pocket Dictionary of Theological Terms*. Intervarsity Press. Downers Grove, Il. 1999. P56.

473 Augustine. *A Treatise On Predestination of the Saints*. Aeterna Press. 2014. P 33.

474 Barrett, Matthew. *Salvation by Grace*.P &R Publishing. Phillipsburg, NJ.2013. P 8-9.

475 Luther, Martin. *The Bondage of the Will*. Translated by J.I. Packer and O.R. Johnston. Baker Academic. Grand Rapids, MI. 1957. P 267-268.

476 Calvin, John. *The Institutes of the Christian Religion*. I.16.12 Pantianos Classics. Coppell, Texas. 2019. P77-78.

477 Calvin, John. *The Institutes of the Christian Religion*. I.16.12 Pantianos Classics. Coppell, Texas. 2019. 344.

478 Winter, Ernst F. (Translator and Editor). *Discourses on Free Will: Desiderius Erasmus and Martin Luther*. Bloomsbury. New York. 2013. P 35-36.

479 Calvin, John. *The Institutes of the Christian Religion*. I.16.12 Pantianos Classics. Coppell, Texas. 2019. P77.

480 What is Common Grace? https://www.gotquestions.org/common-grace.html

481 https://www.gotquestions.org/prevenient-grace.html

482 Calvin, John. *The Institutes of the Christian Religion*. I.16.12 Pantianos Classics. Coppell, Texas. 2019. 344.

483 Luther, Martin. *The Bondage of the Will*. P 267-268.

484 Calvin, John. *The Bondage and Liberation of the Will*. P 114.

485 Calvin, John. *The Bondage and Liberation of the Will*. P 38.

486 Luther, Martin in Desiderius Erasmus and Martin Luther, Discourse on Free Will.Bloomsbury. New Yourk. 2013. P116.

487 Augustine. *A Treatise On Predestination of the Saints* . P 6.

488 Barrett. Salviation by Grace, P 73.

489 Augustine. *A Treatise On Predestination of the Saints* . P 4.

490 Deere, Jack. *Surprised by the Voice of God*. Zondervan Publishing House. Grand Rapids, MI, 1996, p. 53.

491 https://www.inspiringquotes.us › Authors › C. S. Lewis

Chapter 55

492 Swindoll, Charles. *Paul: A Man of Grit and Grace*. Thomas Nelson. Dallas, TX. 2002. P 130.

493 Flew, Antony. *There is a God*. Harper Collins, 2007, p. 158.

494 Wright, N.T. *Simply Christian*. Harper One, New York, 2006.

495 Batterson, Mark. *Whisper: How to Hear the Voice of God*. Penguin, Random House. New York, 2017.

496 Hooper, Walter. *The Collected Letters of C.S. Lewis*. Vol III, Harper Collins, New York, 2007, p. 191.

497 Saucy, Robert L. An Open But Cautious View in Grudem, Wayne A. (ed) *Are Miraculous Gifts for Today*. Zondervan. Grand Rapids, MI, 1996, p. 143.

498 Friesen, Garry. *Decision Making and The Will of God*. Penguin Random House. New York, 2004.

499 Ibid, p. 116.

Chapter 56

500 Walvoord, John F and Zuck, Roy B. the Bible Knowledge Commentary. New Testament edition. Victor Books. Wheaton, IL. 1983. P 16.

501 Lockyer, Herbert, All the Messianic Prophecie of the Bible. Zondervan. Grand Rapids, MI. 1973. P 17.

502 https://www.azbible.com/prophets-in-the-bible.html

503 Lockyer, Herbert. *All the Messianic Prohecies in the Bible*. Zondervan. Grand Rapids, MI. 1973. P 17

504 Lockyer, Herbert. *All the Messianic Prophecies of the Bible*. P 525-527.

505 Bruce, F.F. *The International Bible Commentary*. Zondervan. Grand Rapids, MI. 1979. P 1122.

506 Walvoord, John F and Zuck, Roy B. *The Bible Knowledge Commentary. New Testament edition*. Victor Books. Wheaton, IL. 1983. P 30.

507 Walvoord, John F and Zuck, Roy B. *The Bible Knowledge Commentary. Old Testament edition*. P 1486..

508 Walvoord, John F and Zuck, Roy B. *The Bible Knowledge Commentary. Old Testament edition.* P 1170.
509 *NIV Study Bible.* Zondervan.Grand Rapids, MI. 2008. Notes p 1471.
510 Walvoord, John F and Zuck, Roy B. *The Bible Knowledge Commentary. Old Testament edition.* P 1545. .
511 Bromily, Geoffrey W. (Gen Editor). *The International Standard Bible Encyclopedia.* Eerdmans Publishing. Grand Rapids, MI. Vol 4. P 1186.
512 Bruce, F.F. *The International Bible Commentary.* P 979.
513 Walvoord, John F and Zuck, Roy B. *The Bible Knowledge Commentary. Old Testament edition.* P 878.
514 Walvoord, John F and Zuck, Roy B. *The Bible Knowledge Commentary. Old Testament edition.* P 1569.
515 Bruce, F.F. *The International Bible Commentary.* P 982.

Chapter 57

516 https://davidjeremiah.blog/why-was-daniel-taken-to-babylon/
517 https://davidjeremiah.blog/why-was-daniel-taken-to-babylon/
518 https://www.gotquestions.org/Daniel-eunuch.html; https://davidjeremiah.blog/why-was-daniel-taken-to-babylon/
519 https://en.wikipedia.org/wiki/Daniel_(biblical_figure)
520 https://www.newworldencyclopedia.org/entry/Lives_of_the_Prophets
521 Vincent, Bob. https://www.rbvincent.com/BibleStudies/captivit.htm).
522 https://davidjeremiah.blog/decoding-daniels-seventy-weeks-prophecy/
523 https://davidjeremiah.blog/decoding-daniels-seventy-weeks-prophecy/
524 https://davidjeremiah.blog/decoding-daniels-seventy-weeks-prophecy/
525 https://www.gotquestions.org/seventy-weeks.html
526 https://orwellbible.org/2014/02/18/daniels-prophecy-of-the-seventy-weeks/
527 Norman Cohn, James Tabor, L. Michael White.https://www.pbs.org/wgbh/pages/frontline/shows/apocalypse/explanation/bdaniel.html)
528 *Collins, John J. (1999). "Daniel". In Van Der Toorn, Karel; Becking, Bob; van der Horst, Pieter Willem (eds.). Dictionary of Deities and Demons in the Bible. Eerdmans. ISBN 9780802824912.*
529 Miller, Stephen. *The Apologetics Study Bible*
530 Daniel Introduction. Zondervan Study Bible. Zondervan. Grand Rapids, MI. 2008. P 1774.

531 Pratt, Bill. https://www.toughquestionsanswered.org/2016/07/08/when-was-the-book-of-daniel-written/
532 https://www.britannica.com/biography/Belshazzar
533 https://www.britannica.com/biography/Belshazzar
534 Pratt, Bill. Tough Questions Answered
535 Strong, James. Strong's Expanded and Exhaustive Concordance of the Bible. Thomas Nelson. Nashville, Tn 2010. P157
536 https://www.spiritandtruth.org/teaching/Book_of_Daniel/shared/DanielDiscovered-4.3_Darius_the_Mede.pdf?x=x

Chapter 58

537 https://www.merriam-webster.com/dictionary/amanuensis
538 Leuchter, Mark Chapter 5 The Levite Scribes, Part 1: The Composition of Deuteronomy https://doi.org/10.1093/acprof:oso/9780190665098.003.0007 Pages 155–188
539 https://biblehub.com/hebrew/sofer_5608.htm
540 Englishman's Concordance: https://biblehub.com/hebrew/sofer_5608.htm
541 Strong, James. Strong's Expanded Exhaustive Concordance of the Bible. Thomas Nelson. Nashville, TN. 2010. P774-775.
542 https://www.gospeloutreach.net/613laws.html
543 https://www.newworldencyclopedia.org/entry/Documentary_hypothesis
544 https://study.com/learn/lesson/pentateuch-overview-authorship-timeline.html
545 https://bible.ucg.org/bible-commentary/2%20Kings/The-finding-of-the-Book-of-the-Law/
546 Clayton, Ewan. A History of Writing. https://www.bl.uk/history-of-writing/articles/where-did-writing-begin)
547 https://www.britannica.com/topic/Akkadian-language
548 https://www.historyonthenet.com/mesopotamian-education-and-schools
549 *Schniedewind, William (26 May 2016). "Schools in Ancient Israel". Oxford Bibliographies Online. Oxford University Press https://www.oxfordbibliographies.com/display/document/obo-9780195393361/obo-9780195393361-0222.xml)*
550 https://www.jewishvirtuallibrary.org/writing
551 https://bible.ucg.org/bible-commentary/2%20Kings/The-finding-of-the-Book-of-the-Law/

552 Payes, Jovan. The Role of An Amanuensis in the Letters of Paul. https://biblicalfaith.online/2021/01/14/role-amanuensis-in-the-letters-of-paul/

Chapter 59

553 https://www.britannica.com/place/Roman-Empire
554 https://en.wikipedia.org/wiki/Constantine_the_Great_and_Christianity
555 https://en.wikipedia.org/wiki/Edict_of_Thessalonica
556 https://www.studentsofhistory.com/division-of-the-empire
557 https://www.britannica.com/place/Roman-Empire/Height-and-decline-of-imperial-Rome
558 https://www.britannica.com/place/Byzantine-Empire
559 https://www.britannica.com/event/East-West-Schism-1054
560 http://www.historyworld.net/wrldhis/PlainTextHistories.asp?ParagraphID=etn
561 https://www.britannica.com/topic/Frank-people
562 https://www.wga.hu/tours/gothic/history/holy_rom.html
563 http://law2.umkc.edu/faculty/projects/ftrials/luther/lutherindulgences.html
564 Metaxis, Eric. Martin Luther. Viking. New York, NY. 2017. P 46.
565 http://law2.umkc.edu/faculty/projects/ftrials/luther/lutherindulgences.html
566 Metaxis, Eric. Martin Luther p 99-106.

Chapter 60

567 *NIV Study Bible*. Zondervan, Grand Rapids, MI. 2008
568 Hinds, Arthur. The Complete Sayings of Jesus. https://sarata.com/bible/book/words-of-jesus/csj001.html)
569 *Jesus Saith*; D.O.T. Publishing & Print Shop. Vancouver, WA. 2021.
570 https://www.britannica.com/topic/biblical-literature/The-Synoptic-problem
571 Stein, Robert H. *The Synoptic Problem*. Baker Books. Grand Rapids, MI. 1987. P 48.
572 Tyson, Joseph B. and Longstaff, Thomas R.W. Synoptic Abstract, The Computer Bible,, vol 15. Wooster, Ohio,1978, p 169-171.
573 Stein p 89
574 https://www.britannica.com/print/article/56490.

575 https://www.britannica.com/topic/biblical-literature/The-Synoptic-problem

576 Stein p 163-164

577 Stein p 164

578 Stein p 43

579 Stein p 164-165

580 *History of the Q hypothesis* https://www.newworldencyclopedia.org/entry/Q_Document)

581 Streeter, Burnett H. *The Four Gospels. A Study of Origins Treating the Manuscript Tradition, Sources, Authorship, & Dates.* London: Macmillan and Co., Ltd., 1924.

Printed in the United States
by Baker & Taylor Publisher Services

Printed in the United States
by Baker & Taylor Publisher Services